THE
DIVINE CONCEPTION

Pastor Nichole,

As a long-time listener to your radio broadcasts, I've come to appreciate you as a man of God. I am the former Associate Pastor of <u>Church of Abundant Life</u>. I believe we have a mutual friend in Dr. McCorkle of Southwestern. God bless you.

Gary B Poling

July 25, 2012

CRAIG B. POLENZ

THE
DIVINE CONCEPTION

GOD'S PRODUCING PRINCIPLE FOR
SUPERNATURAL STRENGTH AND VITALITY

TATE PUBLISHING
AND ENTERPRISES, LLC

The Divine Conception
Copyright © 2012 by Craig B. Polenz. All rights reserved.

No part of this publication may be reproduced, stored in a retrieval system or transmitted in any way by any means, electronic, mechanical, photocopy, recording or otherwise without the prior permission of the author except as provided by USA copyright law.

Scripture quotations marked (AMP) are taken from the *Amplified Bible*, Copyright © 1954, 1958, 1962, 1964, 1965, 1987 by The Lockman Foundation. Used by permission.

Scripture quotations marked (CJB) are taken from the *Complete Jewish Bible*, copyright © 1998 by David H. Stern. Published by Jewish New Testament Publications, Inc. www.messianicjewish.net/jntp. Distributed by Messianic Jewish Resources. www.messianicjewish.net. All rights reserved. Used by permission.

Scripture quotations marked (KJV) are taken from the *Holy Bible, King James Version*, Cambridge, 1769. Used by permission. All rights reserved.

All scripture quotations, unless otherwise indicated, are taken from the *New American Standard Bible*®, Copyright © 1960, 1962, 1963, 1968, 1971, 1972, 1973, 1975, 1977, 1995 by The Lockman Foundation. Used by permission.

Scripture quotations are taken from the *Holy Bible, New Living Translation*, copyright ©1996. Used by permission of Tyndale House Publishers, Inc., Wheaton, Illinois 60189. All rights reserved.

Scripture quotations marked (NIV) are taken from the *Holy Bible, New International Version* ®, Copyright © 1973, 1978, 1984 by International Bible Society. Used by permission of Zondervan Publishing House. All rights reserved.

Scripture quotations marked (NKJV) are taken from the *New King James Version*. Copyright © 1982 by Thomas Nelson, Inc. Used by permission. All rights reserved.

Unless otherwise indicated, all scripture quotations in this publication are from the *Good News Translation in Today's English Version*-Second Edition Copyright © 1992 by American Bible Society. Used by Permission.

Scripture quotations marked (YLT) are from *Young's Literal Translation*, Robert Young, 1898. Public domain in the United States. The opinions expressed by the author are not necessarily those of Tate Publishing, LLC.

Published by Tate Publishing & Enterprises, LLC
127 E. Trade Center Terrace | Mustang, Oklahoma 73064 USA
1.888.361.9473 | www.tatepublishing.com

Tate Publishing is committed to excellence in the publishing industry. The company reflects the philosophy established by the founders, based on Psalm 68:11,
"The Lord gave the word and great was the company of those who published it."

Book design copyright © 2012 by Tate Publishing, LLC. All rights reserved.
Cover design by Kate Stearman
Interior design by Lindsay B. Behrens

Published in the United States of America

ISBN: 978-1-61862-005-7
1. Religion / Christian Life / Spiritual Growth
2. Religion / Christian Life / General
12.03.16

Dedication

The Divine Conception is dedicated to my wife who has quietly and patiently endured with me as I researched and compiled this book. She has labored with me to declare the Lord's anointed message of healing, liberty, and sightedness.

He [Jesus] entered the synagogue, as was His custom on the Sabbath day. And He stood up to read.

And there was handed to Him [the roll of] the book of the prophet Isaiah. He opened (unrolled) the book and found the place where it was written,

'The Spirit of the Lord [is] upon Me, because He has anointed Me [the Anointed One, the Messiah] to preach the good news (the Gospel) to the poor; He has sent Me to announce release to the captives and recovery of sight to the blind, to send forth as delivered those who are oppressed [who are downtrodden, bruised, crushed, and broken down by calamity], to proclaim the accepted *and* acceptable year of the Lord [the day when salvation and the free favors of God profusely abound.]'"

Luke 4:16–19 (The Amplified Bible)

Table of Contents

Introduction 11

Part One—*Beginnings*
Chapter One: In the Beginning, God Saw… 23
   Chapter One Evaluation 27
Chapter two: The Eye of the Beholder 31
   Chapter Two Evaluation 36
Chapter Three: Creativity and the Dynamic Process 39
   Chapter Three Evaluation 43
Chapter Four: When the Patriarchs Met God 45
   Chapter Four Evaluation 59
Chapter Five: What's In a Name? 61
   Chapter Five Evaluation 70
Chapter Six: The Prophet of Exceeding Increase 73
   Chapter Six Evaluation 84
Chapter Seven: "On the Mountain of the Lord It
Will Be Provided" 89
   Chapter Seven Evaluation 99
Chapter Eight: "I Have Met El-Roi" 101
   Chapter Eight Evaluation 109

Chapter Nine: Room Enough 111
   Chapter Nine Evaluation 127

Part Two—*Activating God's Anointing*
Chapter One: God's Holy Symphony of Doing. 133
   Chapter One Evaluation. 149
Chapter Two: Reclaiming Your Roots: The Experience
Of Supernatural Muchness 151
   Chapter Two Evaluation. 167
Chapter Three: Ability with God and Men. 169
   Chapter Three Evaluation. 182
Chapter Four: What Would You Do If You Knew
You Could Not Fail? 185
   Chapter Four Evaluation 199
Chapter Five: The Heritage of Israel. 203
   Chapter Five Evaluation 213
Chapter Six: The Secret Things of the Lord 215
   Chapter Six Evaluation 221
Chapter Seven: Commitment Determines Destiny!. 225
   Chapter Seven Evaluation. 236
Chapter Eight: The Wind Ran Out of Breath. 239
   Chapter Eight Evaluation. 246
Chapter Nine: Divine Conceptions: God's Conclusion 251
   Chapter Nine Evaluation 263

Appendix: The Science of "Seeing" 265
Endnotes. 303

Introduction

> Do not conform any longer to the pattern of this world, but be transformed by the renewing of your mind. Then you will be able to test and approve what God's will is—His good, pleasing, and perfect will.
>
> Romans 12:2 (NIV)

What would you do if you knew you could not fail? Have you ever had an "Aha!" moment when you were suddenly awakened from a dark, spiritual stupor as heaven reached down to infuse your soul with mystical insight (a holy intuition)? There is something about such God-moments that are wonderfully invigorating. Like Jacob at Bethel, you looked into heaven and were suddenly changed. "Surely the Lord is in this place; and I knew it not," he exclaimed, trying to frame his experience in the context of mere mortal words (Genesis 28:16, KJV[1]).

My moment of sudden awakening came one Sunday morning after stepping into the pulpit of a church in Fort Worth, Texas. My wife and I had recently left our previous ministry after many years of service. Aimlessly wandering in a spiritual morass of doubt and self-recrimination, we went from place to place in search of a new church—one she and I could call "home." What would we do and where would we go?

Suddenly, in a flash of awareness, I met the Lord and I knew beyond all shadow of doubt that He knew exactly where I was. He held my destiny in the palm of His hand. I've since likened my experience to that of Hagar in the wilderness. She met the Lord near a spring in the desert. "Hagar," He said, calling her by name, "where have you come from, and where are you going?" (Genesis 16:8, NIV). God's question haunts me to this day. It frames my existence because, when faced with my mortal roots and my inherent weaknesses, I realize my hopelessness. Without God's help, my prospects of rising from the morass of mediocrity are slim. Like Isaiah who saw the Lord sitting upon a throne, high and lifted up, I cry, "Woe is me, For I am undone." (Isaiah 6:5, KJV).

I've also come to realize that heaven's inquiry has broader implications. It is heaven's call to all people of every ilk and disposition. The Lord wants each of us to prosper and increase, but we must first carefully consider our beginnings and future intensions. With what's in your hand, have you the wherewithal to finish well? Divinity demands an honest reply. "Where have you come from, and where are you going?"

It's not that God doesn't know the answer, because He does. He wants you and me to personally come to grips with His solution. His question is perhaps one of the most sacred of all inquiries. If you and I can only realize the truth of His inquiry, we can rightly begin to appropriate our heritage in Him. "Where have you come from, and where do you plan to be tomorrow?" Will you be much better off next week than you are today? Be honest. Do your roots (i.e., your upbringing, your past "baggage," and your inherent weaknesses) weigh you down so that you merely exist from one day to the next? "Woe is me! I am ruined!" (Isaiah 5:5, NIV).

From the record of Hagar's life, we know that God saw her comings and goings. He saw Hagar's wretched plight under the heavy-hand of her mistress, Sarai. He saw Hagar's servitude and her misery. Something had to change! But how? What?

At the same time that I was contemplating the answer to these questions, I happened to overhear a conversation between three Christian women who were sitting at a nearby table. I was in a restaurant at the time and was considering Hagar's dilemma at the time. I heard one of the women exclaim, "I need wisdom and revelation."

"Don't we all!" I quietly whispered to myself.

As Hagar contemplated her answer to the Lord's question, a flash of divine insight flooded into her parched, desolate soul. Likewise, in my own eureka-moment when standing in front of the Fort Worth congregation, I too had a sudden spark of rejuvenating insight. All I could do was stand speechless and weep. The crowd within that church building gawked, probably wondering what sort of preacher I was. They could sense I'd experienced something, perhaps an epiphany, but like Paul's companions on the road to Damascus, they knew not what. I had met the God of Hagar's vision, *El Roi*, the "God of Seeing" (Genesis 16:13, The Amplified Bible, AMP).

Flushed with that very special awareness, I didn't know until later that I was also given an extraordinary gift. With my supernatural *knowingness* also came *know-how* (i.e., a requisite capacity and capability) to see it accomplished. This book is all about this dawning awareness. It is what I've come to call *knowingness* with *know-how*; God's *Divine Conception*, His Producing Principle for supernatural strength and vitality.

Through the principles revealed in this book, *The Divine Conception*, I will show you how to discover your own unique awareness of God. You will also learn to make God's blessings work for you, your family, and for those around you. Like Jacob of old, you will be awakened to the realization of God's full bounty. "Surely the Lord is in this place, and I was not aware of it," declared the patriarch at the time of his visitation. "How awesome is this place...[it] is the gate of heaven" (Genesis 28:16–17, NIV). The Amplified Bible's rendition of this passage is particularly insightful. Jacob was afraid when his eyes were suddenly opened. Thus, he declared, "How to be feared *and* reverenced is this place! This is none other than the house of God, and this is the gateway to heaven!" (v. 17).

The Divine Conception explores Jacob's experiences, as well as those of Hagar. We shall also explore the unfolding producing principles of God as revealed to Abraham and Isaac. Additionally, we will examine the beginnings of God's *Israel*; for within the special revelations given to Leah (Jacob's wife), we will find the keys to the gateway of heaven. A gate, Jacob's explicit expression to clarify his divine encounter, is an opening or entrance that permits passage from one place (or realm) to another. Jacob awoke to a new and different reality. *The Theological Wordbook of the Old Testament* says the root idea is "to split open" or "to break through."[2] Together, we shall "break through" into new realms of possibility.[i]

The Lord's producing principles are hallowed ground, being consecrated from the start. Recognizing this, Jacob took the stone from beneath his head and set it up as a pillar (a monument to the vision in his dream). He then poured oil on top of it in dedication, forever marking the place as special.

On that fateful day, Jacob also made a vow. "If God [*Elohiym*] will be with me and will watch over me on this journey I am taking and will give me food to eat and clothes to wear so that I return safely to my father's house, then the Lord will be my God [*Elohiym*] and this stone that I have set up as a pillar will be God's [*Elohiym's*] house, and of all that you give me I will give you a tenth" (Genesis 28:20–22, NIV).

Elohiym is a general reference to god in an ordinary sense. Jacob dedicated himself to the exceeding God—but reservedly! The "if" of his declaration is found in many translations of verse 20 and suggests that Jacob still hadn't made up his mind about the Lord. "If God will be with me ... then," he vowed (NKJV[3]). A man must first realize he is lost before he can be saved. This is the heart of the matter! It's where wholeness with God first begins.

What if Hagar had chosen to stay on the same old path that leads nowhere? What would have become of her and her child? In the Lord's profound question, "Where have you come from, and where are you going?" I believe God is suggesting that it is up to each of us to avail ourselves of His needful change. Rescue and salvation are readily at hand, if only you and I will yield in submission.

---

[i] Our path of discovery is accompanied by many references to mark their worth. They help set forth God's orchestrated revelation of divine increase and productivity. They will buttress your faith and firmly establish the Lord's holy principles within your heart and life.

Admittedly, Hagar's life was a mess! With nowhere to go, she traveled down the no-name road of mediocrity that ultimately leads to death and destruction. It is littered with the dry and brittle bones of many who have wandered there and is simply called the road that leads to Shur (Genesis 16:7).

Been there, done that. Like Hagar, I too have aimlessly drifted through life with clouded eyes full of self-pity and doubt. I am Hagar's cousin, her near relative. Like Hagar, I've traveled along similar paths; heading who knows where with little hope of reprieve.

I *am* Hagar and I've walked in her footsteps.

I *am* Hagar and I've been lost.

I *am* Hagar and have traveled the backroads of life.

But now, like Hagar, I've also met God!

In the Lord's questions is the prospect of hope and divine guidance. Why ask if He was not prepared to lead? Thereafter, God said: "Then you will *know* which way to go, since you have never been this way before" (Joshua 3:4a, NIV, emphasis mine).

Without a doubt, I now know that God sees me and knows my plight. He knows where I am and has determined my destiny. There is no longer any doubt as to my fate because I know I am safely in His hands. *El Roi*, the God Who Sees Me, is the keeper of my soul.

Now it's up to you. It's your turn! Since God is no respecter of people, you too can share in the divine blessings revealed to Hagar. There is no longer any reason to be downcast because the Lord has devised a sure plan of redemption and salvation.

The Divine Conception is the outcome of my encounter with *El Roi* (The Lord Who Sees Me). *The Divine Conception* reveals God's producing principles for supernatural growth, increase, and spiritual strength with vitality. Throughout the book is woven the Lord's question that frames our discussion: "Whence camest thou and whither wilt thou go?" (Genesis 16:8, KJV). "Behold!" is the Lord's challenge (Genesis 16:11, KJV). Our quest is to "see now" (behold with eyes wide-open). Consequently, let us diligently pursue the task that is set before us. In the end, you too shall exclaim, like Hagar: "I have now seen the One Who sees me" (Genesis 16:13, NIV).

So she called the name of the Lord Who spoke to her, "You are a God of seeing," for she said, "Have I [not] even here [in the wilderness] looked upon Him Who sees me [and lived]? Or have I here also seen [the future purposes or designs of] Him Who sees me?" Therefore the well was called *Beer-lahai-roi* [A well to the Living One Who sees me]; it is between Kadesh and Bered.

Genesis 16:13–14 (AMP)[4]

Keil and Delitzsch said in their commentary on the above Scripture:

> In the angel, *Hagar recognized God manifesting Himself to her*, the presence of Jehovah, and called Him, "Thou art a God of seeing; for she said, 'Have I also seen here after seeing?'" Believing that a man must die if he saw God (Exodus 20:19; 33:20), Hagar was astonished that she had seen God and remained alive, and called Jehovah, who had spoken to her, "God of seeing," i.e., who allows Himself to be seen, because here, on the spot where this sight was granted her, after seeing she still saw, i.e., remained alive. From this occurrence the well received the name of "well of the seeing alive," i.e., at which a man saw God and remained alive …
>
> On this ground Delitzsch and others have decided in favour of the interpretation given in the Chaldee version, "Thou art a God of seeing, i.e., the all-seeing, from whose all-seeing eye the helpless and forsaken is not hidden even in the farthest corner of the desert." "Have I not even here (in the barren land of solitude) looked after Him, who saw me?" and Beer-lahai-roi, "the well of the Living One who sees me, i.e., of the omnipresent Providence."[5]

But there's one thing more worth considering as we begin this study of the Lord's *Divine Conception*. "Wouldn't it have been a sad commentary on God if He promised multiplied descendants but gave Hagar none? Similarly, what if He told her to raise up her child and support him, yet failed to provide adequate strength to do so? Indeed, all men are supremely destitute if God's commands are not also divinely enabled. For this reason, with heaven's visions also come requisite capacity and capability to see them through! This is why God said to her in a later visitation, "What aileth thee, Hagar? Fear not..." (Genesis 21:17, KJV). I believe He was challenging her to live up to her previous visitation. She already possessed divine enabling to live and prosper because God's supernatural strength and vitality resided within. His question, "What troubles you, Hagar?" (AMP) suggest she had hidden reserves of strength long ignored or forgotten.

> And God heard the voice of the youth, and the angel of God called to Hagar out of heaven and said to her, "What troubles you, Hagar? Fear not, for God has heard the voice of the youth where he is."
>
> "*Arise, raise up the youth and support him with your hand* for I intend to make him a great nation."
>
> Then God opened her eyes and she saw a well of water; and she went and filled the [empty] bottle with water and caused the youth to drink.
>
> Genesis 21:17–19 (AMP), emphasis added.

According to the above passage, what is required of you and me once enlightened? First, we must realize that within our hands is God's cure for what ails us (i.e. our grief and troubles). Then we must *rise* unto God's appointed tasks. In Hagar's case, her well of refreshment was not far off, it was only a stone's throw away but she had to "rise" unto the Lord's goodness and partake. To her was given the responsibility of "rising" so as to avail herself of heaven's provision (i.e. that which was placed in her hands).

Your prayer and mine should always be, "Lord, open my eyes that I may see. Allow me to regard Your wonders and partake thereof.

And, Lord, grant me the ability to "lift up" the offspring of Your holy intension and support with my hand Your holy charge."

As we begin, you may be wondering what it is that God has placed within your grasp. We shall also discuss this, and much more. *The Divine Conception* will reveal life-changing truths that will set you free. Therefore, diligently follow along with me and, step by step, we shall be wonderfully rejuvenated.

So it was that Hagar, with open eyes, saw her well of provision. She perceived her salvation, and she rose unto it. In that strength, she filled her empty jar with cool water and gave it away to her son. She was divinely empowered to minister to others in keeping with her "beholding."

God's holy intention is realized only as we open our eyes to behold His provision, respond accordingly, and then give it away. It is an awful responsibility to have our eyes opened and yet to refuse the blessing revealed.

Hagar's story is usually read dismissively, with little regard or interest. But the story foretells the destiny of all people who dare rise according to the Lord's design. Hagar opened her eyes with divinely inspired awareness unto a whole new regime of possibilities—a new reality that was pregnant with potential. Thus, she was propelled into God's holy "muchness" (His whole provision).

My life has never been the same since that day when I first encountered the God of Hagar, *El Roi*. When I came to know "the God Who Sees Me" I no longer doubted my future. *El Roi* watches over me to give me strength—divine potency to accomplish His will. Even as God told Hagar to *rise up* and *see to it*, so too has He empowered me. *The Divine Conception* describes this holy symphony of doing, God's means of accomplished greatness. This book will buttress your heavenly experience and bring it to fruition.

Part One of *The Divine Conception* gives practical guidelines that will help you discover your own unique gifting from God. You will learn the important principles of what I call "right seeing" and "right hearing" in the Lord's orchestrated plan of vitality.

Part Two of *The Divine Conception* builds upon the beginning principles of "seeing" and "hearing" and adds the fundamental ingredients of connectedness and active participation. Moses referred to these transformational principles in Deuteronomy 29:29 as "the secret things [that] belong to the Lord our God" (NIV). Jesus called them "the keys of the kingdom of heaven" (Matthew 16:19, NIV). When correctly applied, you too can experience God's supernatural increase with divine vitality: growing and producing a crop that is multiplied thirty, sixty, and even a hundred times. "The secret of the kingdom of God has been given to you," declares the Lord (Mark 4:11a, NIV).

Part One

Beginnings

CHAPTER ONE

In the Beginning, God Saw ...

> In the beginning God created the heavens and the earth. Now the earth was formless and empty, darkness was over the surface of the deep, and the Spirit of God was hovering over the waters.
>
> Genesis 1:1–2 (NIV)

From the desolation and barren waste of chaos, God began to organize. Confusion gave way to the Creator's inspired hands as He looked upon His handiwork. Seven times in the opening verses of the Holy Scriptures, it is written, "God saw..." (Genesis 1:4, 10, 12, 18, 21, 25, 31; NIV). Additionally, seven times we are told He beheld His creation with great pleasure—He saw that it was *good*.

> And God said, "Let there be light," and there was light. *God saw that the light was good,* and he separated the light from the darkness.
>
> Genesis 1:3–4 (NIV), emphasis added

And God said, "Let there be an expanse between the waters to separate water from water." So God made the expanse and separated the water under the expanse from the water above it. And it was so. God called the expanse "sky." ... *and God saw that it was good.*

      Genesis 1:6–8a, 10b (NIV), emphasis added.

Then God said, "Let the land produce vegetation: seed-bearing plants and trees on the land that bear fruit with seed in it, according to their various kinds." And it was so ... *and God saw that it was good.*

      Genesis 1:11–12 (NIV), emphasis added.

And God said, "Let there be lights in the expanse of the sky to separate the day from the night, and let them serve as signs to mark seasons and days and years, and let them be lights in the expanse of the sky to give light on the earth." And it was so. God made two great lights—the greater light to govern the day and the lesser light to govern the night. He also made the stars. God set them in the expanse of the sky to give light on the earth, to govern the day and the night, and to separate light from darkness. *And God saw that it was good.*

      Genesis 1:14–18 (NIV), emphasis added.

God said, "Let the water teem with living creatures, and let birds fly above the earth across the expanse of the sky." So God created the great creatures of the sea and every living and moving thing with which the water teems, according to their kinds, and every winged bird according to its kind. *And God saw that it was good.*

      Genesis 1:20–21 (NIV), emphasis added.

And God said, "Let the land produce living creatures according to their kinds: livestock, creatures that move

along the ground, and wild animals, each according to its kind." And it was so ... *and God saw that it was good.*
Genesis 1:24–25 (NIV), emphasis added.
God saw all that he had made, and it was very good. And there was evening, and there was morning—the sixth day.

Genesis 1:31 (NIV), emphasis added.

Why is *seeing* (*ra'ah* in the original language) emphasized in creation's story? Can it be that seeing (*ra'ah*) somehow plays a vital role in the overall creative process? Why else would it be mentioned seven times in the opening verses of the Bible? In particular, notice the role of God's seeing as emphasized in Genesis 1:31. The Amplified Version of this verse says, "And God saw everything that He had made, and behold, it was very good (suitable, pleasant) *and* He approved it completely. And there was evening and there was morning, a sixth day." Also notice that the same passage emphatically highlights the Lord's satisfaction with those things *seen* (*Strong's* OT:7200).[1] "Behold, it was very good (suitable, pleasant) *and* He approved it completely" (Genesis 1:31b, AMP).

With intelligent design and oversight, the Lord rightly discerned His ordained creation. God's cognition somehow played an essential role in the creative scheme. He affirmed His creative work—God *saw* that it was good!

Vine's Dictionary on *ra'ah* notes that this important verb has several extended meanings.

> *Ra'ah* can refer to "perceiving or ascertaining" something apart from seeing it with one's eyes, as when Hagar saw that she had conceived (Genesis 16:4). It can represent mentally recognizing that something is true: "We saw certainly that the Lord was with thee..." (Genesis 26:28). Seeing and hearing together can mean "to gain understanding": "... Kings shall shut their mouths at him: for that which had not been told them shall they see; and that which they had not heard shall they consider" (Isaiah 52:15).[2]

In the process of shaping the cosmos, the Lord saw His creation and, as inferred by his hearty concurrence, came into active accord with it. From the very beginning, the Holy Writ is clear: God's consciousness is implicit in the origin of all things, then and now. First, at the most subtle levels, "God *saw* that the light was good (suitable, pleasant) *and* approved it" (Genesis 1:4a, AMP). All things began, and still continue, with light and the mechanics of light and energy at their base. This is the subject of later chapters concerning scientific discoveries relating to light and its special properties.

Following His creation of light, the Lord divided it from its close cousin, darkness (Genesis 1:4). He saw that it was good and separated it; giving light its own distinct and separate realm or energetic sphere of influence. By inference, the Creator did the same for "darkness" and it dominion.

After that, God created the vastness above, separating it from the expanse beneath. Time and again, the Creator separated and saw that it was good. In doing so, He fashioned distinctiveness and universal boundaries.

Thus, the Lord's *seeing* was and continues to be the fundamental principle from which all things spring and are fashioned. As identified by Jesus, *seeing* with perception is the first requisite ingredient of conversion and forgiveness of sins (Mark 4:12). To understand this is practical insight for daily living. *The Theological Wordbook of the Old Testament* notes that wisdom is not theoretical and speculative but is practical and based on revealed principles of right and wrong, to be lived out in daily life. It is the "perfect blend of the revealed will of a holy God with the practical human experiences of life."[3]

Chapter One Evaluation

1. Read the first chapter of the Old Testament book of Genesis. Notice how the Bible, time and again, says, "God *saw* that it was good." Why is this statement repeated seven times? What does its repetition suggest? In your estimation, is *The Seeing Principle* an essential element in the creative scheme? Does *seeing* somehow play a role in the shaping, the continuance, and the molding of all things created?

2. Now consider the repeated statements in Genesis that God looked upon His various creations and saw that they were good or very good. Does this suggest that the Creator's recognition (i.e. His creative thoughts) somehow also played a role in the creative scheme? Since we are created in the image of God, does this also suggest that our cognition somehow plays an essential part in the creative scheme?

3. The Scriptures say time and time again, "And God *saw* that it was good" (Genesis 1:10, 12, 18, 21 and 25; NIV). In verse 31 of the same chapter, we are told that God saw *all* that he had made and it was "very good." Everything was included. God looked on His handiwork, evaluated its worthiness (i.e., that it was well-ordered and complete), and then came into agreement with it. Would you agree that God's affirmation was somehow important to the overall creative process? Furthermore, what does it infer regarding your own positive affirmation concerning the many things God has brought into your life? Read 1 Thessalonians 5:16–18.

4. J. Bolton, in *The Biblical Illustrator*, asks, "*Why* was it very good?" If within a group setting, discuss Bolton's answers. First, he says it was very good because it was the offspring of infinite wisdom and power and love. Secondly, Bolton says it was very good because it was guided into existence by Jesus (i.e., God). Thirdly, it was very good because there was no evil in it. Finally, Bolton concludes it was very good because it was like God.[4] Do you agree? What is the impli-

cation of Bolton's fourth supposition? Is Bolton suggesting that creation is somehow invested with God's essence (i.e. His goodness) through the process of seeing and requisite comprehension? Additionally, are wholehearted concurrence with, and affiliation, necessary ingredients of the creative recipe?

5. J. Bolton also asks, "*What* was very good?" "Everything," he answers.[5] Are we sometimes selective in our praise or thanks? Think about it. If everything has the potential of divine "goodness" (bounty, joy, love and latent pleasure), you and I are charged with an awesome prospective. To make such things our own and bring them into our lives, we must begin by looking with God's eyes so as to rightly behold them. Secondly, we must correctly comprehend right associations, relationships, and cohesions. This is wisdom, the revelation of right and wrong to be lived out in daily life. Finally, we must come into absolute, wholehearted agreement and affiliation with God. This is why Jesus instructed His disciples on the matter of faith. He said in Matthew 7:20: "I tell you the truth, if you have faith as small as a mustard seed, you can say to this mountain, 'Move from here to there' and it will move. Nothing will be impossible for you" (NIV). Do you agree?

6. At this point, having only read the first chapter of this book, you may be thinking we've wandered onto "spooky" ground that borders on the metaphysical. For this reason I challenge you to read on. I'll continue to use numerous Biblical references and quotations to calm your doubts and fears. The appendix also shares recent scientific discoveries in quantum mechanics that will further support the principles presented herein. First J. Bolton asked, "*Why* was it very good?" Then he asked, "*What* was very good?" Finally, he asked, "*How* are they [the created works of God] very good?" He answers: "In themselves—in their purposes—in their arrangements." Is everything "very good" still? This

was Bolton's final quandary. Take a moment and honestly evaluate your life. Is everything "very good" according to the Lord's definition? Admittedly, many things have gone wrong awry and are askew because of the introduction of sin. To this, Bolton says: "God is [still] fetching very good things out of the apparent frustration of His plan. He is restoring what is now very bad to be very good."[6] You have a vital role in His creative scheme. God's Producing Principle for supernatural strength and vitality is yours to discover. It is His Divine Conception.

CHAPTER TWO

The Eye of the Beholder

> Thus the heavens and the earth were completed in all their vast array.
>
> Genesis 2:1 (NIV)

Repeatedly, the Creator looked upon His creation, measuring it with a practiced eye. It was good!

> God saw that the light was good.
>
> Genesis 1:4a (NIV)

> And God saw that it was good.
>
> Genesis 1:10b (NIV)

> And God saw that it was good.
>
> Genesis 1:12b (NIV)

And God saw that it was good.

> Genesis 1:18b (NIV)

And God saw that it was good.

> Genesis 1:21b (NIV)

And God saw that it was good.

> Genesis 1:25b (NIV)

God saw all that he had made, and it was very good.

> Genesis 1:31a (NIV)

The Lord assessed the fitness of all He'd made and it was *good* (*towb* in the original language: *beautiful, best, bountiful, cheerful,* and *well-favored*). In God's creative scheme, first He saw, and then He measured. Finally, the Creator actively acquiesced to all things created by coming into vigorous agreement. Seven times, the Lord declared the making of His hands to be "fit." "He saw that everything created was "good" (Genesis 1:4, 10, 12, 18, 21, 25 and 31, NIV). The fact that His acquiescence was affirmed seven times signifies completeness or totality. Zechariah conveys this thought in his vision of God's seven eyes that oversee His creation. "Who [with reason] despises the day of small things...[These seven] are the eyes of the Lord which run to and fro throughout the whole earth" (Zechariah 4:10, AMP).

The first chapter of Genesis is the archetype of the Lord's Producing Principle, that which I call *The Divine Conception*. It is no accident that the Holy Scriptures emphasize the Creator's *seeing* (i.e., *ra'ah* in the original language). Furthermore, the measure of "goodness" (repeatedly emphasized in the first chapter of Genesis) underscores the importance of conscientious assent in the creative process. Knowingness with understanding and agreement is essential in the creation of all things.

But, as pointed out, one thing was still lacking. In addition to the creative principle of seeing with conscientious assent, there was still "no man to work the ground" (Genesis 2:5b, NIV). In accordance with God's holy design, there must always be a conscious participant in the creative scheme. There was no *'adam* (the Hebrew word for mankind) actively *employed* (*'abad*) within the Lord's fields. *'Abad,* in the original text, means, among other things, *to bring to pass* or *do service*.[1] Hence, God shaped man in His own image, making him maximally efficient to bring the creation to its fullness and to keep order. "The Lord God took the man and put him in the garden of Eden to work it and take care of it" (Genesis 2:15, NIV). Thus, the Lord said to Adam, "Be fruitful...fill the earth, and subdue it."

> So God created man in His own image, in the image and likeness of God He created him; male and female, He created them. [Colossians 3:9, 10; James 3:8, 9.] And God blessed them and said to them, "Be fruitful, multiply, and fill the earth, and subdue it [using all its vast resources in the service of God and man], and have dominion over the fish of the sea, the birds of the air, and over every living creature that moves upon the earth."
>
> Genesis 1:27–28 (AMP)

The Lord God looked upon His creation, measured its "goodness," and then came into agreement with it. He finally completed His work by making man in His Own image to use all its vast resources. "And the Lord God took the man and put him in the garden of Eden *to tend* and *guard* (*'abad*) and *keep* (*shamar*) it" (Genesis 2:15, AMP, emphasis mine). *Shamar* means *to hedge about* (*as with thorns*), *i.e. guard; generally, to protect, attend to, etc.*[2] *Shamar* could also be translated as "*be circumspect, take heed,* or *regard* as a watchman."[3]

What is mankind's role in the order of God's creation? Why are we created in the His image—like unto Him? What is the "image" of God? Are we the image of God by virtue of His bodily form? Since God has no outward appearance, and in light of the fact that man's body was formed from the dust of the ground, this is highly unlikely. Keil and Delitzsch's *Commentary on the Old Testament* observes that the words "in our image, after our likeness" are synonymous and are merely combined to add intensity to the thought: "an image which is like Us."[4] Keil and Delitzsch observe:

> There is more difficulty in deciding what the likeness to God consisted of—certainly not in the bodily form, upright position, or commanding aspect of the man, since God has no bodily form, and the man's body was formed from the dust of the ground; nor in the dominion of man over nature, for this is unquestionably ascribed to man simply as the consequence or effluence of his likeness to God. *Man is the image of God by virtue of his spiritual nature.* Of the breath of God by which the being, formed from the dust of the earth, became a living soul.[5]

The Wycliffe Bible Commentary on this same passage notes that God made man distinctly different from the animals already created. He stands on a much higher plateau.

> God created him to be immortal, and made him a special image of His own eternity. Man was a creature with whom his Maker could visit and have fellowship and communion. On the other hand, the Lord could expect man to answer him and be responsible to him.... He was to be God's responsible representative and steward on the earth, to work out his Creator's will and fulfill the divine purpose. World dominion was to be granted to this new creature (cf. Psalm 8:5–7). He was commissioned to subdue (*kabash, tread upon*) the earth and to follow God's plan in filling it with people. This sublime creature, with his unbelievable privileges and heavy responsibilities, was to live and move in kingly fashion.[6]

The above commentaries make it abundantly clear that mankind is the "image" of God by virtue of his spiritual nature. But does "image" of God also extend to likeness in ability, at least in part? It would seem so, since God gave to man the heavy responsibility of *subduing* the earth. "Be fruitful, multiply, and fill the earth, and subdue it [using all its vast resources in the service of God and man]; and have dominion over the fish of the sea, the birds of the air, and over every living creature that moves upon the earth" (Genesis 1:28b, AMP).

Wouldn't it have been a sad joke upon Adam and on all men thereafter if God said "subdue" and "rule" and then did not grant authority, capacity, or capability to do so? Thus, to men, God gave the same measuring eye, according to His own likeness, to do and keep—the eye of the Creator.

As we shall discover in later chapters of *The Divine Conception*, God gave to men His ability to rightly *see* (i.e., *ra'ah*) along with its awesome creative power. The next several chapters shall explore the ramification of this capacity and capability in light of Abraham's revelation. Abraham was the Lord's man who was greatly exalted to be the father of a multitude of people that would follow in the footsteps of their Creator.

The opening chapter of the Bible concludes with one last thought:

> Thus the heavens and the earth were finished, and all the host of them.
>
> And on the seventh day God ended His work which He had made ['*asah*: *Strong's* OT 6213]; and He rested on the seventh day from all His work which He had made ['*asah*].
>
> And God blessed the seventh day, and sanctified it: because that in it He had rested from all His work which God created and made ['*asah*].
>
> These are the generations of the heavens and of the earth when they were created, in the day that the Lord God made ['*asah*] the earth and the heavens,
>
> Genesis 2:1–4 (KJV)

God finished all that He had made (i.e., '*asah*: "accomplished, advance, appoint"[7]). This is the account of the Lord's *doing*.

Chapter Two Evaluation

1. God has empowered mankind "to work the ground" (Genesis 2:5b, NIV). We are made in His image with innate ability to bring forth the earth's increase. The phrase "there was no man to work the ground" suggests that man's "work" is a critical element in the Lord's scheme of doing (*'asah*). It follows that we are divinely equipped to do this "work." Do you agree and, if so, what is your equipping for the work of service?

2. The second chapter of Genesis explains that God made the heavens and the earth and created man in His image to harness (i.e. bring to pass) the earth's full potential. Man's duty is to "work" (till or dress) the same material substance of which he is made. When there was no man to work the ground [*'adamah*], the Lord God formed the man from the dust of the ground [*'adamah*] and breathed into his nostrils the breath of life to make him a living being. What is the earth without man? "Without man, the world would be a school without a pupil, a theatre without a spectator, a mansion without a resident, a temple without a worshipper... 'The earth He hath given to the children of men.' The nature of this gift proclaims the obligation of the receiver. The world is filled with material treasures; develop and use them. The world is fertile with moral lessons; interpret and apply them. The world is full with the presence of God; walk reverently."[8]

3. "Here begins that great system of Divine and human cooperation, which is still in progress," observes J. Parker in *The Biblical Illustrator*.[9] "There were trees, plants, herbs, and flowers, but a gardener was wanted to get out of the earth everything that the earth could yield. By planting, and transplanting, and replanting, you may turn a coarse tree into a rare botanical specimen—you may refine it by development. So man got something for his own pains and

became a sort of secondary creator!"¹⁰ Remember this statement as we slowly wade into the Lord's Holy Symphony of Doing—His producing principle of supernatural strength and vitality. Your challenge and mine is to grasp our various roles within God's scheme of eternity. As His children, we are prepared for works of service and made complete in the faith and in the knowledge of the Son of God. Thus, strive for this—"the whole measure of the fullness of Christ. "Then we will no longer be infants, tossed back and forth by the waves, and blown here and there by every wind of teaching and by the cunning and craftiness of men in their deceitful scheming" (Ephesians 4:13b-14, NIV).

4. Read Ephesians 2:10 which says we are God's workmanship, created in Christ Jesus to work within the ground He has provided for us. The Amplified version of this verse states: "For we are God's [own] handiwork (His workmanship), recreated in Christ Jesus, [born anew] that we may do those good works which God predestined (planned beforehand) for us [taking paths which He prepared ahead of time], that we should walk in them [living the good life which He pre-arranged and made ready for us to live]." Do you live "the good life which has been prearranged by God"; that which I call the Lord's *muchness*? If you don't have this fullness of reality, keep reading. *The Divine Conception* will develop this concept and much more using the patriarchs of Israel as our guides. Through their recorded experiences, we'll rediscover God's fullness as it is intended from the beginning of creation.

CHAPTER THREE

Creativity and the Dynamic Process

> In the beginning, God created (*bara'*) the heavens and the earth.... [He] created (*bara'*) the great creatures of the sea and every living and moving thing with which the water teems, according to their kinds, and every winged bird according to its kind ... [and] God created (*bara'*) man in His own image, in the image of God He created (*bara'*) him; male and female He created (*bara'*) them.
>
> Genesis 1:1; 21; 27 (NIV)

Two different creative processes are seen at work in the creation account. The opening chapter of the Bible records that God "created (*bara,*' Strong's OT:1254) the heavens and the earth" (Genesis 1:1, NIV). Importantly, *bara'* also describes mankind's origin. "So God created [*bara'*] man in His own image, in the image *and* likeness of God He created [*bara'*] him; male and female He created [*bara'*] them" (Genesis 1:27, AMP). Three times, the Hebrew verb *bara'* is used to describe the origins of mankind. The use of *bara'* emphasizes our unique creation (*bara'*) out of nothing (*ex nihilo*).

The second creative protocol is found in Genesis 1:7, 1:16, 1:25, 1:31, 2:3, 2:9, and 2:22. The Hebrew verb *'asah* (*Strong's* OT:6213) is used with the basic connotation of *do* or *make*.[1]

What differences in the creative process do these two words imply? According to *Vine's Expository Dictionary of Biblical Words*, the verb *bara'* is of profound theological significance because only God can "create" in the sense implied by *bara.'*

> Only God can "create" in the sense implied by *bara.'* The verb expresses creation out of nothing, an idea seen clearly in passages having to do with creation on a cosmic scale: "In the beginning, God created the heaven and the earth" Genesis 1:1; cf. Genesis 2:3; Isaiah 40:26; 42:5. All other verbs for *creating* allow a much broader range of meaning; they have both divine and human subjects and are used in contexts where bringing something or someone into existence is not the issue.... A careful study of the passages where *bara'* occurs shows that in the few non-poetic uses (primarily in Genesis), the writer uses scientifically precise language to demonstrate that God brought the object or concept into being from previously nonexistent material.[2]

John Hartley notes, "The OT [Old Testament] uses 'create' *(bara')* restrictively: only God serves as its subject, and the material out of which something is made is never mentioned. The terms 'the heavens' and 'the earth,' being at opposite ends of the spectrum, stand for the totality of what God created."[3]

The Lexical Aid to the Old Testament in the *Hebrew Greek Key Study Bible* notes that *bara'* emphasizes the initiation of the object, not its manipulation thereafter. "[*Bara'* refers to] activity, which can be performed [only] by God. Entirely new productions are associated with *bara'*...."[4] This same lexical aid also notes: "In the account of creation in Genesis, *bara'* (*Strong's* OT:1254) and *'asah* (*Strong's* OT:6213) alternate. *Bara'* conveys the thought of creation [out of nothing] *ex nihilo,* while *'asah*... dealt with *refinement*... the emphasis was on *fashioning* the created objects."⁵ The thought expressed is that God created the earth out of nothing (*ex nihilo*) and then commenced to "manipulate" and "refine" (*'asah*) it. We are made (*bara'*) in God's image and are endowed with ability to *'asah* (refine or manipulate). This is evidenced by the story of Benalel and Oholiab. These prominent craftsmen of the Old Testament were filled with God's Spirit to create (*'asah*) with His own might and power (*'asah, Strong's* OT:6213).

> God has given mankind *'asah*-ability to refine and manipulate His created wonders. For example, the Lord said to Moses, "See, I have chosen Bezalel son of Uri, the son of Hur, of the tribe of Judah, and I have filled him with the Spirit of God, with skill, ability and knowledge in all kinds of crafts—*to make* [i.e., *'asah*] artistic designs for work in gold, silver and bronze, to cut and set stones, to work in wood, and to engage in all kinds of craftsmanship" (Exodus 31:1–5, NIV). Additionally, God also gave skill to Oholiab and other craftsmen to help Bezalel *make* [i.e., *'asah*] all that was commanded by God. Said the Lord, "They are *to make* [i.e., *'asah*] them just as I commanded you"
>
> (Exodus 31:11, NIV), emphasis added).

Strong's definition of *'asah* includes concepts of "accomplishing, advancing, bringing forth and maintaining" so as to have charge of.⁶ Importantly, wisdom, ability, understanding, intelligence, and knowledge are part-and-parcel with God's creative ability (*'asah*). God said concerning Bezalel, "I have filled him with the spirit of God, in wisdom *and* ability, in understanding *and* intelligence, and in knowledge, and in all kinds of craftsmanship" (Exodus 31:3, AMP). The NIV translates this same passage as, "I have filled him with the Spirit of God, *with skill, ability, and knowledge in all kinds of crafts— to make* [*'asah*]" (emphasis mine).

In his book, *The Tao of Physics* (*tao* meaning *way* or *pathway*), Fritjof Capra discusses the two modes of human consciousness: the intuitive, which he describes as "higher" knowledge, and the rational, or "lower" knowledge. According to Capra, rational (lower) knowledge is derived from experience with objects and events in our everyday environment. "It belongs to the realm of the intellect, whose function it is to discriminate, divide, compare, measure, and categorize."[7] He states: "The realm of rational knowledge is, of course, the realm of science, which measures and quantifies, classifies and analyses."[8] But "higher knowledge" is different, in that it has creative potential that lies outside the realm of human intellect. Such insight often comes as an abrupt clarifying insight that adds critical information with life-changing implications.

> Rational knowledge and rational activities certainly constitute the major part of scientific research but are not all there is to it. *The rational part of research would, in fact, be useless if it were not complemented by the intuition that gives scientists new insights and makes them creative.* These insights tend to come suddenly and, characteristically, not when sitting at a desk working out the equations, but when relaxing in the bath, during a walk in the woods, on the beach, etc. During these periods of relaxation after concentrated intellectual activity, the intuitive mind seems to take over and can produce the sudden, clarifying insights which give so much joy and delight to scientific research.[9]

Chapter Three Evaluation

1. Have you ever experienced a sudden, intuitive awareness that can only be described as a *God-Moment*? Often such moments cause us to stop and take note. Try to recall a specific event or time when you and God "connected." Was there a sudden, invigorating awareness or liberation, almost as if shackles had abruptly dropped off? Were new frontiers of possibility suddenly opened? If in a group setting, try to recall your emotions. If alone, write down your thoughts and feelings. Try to remember how God spoke to you or touched you because such eureka-moments are very unique and special. This will help reinvigorate forgotten inspirations and previous anointing.

2. Do you recall the preceding discussion of Hagar's wilderness experience in the desert of Shur? God had given her a very special awareness of *El Roi* ("God Who sees me"). With that revelation she was also given a promise of multiplied descendants and requisite ability to make it happen. But what did she do with it? From the Lord's question on the occasion of their next meeting, it seems Hagar had forgotten her unique enabling. "What aileth thee, Hagar? Fear not..." said God (Genesis 21:17, KJV). Perhaps she failed to appropriate it and make it her own. Perhaps the daily rigors of life had pushed it far from her thought. For whatever reason, she'd shelved her revelation's special relevance. With this in mind, consider your own eureka-moment when you and God "connected." What have you done with it? Have you, like Hagar, shelved your very special awakening? Are you still living in the shadow of its revelation? In this regard, read John 15:1–8. What is the Lord's admonition?

3. In Hagar's later visitation, she was challenged to live up to what God had previously revealed. God's question suggests she already possessed divinely empowered integrity and know-how, but was in trouble for lack of its appropriation.

Jesus once likened Himself to the True Vine and His Father to the Vinedresser. He said any branch in Him that did not bear fruit, or stopped bearing, is cut away (trimmed off and taken away) by the Vinedresser. "He cleanses *and* repeatedly prunes every branch that continues to bear fruit," said Jesus, "to make it bear more *and* richer *and* more excellent fruit" (John 15:2, AMP). In other words, Hagar possessed hidden stores of strength to live and exceedingly prosper. Would God have given her a revelation without an enabling power to see it accomplished? In like manner, would God give you a special revelation without requisite power?

4. At this point you may be struggling to recall your own particular God-Moment. Perhaps you distantly remember a special time of anointing when you and God once met. Maybe you were kneeling at a quiet altar or were within your prayer closet. Perhaps it was a special word from God or maybe a rejuvenating, life-changing flash of intuitive insight into a Biblical passage. Whatever it was, do you recall your new sense of purpose? Often there was a wellspring of joy or a very deep, profound serenity? If possible, try to verbalize your experience or jot it down. At first you may find this difficult. Hagar found it difficult to verbalize and, hence, could only describe her encounter as, "I have met the God Who sees me!"

5. Our duty is to refine or fashion God's creation. This chapter's challenge is to revisit your special awareness and find again what's been given into your hands to do (*'asah*). Revive your God-Moment and its wonder. "Listen to me, you who pursue righteousness and who seek the Lord," [says the Lord]: "Look to the rock from which you were cut and to the quarry from which you were hewn; look to Abraham, your father, and to Sarah, who gave you birth. When I called him, he was but one, and I blessed him and made him many" (Isaiah 51:1–2, NIV). In the next several chapters we shall do as instructed and "look to Abraham" as our example.

CHAPTER FOUR

When the Patriarchs Met God

> Then he [Abram] proceeded from there to the mountain on the east of Bethel, and pitched his tent, with Bethel on the west and Ai on the east; and there he built an altar to the Lord and called upon the name of the Lord.
>
> Genesis 12:8 (NASU)[1]

> For you shall go out with joy, and be led out with peace; the mountains and the hills shall break forth into singing before you, and all the trees of the field shall clap their hands. Instead of the thorn shall come up the cypress tree, and instead of the brier shall come up the myrtle tree; *and it shall be to the Lord for a name*, for an everlasting sign that shall not be cut off.
>
> Isaiah 55:12–13 (NKJV), emphasis mine.

"Leave your country, your people, and your father's household and go to the land I will *show* you" (Genesis 12:1, NIV, emphasis added), commanded the Lord. Thus began a new way of life for the man named Abram. A covenant relationship was hatched between him and the Lord. First, God promised to *show* (i.e., *ra'ah*) him the way and then pledged to bless him with greatness. "Leave your country, your people and your father's household and go to the land I will show you," declared the Lord. "*I will make you into a great nation and I will bless you; I will make your name great; and you will be a blessing*" (Genesis 12:1–2, NIV). Then the Lord added an extra special favor. "I will bless those who bless you, and whoever curses you I will curse," said God; "and all peoples on earth will be blessed through you" (v. 3, NIV).

The next several chapters will explore the meaning of blessedness in God. What does it mean and what are its prerogatives? It's important to understand that the divine promise given to Abram was not just for him and his family but for "all the families *and* kindred of the earth be blessed [and by you they will bless themselves]" (Genesis 12:3b, AMP). For this reason, the apostle Paul cautions us to mull over and consider on a personal level everything that happened to Abraham. "Consider Abraham," he warns, "[because] 'He believed God, and it was credited to him as righteousness.' Understand, then, that those who believe are children of Abraham. The Scripture foresaw that God would justify the Gentiles by faith, and announced the gospel in advance to Abraham: 'All nations will be blessed through you.' So those who have faith are blessed along with Abraham, the man of faith" (Galatians 3:6–9, NIV).

The Lord swore His everlasting allegiance to Abram, the man who was eventually to be called Abraham. God promised blessing "with abundant increase of favors" (Genesis 12:2, AMP); that which I call "muchness." With only this assurance of continuing fidelity, Abram pursued his holy prerogative. He knew what he knew and that was enough for him. Heaven help us to be more like Abram. We must each grab hold of that which God has specifically given us and run with it, no matter what!

We casually skip over the events of the first verses of Genesis 12, failing to put ourselves in the man's shoes. Can you imagine Abram's inner turmoil when asked to abandon all ties to this world and move on lock, stock, and barrel? Consider the toll on his family and their apprehension. Abram was seventy-five years old. His life was already well-established; it was no small thing for him to simply pull-up stakes and leave it all behind. He would literally have to begin again and start over.

Around Abram swirled a storm of controversy. Those who didn't know him probably thought he'd lost his mind. Many well intentioned friends and relatives undoubtedly argued against his fanciful vision and questioned his judgment. One can only imagine their skepticism and convincing, logical arguments for staying put.

From Abram, we learn important lessons regarding the supernatural and all things divine. In most cases, those people closest to you will not understand your holy insight because such things are unique and uniquely known. Naysayers will question your judgment and others will talk to you of sensibility. Friends will tenderly pat you on the arm and warn you against such radical views. Some will even curse your folly. Therefore, learn from Abram and, despite all arguments to the contrary, tenaciously hold to your beliefs—your special knowingness. Abram knew what he knew, and that was enough for him!

Against all odds and in opposition to every logical sensibility, Abram packed his bags and went forth. The scriptures simply say, "So Abram departed, as the Lord directed him" (Genesis 12:4a, AMP). What an understatement! Am I right? It is much easier said than done.

What would you have done? Better yet, what have you done? To be painfully honest, we often who have heard from God often hesitate because of the perceived cost. We weigh the odds and wager against God. We decide it's more than we can bear. But be warned, if you and I are to follow the dictates of Paul as prescribed in Galatians 3:6–9, we must be prepared to take God at His word and follow Him unreservedly.

Does God expect you to wholeheartedly turn your back on everything you know and rely and simply pack your bags to move on? Yes, but only if He has specifically told you so. Like Abraham, we are assured of the outcome because "those who have faith are blessed along with Abraham" (Galatians 3:9, NIV). In addition, God's gifts and His call are irrevocable. That is, "He never withdraws them when once they are given, and He does not change His mind about those to whom He gives His grace or to whom He sends His call" (Romans 11:29b, AMP). That which God has specifically given to each of us should never be neglected or regretted. It is for this reason that I spend so many hours each week writing about and expounded on these precious truths. Like you, I too have a daily task to which I am called. It is what God has given me to do.

What, then, is in it for you if you wholeheartedly and unreservedly pursue that which God has given to you without regret? It's what the Lord promised Abram. "I will bless you [with abundant increase of favors] and make your name famous *and* distinguished, and you will be a blessing [dispensing good to others]. And I will bless those who bless you [who confer prosperity or happiness upon you" (Genesis 12:2b-3a, AMP).

In another day and time, Jesus said to those who were with Him, "Let us cross over to the other side" (Mark 4:35, NKJV). But to cross over to the other side, Jesus and His disciples had to first rise unto the appointed task. We can never expect significant gains while lounging in our beds. I've quoted this before because it is a favorite limerick from my childhood. Someone once wrote, "There once was a fellow named Ned who dined before going to bed; on pickles and ham, lobster and jam. And when he awoke, he was dead." Don't wait too long or put-off the things of God.

Can you imagine the many reasonable and logical objections to Jesus' immediate departure? After all, it was getting late and the sun was setting. The disciples could have said, "Shouldn't we wait until tomorrow and get a fresh start?" There are many objections to "crossing over" when in the darkness of night. But, much to their credit, not one word of dissension or reservation is expressed in the Scriptures. Despite every reasonable argument to the contrary, I believe the disciples saw the Lord's steadfast determination to cross over to the other side. End of discussion!

Countless arguments cause you and me to delay and thereby stumble. Many have tarried; never to begin again! Consider Abraham! He believed God despite the many arguments to the contrary, and it was credited to him as righteousness" (Galatians 3:6). Don't delay! Rise unto your appointed tasks.

> That day when evening came, he said to his disciples, "Let us go over to the other side." Leaving the crowd behind, they took him along, *just as he was*, in the boat.
>
> Mark 4:35–36 (NIV), emphasis mine.

Leaving the crowd behind, the disciples took Jesus *just as He was*. First, take your cue from the beginning words of Mark 4:36 (NIV). It's often necessary to leave the crowd behind when pursuing God. Furthermore, the same verse explains that Christ's disciples took Him "just as He was." They didn't try to encumber Him with their preconceived notions, ideas, or opinions. They simply *took Him as He was*. We would all do well to learn these lessons.

As instructed, the devoted band of disciples dutifully got into the boat with Jesus. They pushed off for distant shores, not knowing that a great storm was about to furiously break forth upon them.

> A furious squall came up, and the waves broke over the boat, so that it was nearly swamped. Jesus was in the stern, sleeping on a cushion. The disciples woke him and said to him, "Teacher, don't you care if we drown?"
>
> Mark 4:37–38 (NIV)

Terrible, unexpected storms are not uncommon when we finally decide to get in the boat with Jesus. All believers have experienced them. It is for this reason that most men row close to shore. But Mark's narrative reveals otherwise; the men with Jesus rowed far from shore, daring to cross by the shortest route possible. There is no beating around the bush with Jesus. After all, did not the Lord say, "Let us go over to the other side" (Mark 4:35, NIV)?

Being with Jesus, these experienced men of the sea did not expect such a fierce storm. They were blindsided and caught off guard by the furious squall. They rowed, they bailed, they strained against the giant seas, and they feared. No matter how much they struggled, however, they could not cross in the power of their own might. At any moment, their fragile craft was on the verge of capsizing and being torn asunder. They rowed some more, they bailed as fast as they could, they strained against the giant seas, and they greatly feared!

"Jesus, don't you care if we drown?" cried the men with Jesus. They woke Jesus, Who was nestled in the slumber of faith. The genuineness of one's faith is often revealed by its tranquility when tested.

So it was that Jesus arose to meet the storm on His own terms. He did not confront the storm while lying in the stern of the boat. There must always be a certain amount of rising unto the tasks of God. "He got up, rebuked the wind, and said to the waves, 'Quiet! Be still!' Then the wind died down, and it was completely calm. He said to his disciples, 'Why are you so afraid? Do you still have no faith?'" (Mark 4:39–40, NIV).

The Amplified Bible's rendition of this same passage says Jesus rose and told the sea to be muzzled.

> And He arose and rebuked the wind and said to the sea, "Hush now! Be still (muzzled)!" And the wind ceased (sank to rest as if exhausted by its beating) and there was [immediately] a great calm (a perfect peacefulness). He said to them, "Why are you so timid and fearful? How is it that you have no faith (no firmly relying trust)?"
>
> Mark 4:39–40 (AMP)

Returning to Abram's story, the scriptures simply say he departed according to the word of the Lord. Abram didn't know where he was going. Neither did he know his journey's duration. He sojourned with God by faith. With stubborn determination, Abram steadfastly pursued his vision. He knew what he knew—and that was enough!

In the end, the Bible simply says, "and they arrived there" (Genesis 12:5, NIV). The KJV says, "and into the land of Canaan they came." Thank God for these final words. "Count the cost!" warned Jesus, because it's worth it in the end.

> And whoever does not bear his cross and come after Me cannot be My disciple. For which of you, intending to

build a tower, does not sit down first and count the cost, whether he has enough to finish it—lest, after he has laid the foundation, and is not able to finish, all who see it begin to mock him, saying, "This man began to build and was not able to finish."

Luke 14:27–30 (NKJV)

Consider Abraham because we learn valuable lessons from him on *fleshing out* our special knowingness and knowhow in God. First, like Abraham, we must begin well. This requires that we hold fast to our God-given proficiency, no matter what. Despite all arguments to the contrary, and in spite of the odds or the opposition, Abram steadfastly pursued his Godly vision. Furthermore, he did not stop until he finally arrived at his journey's appointed end. Declares the writer of Hebrews, "Let us hold unswervingly to the hope we profess, for He Who promised is faithful" (Hebrews 10:23, NIV). Abram struck forth for an unknown destination; following an unfamiliar path at the Lord's behest. "Get thee out of thy country, and from thy kindred, and from thy father's house," said the Lord, "unto a land that I will shew thee" (Genesis 12:1, KJV).

What is true and right for you? First, be sure to measure your vision or special knowingness against the Bible for it is your only sure test. Be assured that God will never contradict Himself. "If a house is divided against itself, that house cannot stand," said Jesus (Mark 3:25, NIV). Consequently, always test your experience by the Word of God. "If you hold to My teaching, you are really My disciples," said Christ, "then you will know the truth, and the truth will set you free (John 8:31–32, NIV). The privilege of true Christian discipleship is that we know the truth and what proves it to be so. Additionally, Christ's truth brings a transforming sense of freedom to the human experience.

There is one thing more you must understand when pursuing God and your inspired vision. Always expect opposition regarding it because, even though it is completely compatible with God's revealed Word, it is incompatible with the world. As was once said of Amos' inspired message, "The land cannot bear all his words" (Amos 7:10b, NIV).

Consider Abraham. Because of his vision, he incurred the wrath of foreign rulers (Genesis 12:15; 20:2), beloved friends and relatives turned their back on him (Genesis 13:7), and wicked men envied him. However, despite the odds and every opposition, Abram continued to believe God. Even when his wife laughed, perhaps in disbelief, he held to his convictions (Genesis 18:12).

Even Abram sometimes had moments of weakness. Genesis 15: says, "*After this*, the word of the Lord came to Abram in a vision: 'Do not be afraid, Abram' [said God]. 'I am your shield, your very great reward.' But Abram said, 'O Sovereign Lord, what can you give me since I remain childless and the one who will inherit my estate is Eliezer of Damascus?' And Abram said, 'You have given me no children; so a servant in my household will be my heir.' Then the word of the Lord came to him: 'This man will not be your heir, but a son coming from your own body will be your heir.' He took him outside and said, 'Look up at the heavens and count the stars—if indeed you can count them.' Then He said to him, 'So shall your offspring be.' Abram believed the Lord, and he credited it to him as righteousness" (Genesis 15:1–6, NIV, emphasis mine).

Have you ever suffered an "after this" moment as did Abram (Genesis 15:1, NIV)? It seems he was momentarily fearful and doubted. However, despite all odds and contrary opinions, Abram "believed God, and it was credited to him as righteousness" (Romans 4:3, NIV). He remembered his special calling and refused to conform to the pattern of the world around him. Consequently, he was transformed by the renewing of his mind and, in the end, was able to test and approve what God's will was—the Lord's good, pleasing and perfect will (Romans 12:2). Consider Abraham!

Also, with revelation also comes proficiency (i.e., capacity and capability) to see it accomplished. Thus, God once again appeared to Abram and declared, "to your descendants I will *give* this land" (Genesis 12:7a, NIV, emphasis mine). Previously, the Lord had promised to *show* Abram the land (Genesis 12:1). This time, however, God declared to make it his own possession. "I will give this land to your posterity," declared God (Genesis 12:7, AMP)

From Abraham we also learn that revelation (spiritual awakening and revival) is almost always progressive...gradually unfolding as we leave behind our natural affections, affinities, and afflictions. "Go for yourself [for your own advantage] *away from your country*, from your relatives and your father's house, to the land that I will show you," declared God (Genesis 12:1, AMP). There are many things that restrain us from fully realizing God. We must, therefore, separate ourselves from them. Thus, when Lot chose to adopt the ways of Sodom rather than those of Jehovah, Abraham (Lot's uncle) said to him, "Is not the whole land before you? Separate yourself, I beg of you, from me. If you take the left hand, then I will go to the right; or if you choose the right hand, then I will go to the left" (Genesis 13:9, AMP). Consider Abraham!

So it was that when Abram was first called, he departed as the Lord directed him. Only then did divine insight begin to unfold; as he lived it, day-by-day, moment-by-moment, and from glory to glory. Matthew Henry comments:

> They went forth to go into the land of Canaan...they held on their way, and, by the good hand of their God upon them, to the land of Canaan they came, where by a fresh revelation they were told that this was the land God promised to show them. They were not discouraged by the difficulties they met with in their way, nor diverted by the delights they met with, but pressed forward. Those that set out for heaven must persevere to the end, still reaching forth to those things that are before. That which we undertake in obedience to God's command, and a humble attendance upon his providence, will certainly succeed, and end with comfort at last."[2]

Abram did not know all things about the Lord. In fact, he was spiritually naïve with regard to most things concerning his God. But such as he knew, he lived. He journeyed in this knowingness and it became the beginning of his strength.

> So he built an altar there to the Lord, who had appeared to him.
>
> Genesis 12:7b (NIV)

We lightly skip over verse 7 of Genesis 12 and miss its relevance regarding our own Christian experience. Abram's praise and worship was very specific and to the point. He did not praise a god. Neither did he praise God, in general. His praise was poignant and succinct. Abram worshipped the Lord he knew—the Lord Who appeared to him. Abram did not know all things about God but such as he knew and understood, he worshipped.

The importance of Abram's altar is made all the more plain in the next verse which says he went on from there toward the hills east of Bethel and pitched his tent. With Bethel on the west and Ai on the east, "he built an altar to the Lord *and called on the name of the Lord*" (Genesis 12:8, NIV). First, he built an altar to the Lord Who had appeared to him and then called on Him by name. Consider Abraham! His praise was poignant and to the point. Is yours? It was not nearly good enough for him to build an altar and worship the Lord *in general*. He worshipped very specifically according to his particular knowingness. Thus, so too should we praise.

The custom of calling on God *by His name* goes all the way back to the first man. It was not a new practice but was known from the beginning. When Adam's son, Seth, was born, Adam called upon God by "the name of the Lord" (Genesis 4:26; NIV, KJV, AMP).

> To Shet too was born a son, whom he called Enosh. That is when people began to call on the name [i.e., *shem*] of Adonai.
>
> Genesis 4:26 (CJB–*The Complete Jewish Bible*)

In the language of the Bible, *shem* (*Strong's* OT:8034) refers to an appellation, "as a mark or memorial of individuality; by implication honor, authority, character."[3] From the very beginning, men called upon God according to His revealed character or nature, that which they knew. Thus, Abram repeatedly called upon the revealed nature of his God (Genesis 12:8; 13:4; 21:33) according to his specific knowingness of it. So too did his son after him. Genesis 26:25 says Isaac built an altar and called on the name of the Lord.

With this in mind, I once again ask you to carefully consider your practice of praise. Consider Abraham! If he called upon the name of the revealed Lord as he knew it, so too should you and I. I believe it is for this reason that God declared we should never misuse His name. "The Lord will not hold anyone guiltless who misuses His name (Exodus 20:7b, NIV).

> You shall not use *or* repeat the name of the Lord your God in vain [that is, lightly or frivolously, in false affirmations or profanely]; for the Lord will not hold him guiltless who takes His name in vain.
>
> Exodus 20:7 (AMP)

For all the above reasons, the angel of the Lord was very succinct when it came to the name by which God's son would be called. "You are to give him the name Jesus, because he will save his people from their sins," declared the angel (Matthew 1:21, NIV). Why is God so particular about His name? I believe it is because associated power lies within its scope. So it was that the son's of Levi (Israel's priests) were to "pronounce blessings *in the name of the Lord* and to decide all cases of dispute and assault" (Deuteronomy 21:5, NIV, emphasis added). This is the primary principle of praise.

The revealed name and character of God must always be in our heart. It was for this reason that King David desired to build the temple in Jerusalem. The Lord said to him, "Whereas it was in your heart to build a temple *for My name, you did well that it was in your heart*" (1 Kings 8:17–18, NKJV, emphasis mine).

While the Scriptures are silent as to the exact name used by Abram when calling upon God, the text infers that he worshipped according to his own unique revelation of God—the revealed nature of the Lord that he knew. This is made plain when he later saw God in a new light—as *Jehovah-jireh.*

> Abraham looked up and there in a thicket he saw a ram caught by its horns. He went over and took the ram and sacrificed it as a burnt offering instead of his son. So Abraham called that place The Lord Will Provide. And to this day it is said, "On the mountain of the Lord it will be provided."
>
> Genesis 22:13–14 (NIV)

By what name did Abraham praise God when worshipping in the place he called *The Lord Will Provide*? Do you suppose he worshipped a god? Did he worship God, in general? I believe not. It makes sense that he worshipped very specifically—poignantly praising *The God Who Sees to It*. Furthermore, the Scriptures tell us that God responded accordingly. He called to Abraham from heaven a second time and said, "I swear by Myself..." I believe His oath was in keeping with His revealed nature that was appropriate to that time, *Jehovah-jireh*. "I [*the Lord Who Provides*] will surely bless you," declared God (Genesis 22:17, NIV).

Thus, when Abraham looked up and glanced around, he saw a ram caught in a thicket by its horns. Why hadn't he seen it before? I believe it was because the ram was freshly revealed to him by his Lord, the God of Provision.

Taking the ram, Abraham offered it up for a burnt offering and an ascending sacrifice! Abraham then called the name of that place *The Lord Will Provide*. Importantly, the Scriptures tell us: "And it is said to this day, on the mount of the Lord it will be provided" (Genesis 22:14b, AMP). The suggestion is that that divine aspect of God's provision is still present for all who find it.

The Lord's response to the man's praise is especially important. The Angel of the Lord called to Abraham from heaven a second time and said, "I have sworn by Myself... that since you have done this and have not withheld [from Me] or begrudged [giving Me] your son, your only son, *in blessing I will bless you and in multiplying I will multiply your descendants like the stars of the heavens and like the sand on the seashore. And your seed (Heir) will possess the gate of His enemies* ((Genesis 22:17, AMP). Thereafter, Abraham praised and worshipped *Jehovah-jireh* (*the Lord Who Provides*) and God responded accordingly. Consider Abraham! He lived in keeping with that which was in his heart and God blessed him with exceeding multiplication and increase (i.e. muchness). Furthermore, *Jehovah-jireh* (*the Lord Who Provides*) also gave Abraham requisite power to live within the scope of his revelation. As we shall later see, he possessed an uncanny ability to "see to it."

When God is specifically praised in keeping with a particular knowingness, expect His specific response. Hence, Abraham did not bow before a nebulous, indefinable god. He *knew* and was *known* by *Jehovah-jireh*. *Jehovah-jireh* was in his heart. *Jehovah-jireh* was a part of his being. Consider Abraham!

Now we come to the part where the rubber meets the road … how do *you* call upon the Lord? Do you call upon Him by name, according to the name and character that you've personally come to know? By what name do you praise Him? People throughout the ages have known God in a variety of ways, according to their varied revelations. Melchizedek knew Him as "God Most High," *El Elyown* (Genesis 14:20, NIV). To Hagar, He was the Seeing God, *El-Roi*. She gave this name to the Lord who spoke to her, saying: "You are the God who sees me. I have now seen the One who sees me" (Genesis 16:13, NIV). To Jacob, He was "The Mighty God of Israel," *El Elohe Israel*. For a hundred pieces of silver, Jacob bought a plot of ground where he pitched his tent. There he set up an altar and called it *El Elohe Israel* (Genesis 33:19–20, NIV). Moses also built an altar, calling it The Lord is my Banner [*Jehovah-nissi*]. He said, "For hands were lifted up to the throne of the Lord" (Exodus 17:15–16a, NIV). Gideon called upon God according to the name, "The Lord Is Peace," (*Jehovah-shalom*). He asked, "Lord, how can I save Israel?" The Lord answered, "I will be with you, … Peace! Do not be afraid" (Judges 6:16b&24 NIV).

Each of the saints called upon God according to his own unique *knowingness* of His holy character.

With Whom do you identify?
With Whom are you identified?
To Whom are you devoted?
Who do you praise?

The International Standard Bible Encyclopedia makes an interesting comment concerning the name Yahweh. Yahweh, it notes, is "the name most distinctive of God as the God of Israel…[and] was not first made known at the call of Moses (Exodus 3:13–16; 6:2–8), but, being already known, was at that time *given a larger revelation and interpretation*: God, to be known to Israel henceforth under the name 'Yahweh' and in its fuller significance, was the One sending Moses to deliver Israel."[4]

"Can God be known?" asks the writer of *The New Unger's Bible Dictionary*. According to this dictionary on the subject of God, the writer maintains: "The Scriptures declare that God is incomprehensible (see Job 11:7; 21:14; 36:26; Psalm 77:19; Romans 11:33). Perfect or complete knowledge of God is not attainable by man upon the earth. But equally true is that the Scriptures represent God as revealing Himself to man and that a sufficient, though limited, measure of true knowledge of God is put within the reach of human beings. The important distinction to be maintained at this point is that between partial and perfect knowledge. We cannot comprehend God, and yet we can truly know Him. Our blessedness, our eternal life even, is in such knowledge (see Matthew 11:27; John 17:3; Romans 1:19–20; Ephesians 1:17; Colossians 1:10; 1 John 5:20)."[5]

Chapter Four Evaluation

1. Have you ever shared your special revelation of God with others? How did they respond? Were they skeptical and disbelieving? Did those who heard your testimony stare at you with blank, unknowing eyes? If so, do not be discouraged. Reread the story of Joseph, the man known for his dreams (Genesis 37). Did his brothers share his wonder? What was his father's response? The Word of God says when he told his father his dreams, his father rebuked him but "kept the matter in mind" (Genesis 37:11, NIV). What would have become of his family and of all of Israel had he become discouraged and shelved his special anointing from God?

2. Recall your special God-Moment when heaven and earth met at your doorstep. What have you done since that fateful day of sudden *seeing*? Have you energized your divine cognition through emotional affiliation and intention, or have you allowed it to die through neglect? Have you "tended" and "kept it" according to the intent of Genesis 2:15? This passage says God "put man into the Garden to *tend* and *guard* and *keep* it" (AMP, emphasis added). What's become of your holy inspiration?

3. The injunction of Galatians 3:6 is that we consider Abraham. Like Abraham, does your personal praise reflect your inspired awareness of God? By what name do you call upon the Lord?

4. Learn from the great patriarchs of Israel who worshipped purposely according to their particular awareness and cognition of God. Read Genesis 12:8 and Genesis 13:4. What was special about Abram's altar? What does Genesis 22:13–14 say about Abraham's special altar where he met *Jehovah-jireh* (*the Lord Who Provides*)? In your estimation, did he worship God generally or specifically at that altar? Furthermore, why do the Scriptures say that they place of visitation where Abram met God was special? Does the passage suggest

that God's presence somehow invested that place with special anointing?

5. Lastly, read Joshua 22:21–23. The loyalty of the tribes of Reuben, Gad and the half-tribe of Manasseh was called into question. Some within Israel questioned their religious and spiritual integrity. Notice that their answer centered around their altar. "The Mighty One, God, the Lord," they said, "He knows! And let Israel know! If this has been in rebellion or disobedience to the Lord, do not spare us this day. If we have built our own altar to turn away from the Lord to offer burnt offerings and grain offerings, or to sacrifice fellowship offerings on it, may the Lord Himself call us to account" (Joshua 22:21–23, NIV). Obviously, the altar was of special significance to God's people. What does this say about our own altars? What does it say about your altar? Keep reading because we have much more to learn about the significance of altars and, specifically, *your* altar.

CHAPTER FIVE

What's In a Name?

> Therefore if anyone is in Christ, he is a new creature; the old things passed away; behold, new things have come.
>
> 2 Corinthians 5:17 (NASU)

> He who has an ear, let him hear what the Spirit says to the churches. To him who overcomes, to him I will give some of the hidden manna, and I will give him a white stone, and *a new name* written on the stone *which no one knows but he who receives it.*
>
> Revelation 2:17 (NASU), emphasis added.

In matters of faith and belief we are urged to "consider Abraham" (Galatians 3:6b, NIV). The Amplified Bible says: "Thus Abraham believed in *and* adhered to *and* trusted in *and* relied on God, and it was reckoned *and* placed to his account *and* credited as righteousness (as conformity to the divine will in purpose, thought, and action)." He knew what he knew and that was enough. Although he sometimes faltered, Abraham tenaciously clung to his divine promise of strength and well-being. Even when he was an old man and still without an heir, God said to him, "I am God Almighty; walk before me and be blameless" (Genesis 17:1b, NIV). But then He added, "I will confirm My covenant between Me and you and will greatly increase your numbers" (v. 2). Another version says God promised *exceeding* multiplication (NKJV).

But there was a matter that first had to be settled. When the Lord made this promise, the man was still called *Abram*. As such, he was still too limited in capacity and capability to live-up to his revelation. As *Abram*, he could not naturally appropriate the fullness of God's manifest destiny—His vigor and vitality. He was incapable of the Lord's *muchness*. Indeed, the *exceedingness* of God, with its consequent supernatural ability to multiply, was as far from Abram's grasp as were the stars of heaven. He was incapable of *beholding* the wonders of God's holy prerogative.

Hence, Abram had to wonderfully and divinely enlarged and transformed. So God said to the man: "As for Me, behold, My covenant is with you, and you shall be a father of many nations. No longer shall your name be called *Abram*, but your name shall be *Abraham*; for I have made you a father of many nations. *I will make you exceedingly fruitful*; and I will make nations of you, and kings shall come from you" (Genesis 17:4–6, NKJV, emphasis added).

The name *Abram*, in and of itself, was a good name. It meant *exalted father*. But it was not nearly good enough for God because it harkened back to Terah, Abram's mortal father. As such, the man's given name tainted him from birth with a natural lowness that was unbecoming of God. But as *Abraham*, the man's prospects hearkened unto God's manifest and limitless possibility. The name *Abraham* delineated a potentiality of divine increase with *muchness*. As God had said, "I will make you *exceedingly* fruitful," declared the Lord (Genesis 17:6, NKJV, emphasis added).

The Jamieson, Fausset, and Brown Commentary on Genesis 17:5 notes that in Eastern countries, the name given in infancy sometimes sets the course of life.

> A change of name is an advertisement of some new circumstance in the history, rank, or religion of the individual who bears it....The altered form may express the difference in the owner's state or prospects. It is surprising how soon a

new name is known and its import spread through the country. In dealing with Abraham and Sarai, God was pleased to adapt His procedure to the ideas and customs of the country and age. There was no way, according to prevailing notions, in which the divine promise would be so well remembered and the splendid prospects of the patriarch become more widely known than by giving him and his wife new names, significant of their high destiny. Instead of Abram = *Ab* or *Abba, father*, and *ram, high, a high father*, he was to be called Abraham = *Ab-rab-hamon*, father of a great multitude; and this has been verified, whether he is considered as the ancestor of the Jews, Arabs, etc., or as the Father of the Faithful.[1]

"You are *Abram* and we will not call you otherwise!" argued the man's many skeptics who knew him all too well. But Abraham was insistent, despite the fact that his body belied him. He was ninety-nine years old at the time.

Behind his back people called him presumptuous and pompous. They most certainly laughed, pointed fingers, and made him the brunt of their jokes. Without his same unique vision, everything Abraham argued for was unreasonable to their reasoning minds. This was especially so since Abraham's wife, Sarah, was ten years his younger and well beyond her childbearing years.

"It is who and what you are!" they argued. "Your name defines you," they said. "You are *Abram*, Exalted Father, and that's good enough. Live with it, and live by it. Your fanciful vision is only a figment of your pompous imagination. You've become a laughing stock!"

But despite the many arguments to the contrary, Abraham knew what he knew. He was gifted by God to be a father of great multitudes and, consequently, tenaciously held to his beliefs and his new name with its implied abilities. Inwardly, he knew he was no longer *Abram*. He was *Abraham*! In faith he believed that the unfolding of his new name would follow; that the progressive revelation of his new disposition would eventually become manifest.

Abraham was now who and what he was. He would be nothing less than what God called him. "I am who I am," he stubbornly persisted. "To call myself anything less would be a sin!"

Consider Abraham and never call yourself anything less than does God!

From that day forward, the Scriptures no longer refer to man by his former appellation, the name that was given to him at birth. As far as he and God were concerned, he was no longer *Abram* but *Abraham*. A new creation had been birthed with supernatural ability. Praise God!

Admittedly, the name *Abram* was a great and wonderful name. It meant *exalted father*. But the name *Abram* was also associated with the man's natural self and all its inherent flaws and frailties. Consequently, the man went forth, not as *Abram*, but as *Abraham*. The new name signaled a richer and higher character and destiny. To rise up as *Abram* was good, but to arise as *Abraham* was divine! It was in the capability of *Abraham* that the man would emerge *exceedingly* unto his new destiny of multiplied increase.

We must each come to grips with the realization that our inherent nature is weak and flawed. It is only as we come to this understanding that we can begin to step into our divinely appointed muchness as heirs of Abraham.

I opened this chapter with two scriptures. The first (2 Corinthians 5:17), testifies that any person who is grafted into Christ is a new creation (a new creature altogether). "The old [previous moral and spiritual condition] has passed away. Behold, the fresh *and* new has come!" (AMP). What then shall I call you if this is true?

The second verse that opens this chapter is Revelation 2:17. It confirms that we must have an ear toward that which the Spirit of God is saying to us.

> He who is able to hear, let him listen to *and* heed what the Spirit says to the assemblies (churches). To him who overcomes (conquers), I will give to eat of the manna that is hidden, and I will give him a white stone with a new name engraved on the stone, which no one knows *or* understands except he who receives it.
>
> Revelation 2:17, AMP

We each have a new name written in glory. Consequently, if we rightly look to Abraham as our guide and never call ourselves anything less than does God, we will be able to lift ourselves up from the doldrums of our present situation. A whole new reality waits; one that is divinely appointed.

Even now you may be wondering by what name God calls you. This is the subject of later chapters and, specifically, deals with the matter of hearing as intoned by the Revelator in Revelation 2:17.

Nelson's Illustrated Bible Dictionary gives valuable insight into the biblical use of names.

> Personal names (and even place names) were formed from words that had their own meaning. Thus, the people of the Bible were very conscious of the meaning of names. They believed there was a vital connection between the name and the person it identified. *A name somehow represented the nature of the person... in the giving or taking of new names, often a crucial turning point in the person's life has been reached.* Simon was given the name Peter because, as the first confessing apostle, he was the "rock" upon which the new community of the church would be built (Matt. 16:18). Saul was renamed Paul, a Greek name that was appropriate for one who was destined to become the great apostle to the Gentiles.[2]

This same dictionary also notes that the connection between a name and its reality is especially significant when the name refers to God.

> The connection between a name and the reality it signified is nowhere more important than in the names referring to God. The personal name of God revealed to Moses in the burning bush—I Am Who I Am—conveyed something of His character (Exodus 3:14). According to Exodus 34:5–6, when the Lord "proclaimed the name of the Lord," He added words that described His character. The name of the Lord was virtually synonymous with His presence:

"For your wondrous works declare that your name is near" (Psalm 75:1). To know the name of God is thus to know God Himself (Psalm 91:14).[3]

Finally, the author John Hartley writes:

> In that culture, a change in name meant a change in either one's character or one's destiny. God defined the purpose of the name change, declaring that he would make Abraham very fruitful with the result that nations and kings would come from him. The terms "greatly increase" and "be fruitful" echo God's command to Adam (Genesis 1:28), which God reaffirmed to Noah (8:17; 9:1, 7). The connection between these blessings indicates that God empowered Abraham to fulfill the divine purpose begun in creating Adam and delivering Noah.[4]

Fruitfulness (v. 6) is wonderful but pales in comparison to God's supernatural increase. The full realization of this, the Lord's inherent *image* (Genesis 1:27), awaits our discovery. "This is My covenant which you shall keep, between Me and you and your descendants after you," said God to Abraham (Genesis 17:10a, NKJV). Henceforth, Abraham began to realize a difference. Old things began to pass away, fading into oblivion; while new and effervescent blessings from God came forth.

> Therefore, if anyone is in Christ, he is a new creation; old things have passed away; Behold, all things have become new. Now all things are of God, Who has reconciled us to Himself through Jesus Christ, and has given us the ministry of reconciliation, that is, that God was in Christ reconciling the world to Himself, not imputing their trespasses to them, and has committed to us the word of reconciliation.
>
> 2 Corinthians 5:17–19 (NKJV)

Moreover, the Scriptures tell us that even as the Lord changed Abram's name, He also changed Sarai's name. What's more, He also gave her divine ability in keeping with her new name and her husband's promise so as to accomplish His purposes.

> Then God said to Abraham, "As for Sarai your wife, you shall not call her name Sarai, but Sarah shall be her name. And I will bless her and also give you a son by her; then I will bless her, and she shall be a mother of nations; kings of peoples shall be from her."
>
> Genesis 17:15–16 (NKJV)

The name *Sarah* denotes a heritage of royalty. She was supernaturally endowed to be a *princess* of multitudes—the mother of nations. Kings issue forth from her womb because anything less would not have been in keeping with God's holy design and purpose.

Abraham was one hundred years old, and Sarah was ten years younger when she finally conceived. We can only imagine the joy of those gathered with her as the time approached. I can only imagine her laughter when Sarah breathed a great sigh of relief and said, "Finally!" Against all hope, Abraham and Sarah dared to hope. Barak Obama referred to this as *the audacity of hope*. Despite all odds, Abraham and Sarah believed. Who would have ever thought?

> Against all hope, Abraham in hope believed and so became the father of many nations, just as it had been said to him, "So shall your offspring be." Without weakening in his faith, he faced the fact that his body was as good as dead—since he was about a hundred years old—and that Sarah's womb was also dead. Yet he did not waver through unbelief regarding the promise of God, but was strengthened in his faith and gave glory to God, being fully persuaded that God had power to do what he had promised. This is why "it was credited to him as righteousness."
>
> Romans 4:18–22 (NIV)

Consider Abraham! Have an audacious hope that refuses to give up despite all odds and arguments to the contrary?

Consider Abraham because you are his spiritual heir and he is the father of a multitude (Galatians 3:7–9).

When the apostle Paul first penned the words, "Consider Abraham" (Galatians 3:6a, NIV), perhaps he was thinking of the prophet Isaiah. Centuries before Christ, Isaiah hearkened to the people. "Listen to Me, you who follow after righteousness," he prophesied. "You who seek the Lord: Look to the rock from which you were hewn, and to the hole of the pit from which you were dug. *Look to Abraham... for I called him alone, and blessed him and increased him*" (Isaiah 51:1–2, NKJV), emphasis added).

Look to Abraham because from him we learn of God's blessedness. Understand that those who believe are children of Abraham. "The Scripture foresaw that God would justify the Gentiles by faith, and announced the gospel in advance to Abraham: "All nations will be blessed through you." So those who have faith are blessed along with Abraham, the man of faith" (Galatians 3:8–9, NIV).

Christ is our witness in this matter. One day, on a Sabbath, Jesus was teaching in one of the synagogues. A woman was there who had been crippled by a spirit for eighteen years. She was bent over and could not straighten up at all. When Jesus saw her, He called her forward and said to her, "Woman, you are set free [released] from your infirmity" (Luke 13:12b, NIV). Then He put his hands on her, and immediately she straightened up and praised God.

The synagogue leaders were indignant because Jesus healed on the Sabbath, but Jesus said in rebuttal: "You hypocrites! Doesn't each of you on the Sabbath untie his ox or donkey from the stall and lead it out to give it water? *Then should not this woman, a daughter of Abraham*, whom Satan has kept bound for eighteen long years, be set free on the Sabbath day from what bound her?" (Luke 13:15–16, NIV, emphasis mine).

Abraham was God's steward of *miraculous fruitfulness. Multiplied increase* was his to govern; it was placed in his hands to "do" (Deuteronomy 2:7; Joshua 2:24; 6:2). This did not make him a god. Neither did he know all things about God. But that which he knew, he was required to work.

Abraham was divinely equipped by *Jehovah-jireh* (the Lord Who Will See to It). "Walk before Me and be blameless," declared the Lord (Genesis 17:1). God gave him the ability to walk and be blameless. In like manner, you and I are to also walk; similarly enabled with ability.

Consider Abraham for God blessed him and increased him. He lived in keeping with his new name—a destiny of holy sufficiency and endowed fullness. *Adam Clark's Commentary* on Genesis 17:1 says:

> This is the state in which man was created, for he was made in the image and likeness of God. This is the state from which man fell, for he broke the command of God. And this is the state into which every human soul must be raised, who would dwell with God in glory.[5]

You and I are made in the image and likeness of God (Genesis 1:26, NIV). God has said to us, "Be fruitful and increase in number; fill the earth and subdue it. Rule..." (Genesis 1:28, NIV). "Unto every one of us is given grace according to the measure of the gift of Christ... some [as] apostles; and some, prophets; and some, evangelists; and some, pastors and teachers; for the *perfecting* [*katartismos*, Strong's NT:2677] of the saints, for the work of the ministry, for the edifying of the body of Christ" (Ephesians 4:7, KJV, emphasis added). God's people are *prepared* (NIV) and *equipped* (NKJV) for works of service so that Christ's body is built up. The Greek *katartismos* (NT:2677) is from *katartizo* (*Strong's* NT:2675) which means to *complete thoroughly*, i.e., *repair* (literally or figuratively) or *adjust*.[6] This is our heritage.

Chapter Five Evaluation

1. Abraham knew what he knew, and that was enough for him. He tenaciously held to his revelation of God, his new name, and its requisite nature. Inwardly, he knew he was no longer *Abram*. He was *Abraham* despite the many arguments to the contrary. If you are struggling to discover God's will for your life, read Galatians 3:6–9 and follow its direction. Consider Abraham and learn from him of faith and righteousness. ed

2. When writing to the church in Rome, Paul counseled the believers to think of themselves with sober judgment in keeping with the measure of *faith* given them (Romans 12:3). "Faith," writes William Hendriksen, "is here used in the more usual sense of the trust in God by means of which an individual lays hold on God's promises. In the present context, however, the apostle is not thinking in quantitative terms (a large or a small amount of faith). He is thinking rather of the various ways in which each distinct individual is able to be a blessing to others and to the church in general by using the particular gift with which, in association with faith, God has endowed him or her."[7] What is your particular gift from God? Are you actively employing it with faith?

3. Hendriksen adds: "It is clear that Paul believes that not only ministers, elders, and deacons have gifts, but every believer has one or more divinely bestowed gifts or endowments. The apostle shows how these *charismata* should be used to benefit the church and, in fact, men in general."[8] Once again, I encourage you to consider Abraham.

4. We are new creations in and through the agency of God's Holy Spirit. He has laid up new names in glory for all His saints. "He who has an ear, let him hear what the Spirit says to the churches. To him who overcomes, I will give some of the hidden manna. I will also give him a white stone with a new name written on it, known only to him who receives it" (Revelation 2:17, NIV). Do you still identify yourself with

who and what you were prior to God's great salvation and deliverance, or are you living according your newly created nature and its corresponding inspiration? By what name (i.e., nature and character) are you now identified? Consider Abraham and refuse to call yourself anything less than does Almighty God. *Dare to behold!*

CHAPTER SIX

The Prophet of Exceeding Increase

> Now return the man's wife, *for he is a prophet*, and he will pray for you and you will live. But if you do not return her, you may be sure that you and all yours will die.
>
> Genesis 20:7 (NIV), emphasis added.

After Abram had faithfully left everything behind to walk with God, the Lord appeared to him and said, "To your offspring I will give this land" (Genesis 12:7, NIV). But then tragedy struck and a severe famine forced Abram to abandon his new home and seek shelter in Egypt. Because he was stranger in that land, and in fear of his life, Abram lied about his lovely wife saying she was his sister. When his duplicity was discovered, Abram and his family were sent packing in disgrace. The man of promise slunk back to Canaan; returning to the place where he'd previously pitched his tent.

But in keeping with Lord's promises, Abram and his family returned from Egypt greatly enrich. The family fortunes had grown and Abram was rich in livestock, in silver, and in gold.

Then began a whole new set of problems; their possessions were so great that land was unable to support the combined herds of Abram and his nephew, Lot. Strife broke out between their herdsmen forcing Lot to make a fateful decision. Having forgotten the Lord's blessings of multiplied increase, he lifted his eyes toward the plain of Jordan and liked what he saw. It was a well-watered plain and, in many ways, reminded him of Egypt. So Lot struck-out on his own; swallowing the old lie that the grass is greener on the other side. Lot journeyed east and separated himself from his uncle. Lot made the cities of the plain his dwelling place and pitched his tents as far as Sodom. Abram was devastated.

There is a side-note concerning Lot's chosen homestead that is also important to our story. Genesis 13:13 notes that the men of Sodom were exceedingly wicked and sinful against the Lord. The Sodomites were not just a little bit "wicked"; they were openly and appallingly evil. To his shame, Lot chose to identify himself with them and pitched his tent with its door toward their wickedness.

Abram was undoubtedly disheartened by the tragic turn of events. Not only had he been run out of Egypt and humiliated; now he was estranged from his beloved nephew.

So it was that God once again found Abram. "Lift up your eyes from where you are and look north and south, east and west," said God to him. "All the land that you see I will give to you and your offspring forever. I will make your offspring like the dust of the earth, so that if anyone could count the dust, then your offspring could be counted. Go, walk through the length and breadth of the land, for I am giving it to you" (Genesis 13:14b-17, NIV).

Within this short discourse is God's framework for peace and tranquility. First, God told the man to lift up his eyes from his tragic circumstances. Good beginnings start with true and right *sight—seeing* from God's perspective. We must avert our eyes from despondency that often besets us.

Then the Lord gave Abram another principle to live by. In His divine scheme of restoration, God said, "All the land that you see I will give to you and your offspring forever. I will make your offspring like the dust of the earth, so that if anyone could count the dust, then your offspring could be counted" (Genesis 13:15–16, NIV). Abram *heard* the divine pronouncements with implied understanding. This is the Lord's second principle of blessing. It involves our hearing with ears that are unstopped.

But the Lord wasn't finished. He continued, saying; "Go, walk through the length and breadth of the land, for I am giving it to you" (Genesis 13:17, NIV). In this short passage we find God's final two principles of restoration and blessing. We must make that which has been promised our own. This requires requisite action and affiliation. We must fully claim that which is ours in God and *go forth* with confidence that He will see to it. Praise is extending one's open hand to the Lord without reservation. Nothing is ours until we literally walk the length and breadth of God's Word! As Dr. Paul Yonggi Cho, pastor of the world's largest church, put it: "Miracles come not by blindly struggling. There are laws in the spiritual realm, and you have endless resources in your heart. God is dwelling within you; but God is not going to do anything for you without coming through your own life. God ... co-operate[s] with you to accomplish great things."[1]

Bolstered by his revelation, Abram moved his tent signaling his intention to once rise up with God at his side. As the Psalmist sings: "Bless the Lord, O my soul: and all that is within me, bless His holy name. Bless the Lord, O my soul, and forget not all His benefits: Who forgiveth all thine iniquities; Who healeth all thy diseases; Who redeemeth thy life from destruction; Who crowneth thee with lovingkindness and tender mercies; Who satisfieth thy mouth with good things; so that thy youth is renewed like the eagle's" (Psalm 103:1–5, KJV)

But even as we are rejuvenated in God, we must always remember that evil lurks in the dark shadows that surround us. Not long thereafter a man came staggering into Abram's camp. Four kings had banded together to make war against the five allied kings in the region of Sodom and Gomorrah. It was four kings against five but the four prevailed and carried away all the goods of the latter. They also carried off Abram's nephew, his family, and all Lot's possessions.

When Abram heard that his relative had been taken captive, he amassed an army of trained men. He pursued the kings and, when it was night, Abram reaped his vengeance. He routed the four kings and reclaimed his relatives and their belongings. Soon thereafter, Melchizedek, the king of Salem, met Abram. "Blessed be Abram by God Most High, Creator of heaven and earth," [he declared]. "And blessed be God Most High, who delivered your enemies into your hand" (Genesis 14:19–20, NIV). Either now or in the hereafter, this is always the outcome of living the transformed life of freedom in Christ Jesus! If the Son has set us free, we are free indeed (John 8:36b). Blessed be God Who delivers our enemies into our hands!

Within the story of Lot's salvation we discover that God cooperates with you and me to accomplish great and mighty things. The working of His mighty power begins with enlightened eyes and unstopped ears to as to understand. We must know beyond all shadow of doubt what is the hope of our calling—the riches of the glory of His inheritance. To do this, we must grab hold of His exceedingly great power that is extended towards us who believe (Ephesians 1:18–20). We must walk the length and breadth of His land!

So now we come to the pivotal part of this chapter. It is founded upon three words found in Genesis 15:1. They signal a change of mood. The Word of God says, "After these things..." (NKJV, AMP).

The words "after these things" summon our attention because something new is about to happen. It was only "after these things" that the word of the Lord came to Abram in a clear and present vision. "Fear not, Abram," [declared the Lord], "I am you Shield, your abundant compensation, *and* your reward shall be exceedingly great" (Genesis 15:1, AMP).

Don't miss the relevance of the above passage because it introduces essential concepts in our discussion of God's kingdom productivity. It seems that fear was holding Abram back from realizing the full potential of God's multiplied increase and vitality. What is your nemesis? What holds you back?

So it was that the Lord warned Abram against fear. As defined by Franklin D. Roosevelt in his 1933 inaugural address, he said fear is a nameless, unreasoning, unjustified terror which paralyzes needed efforts to convert retreat into advance. "The only thing we have to fear is fear itself," he declared.

Importantly, the Lord called His servant by name, *Abram*. In essence, He was recognizing the man's inherent weakness. Just as He saw Hagar and her innate flaws, so too did God know and recognize (i.e. see) Abram as he was; a naturally-flawed individual in need of being remade. Consequently, God met *Abram* just as he was!

The Lord's revelations are often progressive. They take us from where we are, turn us about, and then set on the right track. In many cases, small beginnings are usually par for the course. Therefore, it was necessary for Abram to grasp that God was always with him as a shield of protection.

In his early stages of spiritual development, Abram knew precious little about the Lord. But, such as he knew, he lived! This is the way we all must begin if we are to turn our world upside down. Take that which you know, as small or insignificant or illogical as it may seem, and fully make it your own. Jesus emphasized this in His parable of the mustard seed. "What shall we say the kingdom of God is like, or what parable shall we use to describe it?" asked Jesus. "It is like a mustard seed, which is the smallest seed you plant in the ground. Yet when planted, it grows and becomes the largest of all garden plants, with such big branches that the birds of the air can perch in its shade" (Mark 4:30–32, NIV).

"Do not be afraid, Abram," [said the Lord]. "I am your shield, your exceedingly great reward" (Genesis 15:1b, NKJV). Apparently, something was coming that would shake Abram to his core. Furthermore, by introducing Himself as Abram's shield, God was speaking in tangible terms of assurance that the man could understand. The Lord did not speak in high, lofty theological terms that were beyond the man's comprehension. The ability to contextualize and put into perspective our Godly vision is absolutely essential to its fleshing out. Consequently, the Lord opens the eyes of our heart that we may be totally enlightened as to the hope of His calling. His desire is that we wholly experience "the riches of his glorious inheritance in the saints, and His incomparably great power for us who believe" (Ephesians 1:19a, NIV).

When promising Abram His continuing fidelity, God then gave an additional word of encouragement. Don't miss it! The Lord said, "I am...your *exceedingly* great reward," (Genesis 15:1b,

NKJV, emphasis mine). Abram's benefit not only included promised protection but also exceptionally great reward which is described earlier as the Lord's *muchness*.

Skeptically, Abram questioned, "Lord God, what will You give me, *seeing* I go childless, and the heir of my house is Eliezer of Damascus? *Look*," [Abram challenged], "You have given me no offspring; indeed one born in my house is my heir!" (Genesis 15:2–3, NKJV, emphasis mine). Notice that Abram twice referred to aspects of *seeing* in his response. "What will you give me, *seeing* I go childless," he said. For emphasis, he then added, "*Look!*" to make his point. Abram knew that his promised "muchness" was irrevocably linked to the concept of *seeing*. Thus, he challenged the Lord to *look* upon his bleak condition.

What was the Lord's response? Did He chastise the man for his pettiness or pitiful complaints? No. In fact, it was quite to the contrary. He redirected the man's attention; telling him to look up towards heaven (Genesis 15:5a). "*Look (nabat) now!*" said God. Don't put it off!

As I was preparing this book for publication, the news media had just announced a rare celestial event was soon coming. The very next morning, beginning about 1:30 a.m., the full moon would be totally eclipsed. This event only rarely happens, and the media proclaimed its advent. I set my alarm and crawled from my bed early the next morning. I wanted to see it. It was a cold, wintry night. I stepped into my slippers and donned a warm coat. Going downstairs with my faithful dog at my side, I went out the back door to witness the remarkable happening. I arrived outside and looked up. Behold...it was cloudy! Much disappointed, I went to bed but couldn't go back to sleep. The much-heralded event was missed for lack of my ability to see it. But it was not so with Abram. With divinely inspired eyes, he looked up into the heavens and saw as never before.

Abram was instructed by God to look attentively (*nabat*) so as to rightly behold the revelation of God's promises. *Nabat*, as used in the original language of the Bible, means *look intently at*; by implication, *to regard with pleasure, favor, or care*.[2] Our responsibility is to look with favor and with great care.

Suddenly, with divinely empowered eyes the see, the heavens were majestically opened and the man, conjoined with God, looked and saw. Borrowing a phrase from Paul's letter to the Ephesians, the eyes of Abram's heart were enlightened so that he might know the hope of that to which he was called.

> [For I always pray to] the God of our Lord Jesus Christ, the Father of glory, that He may grant you a spirit of wisdom and revelation [of insight into mysteries and secrets] in the [deep and intimate] knowledge of Him, by having the eyes of your heart flooded with light, so that you can know *and* understand the hope to which He has called you, and how rich is His glorious inheritance in the saints (His set-apart ones).
>
> Ephesians 1:17–18 (AMP)

Wouldn't it have been appalling if God said "look," but then gave the man no ability to do so? God's command to Abram was to take a careful, sustained look. *Vine's Dictionary* on this important Hebrew verb says *nabat* is commonly used for physical *looking* (Exodus 3:6) but is also used figuratively in the sense of spiritual and inner apprehension.[3] Keil and Delitzsch observe that there is a transition from the outward sphere of the senses to the inward, spiritual sphere of vision.[4] In essence, Abram looked up and saw the stars from God's perspective. They provided a new framework of reference for him to help contextualize and understand. Hence, he "looked" into the heavens, beheld the multitude of stars, and knew that he could not count them. No man of ordinary strength could accomplish what God had devised!

I believe Abram began to sense the purpose of his visitation. Hence, he said, "O Sovereign Lord, how can I *know* that I shall gain possession of it [the land and all that is promised]" (Genesis 15:8, NIV, emphasis mine). His visitation concerned his *knowingness.* Thus, as he looked upward, Abram knew that he knew that he knew that all things would work out in the end. Abram saw and heard, and then he believed with willful intension. Finally, he went forth to live the dream, bringing it to fruition.

Most sermons on Genesis 15 rarely discuss the valid and honest question posed by Abram. It was raw and steeped in admitted weakness; but, from the text, we see that God wasn't shy to answer. Abram sincerely want to know, "What" and "Who" (Genesis 15:2, NIV), and "how can I *know* for sure?" (Genesis 15:8, NIV, emphasis mine). *The Bible in Basic English* frames his question: "O Lord God, how may I be certain that it will be mine?" (Geneses 15:8, BBE). The Amplified Bible's translation says he asked, "Lord God, by what shall I know that I shall inherit it?"

The above questions (Abram's "what," "who" and "how") are some of the Bible's most intriguing puzzles. They frame this discussion on *knowingness* and take center stage in the realization of God's productivity with promising increase. They were Abram's greatest concern and should be ours as well. How can we *know* for sure? As for me, I want to know for sure that my vision, my special epiphany, and my intuitive insight is really from God? What? How? Who? They are all valid questions and are answered in Genesis 13. First, God told Abram to lift up his eyes from his present circumstances and look north and south, east and west (v. 14). Secondly, Abram had to rightly hear; discerning what God has promised (v(v). 15–16). Lastly, Abram was instructed to go and make the land his own by walking its length and breadth. His active agreement and affiliation were required.

Warren Wiersbe says Abram's question was not a sign of unbelief but a request for a token of assurance.[5] From time to time, we all need God's reassurance that all is well and that He is still in control. Often, we need an assuring word to shore up our faith.

Consider Abraham!

Abram said, "O Sovereign Lord, how can I to know that I will gain possession of it?" (Genesis 15:8, NIV).

Since the foundation of success was already given (Genesis 13:14–17), the Lord gave Abram a sign of assurance. He said to him, "Bring me a heifer, a goat and a ram, each three years old, along with a dove and a young pigeon." Abram brought all these, cut them in two and arranged the halves opposite each other; the birds, however, he did not cut in half.

But the Lord delayed in His coming until the setting of the sun. A deep sleep overcame Abram, and a horror (i.e. a terror, a shuddering fear) of great darkness assailed and oppressed him. At such times of waiting and dread, I recall the words of Habakkuk. "For the revelation awaits an appointed time," [he declared]; "it speaks of the end and will not prove false. Though it linger, *wait for it*; it will certainly come and will not delay" (Habakkuk 2:3, NIV, emphasis added). Thus, the Lord came to Abram and said, "Know [*yada'*] positively [beyond all shadow of doubt]" (v. 13a, AMP). *Yada'* properly means to ascertain by seeing and is rendered in Scripture, "comprehend" and "discern." Out of the horror of that darkness a great light shone and the words of God forever whispered in Abram's ears..."Know for certain! Know for certain!" (Genesis 15:13a, NIV).

Then an even thicker darkness enveloped the man and Abram saw a smoking oven and a flaming torch pass between the pieces of the sacrifice. On the same day the Lord made a covenant (a promise or pledge) with him, saying, "To your descendants I have given this land..." According to McClintock and Strong, "When God blesses, he bestows that virtue, that efficacy, which renders his blessing effectual, and which his blessing expresses. His blessings are either temporal or spiritual, bodily or mental; but in everything they are productive of that which they import. God's blessings extend into the future life, as his people are made partakers of that blessedness which, in infinite fullness, dwells in himself."[6]

Earlier we debated the issue of God's statement "after these things..." (Genesis 15:1a, NKJV). I noted that the phrase "after these things" summons our attention and signals a turn of events. Thus, the word of the Lord came to Abram. "Fear not, Abram," [said the Lord], "I am you Shield, your abundant compensation, *and* your reward shall be exceedingly great" (Genesis 15:1, AMP). Then, and at the ripe old age of ninety-nine years old, God changed the man's name from *Abram* to *Abraham* and gave him a son, Isaac.

Thereafter, Abraham journeyed south and dwelt in Gerar. But, as before, he said of Sarah his wife, "She is my sister." (Genesis 20:2,

AMP). Abimelech, the king of Gerar, saw Sarah and took her into his harem.

But God intervened and came to Abimelech in a dream. "Behold, you are a dead man because of the woman whom you have taken as your own, for she is a man's wife. But Abimelech had not come near her, so he said, "Lord, will you slay a people who are just *and* innocent? Did not the man say she was his sister? And she herself said, 'He is my brother.' In integrity of heart and innocency of hands I have done this" (v. 5, AMP).

"Yes, I know you did this in the integrity of your heart," declared the Lord. "It was I Who kept you back *and* spared you from sinning against Me. Therefore I did not give you occasion to touch her."

Now God said something that is most important to our story. It is the underlying theme of *The Divine Conception* and concerns our own empowerment in and of the Lord. Pay close attention to what happens next.

God said to Abimelech, "So now restore to the man his wife, *for he is a prophet*, and he will pray for you and you will live. But if you do not restore her [to him], know that you shall surely die, you and all who are yours" (v. 7, AMP, emphasis mine).

Earlier I quoted McClintock and Strong who recognized that when God blesses, He also bestows virtue and efficacy. This renders His blessing effectual and productive. They are lifelong gifts and we are their steward. As heirs of Abraham, we are partakers of God's blessedness which, in infinite fullness, dwells in the Lord Himself.

So it was that Abimelech rose early the next morning and called all his officials. He told them all the things he knew (*yada'*) because God had told him and they were very much afraid.

"What have you done to us?" said Abimelech to Abraham. "How have I offended you that you have brought such great guilt on me and my kingdom? You have done things to me that should not be done."

Then Abimelech took sheep and oxen and male and female slaves and gave them to Abraham and restored to him Sarah his wife.

And Abimelech said, "Behold, my land is before you; dwell wherever it pleases you." And to Sarah he said, "Behold, I have given this brother of yours a thousand pieces of silver [the price of redemption]; see, it is to compensate you [for all that has occurred] and to vindicate your honor before all who are with you; before all men you are cleared *and* compensated" (v(v) 15–16, AMP).

In the eyes of God, Abraham was His prophet. But in what sense was he a prophet? The answer is discovered in Abraham's effectual prayer. When he prayed to God, the Lord listened to him and healed Abimelech and his wife and all his female slaves. They once again bore children because the Lord had closed fast the wombs of all in the household of Abimelech because of Sarah, Abraham's wife.

Why should you and I diligently "consider Abraham" (Galatians 3:6a, NIV)? In Genesis 18:19 we find our answer. When God was about to destroy Sodom and Gomorrah because of their great wickedness, He said, "Shall I hide from Abraham that thing which I do; seeing that Abraham shall surely become a great and mighty nation, and all the nations of the earth shall be blessed in him? *For I know* [*yada'*] *him* ..." (Genesis 18:17–19a, KJV, emphasis added). Then God added, "For I know him, that he will command his children and his household after him, and they shall keep the way of the Lord, to do (*'asah*) justice and judgment; that the Lord may bring upon Abraham that which he hath spoken of him" (v. 19, KJV).

Knowing these things, how do you propose to respond? I love what Ayn Rand, the well-known Russian-American novelist and philosopher, once said. "You can ignore reality," she declared, "but you can't ignore the consequences of ignoring reality."

Chapter Six Evaluation

1. Are you struggling for a sense of direction? Perhaps you are unsure of the Lord's calling on your life. If so, I urge you to rediscover who and what you are in God. Begin by remembering your special time of inspiration or cognition when God met you in a very *real* way. Recall your emotions and your sense of peace or freedom. In doing so, you will also catch a glimmer of your special knowingness. Then, you should measure it against the revealed will of God in the Holy Scriptures. Does your vision, your dream, or your inspiration line up with Christ's stated purpose in Luke 4:16–20? Additionally, read James 1:25 that says the perfect law of God gives freedom and blessing. Your *Ah-ha* moment should always lead to liberty, purity, joy, and love? This is always God's intent and anything less or contrary may not be of Him.

2. Read Genesis 20. Abraham said to himself, "Surely there is no reverence *or* fear of God at all in this place, and they [the Philistines] will slay me because of my wife" (Genesis 20:11, AMP). Consequently, he said of Sarah, "She is my sister" (Genesis 20:2, NIV, AMP). Unknowing of Abraham's duplicity, the Philistine king took Sarah into her harem to be his wife. But before he could come near her, God came to Abimelech in a dream. "Behold," He said, "you are a dead man because of the woman ... for she is a man's wife" (Genesis 20:3, AMP). Abimelech cringed. "Lord, will you slay a people who are just *and* innocent? Did not the man tell me, 'She is my sister?' And she herself said, 'He is my brother.' In integrity of heart and innocency of hands I have done this" (v(v). 4–5, AMP). God didn't argue this point; focusing instead on the solution. "So now restore the man his wife, *for he is a prophet*, and he will pray for you and you will live. But if you do not restore her [to him], know that you shall surely die, you and all who are yours" (Genesis 20:7, AMP). God considered Abraham to be His prophet. But in what ways was he the

Lord's prophet? I believe the answer was in the man's special knowingness. He was a prophet in the sense of the amazing truths revealed to him. Such things are meant to be shared and ministered. In this regard, what is your responsibility regarding those things you specifically revealed to you? Even though Abraham lived below his high calling (at least for a time), he was still God's divinely-empowered agent of change. As the Lord's prophet, he had within him the power to *do* as well as *speak* the revelations of God. He had within him a spark of divine know-how with accompanying supernatural strength to overcome curses of decrease and decline. Abraham possessed inspired ability that afforded prosperity and increase, not only for himself and his family, but also for others. Now it's your turn! Armed with your special insight, you also can stand against and overcome even the worst plagues that beset mankind. As always, I encourage your to get in touch with who and what you are in God. What makes you special in the eyes of the Lord?

3. The Apostle Paul admonishes us to "Consider Abraham!" (Galatians 3:6a, NIV). Abraham believed God, and it was credited to him as righteousness. In like manner, God has also justified you and me by faith. Thus, He said to Abraham, "All nations will be blessed through you" (Galatians 3:8, NIV). Consider Abraham because if we are of like faith with Abraham, we are also blessed.

4. Don't be surprised if others are skeptical of your divinely inspired *knowingness* and its accompanying requisite power. Most people will not readily understand or appreciate your special appointment or inspiration because such things are uniquely yours. No matter what your tests or trials, never call yourself anything less than does God. Reread the story of Joseph beginning in Genesis 37:1. Notice the reaction of Joseph's uncomprehending kindred to his sacred gift (the ability to dream and interpret dreams). They treated him with scorn and resentment. What is our lesson? Read

Joseph's story to its end for it reveals special blessings for all people who tenaciously hold to God's revealed truths.

5. Do you agree that revealed knowledge carries with it a responsibility to minister? From such Old Testament saints as Abraham and Joseph we learn that God gives ability (empowerment) to see His will accomplished? Can you give examples of this in your own life?

6. Abraham was undoubtedly astounded by the turn of events in Gerar (Genesis 20). He knew that he was changed by God's revelation and special insights, but it seems he didn't considered himself to be an ambassador of them. A prophet is one who is divinely enabled *to do* (*'asah*) and *speak* the revelations of God. Thus, Abraham had within him the divine know-how of supernatural strength to overcome curses of decrease and decline. He possessed inspired ability that afforded prosperity and increase, not only for himself and his family, but also for others. Do you agree?

7. Give God a chance! The Lord said to Abram, "I will confirm (i.e. validate) My covenant between Me and you…" (Genesis 17:2, NIV). Allow Him to corroborate your special cognition. But to do this, you must follow the Lord's holy template as outlined in Genesis 13:14–18. Once again, what are the four vital principles of revelation and empowerment revealed there?

8. We must each "walk-out" (give legs to) our special appointments. In this regard, the Lord told Abram to "Go [and] walk through the length and breadth of the land" (Genesis 13:17a, NIV). In this regard, we must come into absolute agreement with our special cognition (inspired knowingness). Therefore, measure everything according to the standard of God's written Word, the Holy Bible. Remember Christ's response when thrice tempted. Each time, He said, "It is written!" (Matthew 4:4, 6, 7&10). "It is no coincidence that Jesus's temptation immediately follows his baptism," say the

authors of *The New American Commentary*. "Many of God's people have had similar experiences. Right after conversion or some other significant spiritual event, precisely when a certain level of victory or maturity seems to have been attained, temptations resume more strongly than ever (cf. Elijah in 1 Kings 19:1–18 and Paul in Romans 7:14–25)."[7]

9. Abraham was the Lord's prophet of exceeding increase. As such, he had within him the ability to save Abimelech and minister to Abimelech's entire nation. He could effectively counter the declared curse of decrease. However, Abraham had to live-up to his divine potential and minister accordingly. Likewise, Abimelech had a responsibility to humble himself and restore Sarah to her husband. God never forces His will upon you or me. Therefore, "consider Abraham" (Galatians 3:6, NIV) and do not neglect the unfolding of divinely-appointed tasks. In this is true success. Consequently, Abraham prayed for the king and his nation, and the Lord healed Abimelech, his wife, and all his female servants. They again bore children; "for the Lord had closed up all the wombs of the house of Abimelech because of Sarah, Abraham's wife" (Genesis 20:18, NKJV). Consider Abraham for he believed God and it was credited to him as righteousness. Revealed knowledge carries with it corresponding ability. It is the greatest possession a person can have. According to *Nelson's Illustrated Bible Dictionary*, such knowledge "cannot be gained by unaided human reason (Job 11:7; Romans 11:33). It is acquired only as God shows Himself to man in nature and conscience (Psalm 19; Romans 1:19–20)."[8] *The International Standard Bible Encyclopedia* observes that God's knowledge is "absolute, unerring, complete, intuitive, embracing all things, past, present, and future, and searching the inmost thoughts of the heart (Psalm 139:1, 23); whereas man's is partial, imperfect, relative, gradually acquired, and largely mixed with error. Now we see in a mirror darkly... in part" (1 Corinthians 13:12).[9]

CHAPTER SEVEN

"On the Mountain of the Lord It Will Be Provided"

> Abraham looked up and there in a thicket he saw a ram caught by its horns. He went over and took the ram and sacrificed it as a burnt offering instead of his son. So Abraham called that place The Lord Will Provide. And to this day it is said, "On the mountain of the Lord it will be provided."
>
> Genesis 22:13–14 (NIV)

Bitter memories of his encounter with Abimelech haunted Abraham. "What have you done to us?" said the king. "How have I wronged you that you have brought such great guilt upon me and my kingdom? You have done things to me that should not be done" (Genesis 20:9, NIV).

Abraham had foolishly forsaken his anointed calling in God. Furthermore, he neglected the Almighty God Who was his shield. Abimelech's question is worthily asked, not only of Abraham, but of all men and women of knowingness and know-how. "What have you done?" In other words, do not neglect holy duties and divine callings. Do things rightly as ought to be done! Never let it be asked of you, "What have you done with your divine calling and gifting?"

Abraham was the Lord's prophet of increase with a supernatural ability to administer God's muchness and vitality. As such, he could intercede on man's behalf to overcome barrenness and death (Genesis 20:7). God does not hide what He will do, and it was Abraham's sacred duty as His "seer" to live and proclaim the Lord's holy intentions (Numbers 12:6). Abraham could literally go forth as God, in His name and by His authority (Exodus 7:1). According to *Easton's Bible Dictionary*:

> Prophets were the immediate organs of God for the communication of his mind and will to men (Deuteronomy 18:18, 19)...The foretelling of future events was not a necessary but only an incidental part of the prophetic office. The great task assigned to the prophets whom God raised up among the people was "to correct moral and religious abuses, to proclaim the great moral and religious truths which are connected with the character of God, and which lie at the foundation of his government."[1]

Abraham's mediation meant that Abimelech, his family, and his nation, would live and be healed. The alternatives of ignoring God and restraining Sarah were too terrible to contemplate—"You shall surely die, you and all who are yours!" declared the Lord (Genesis 20:7b, AMP).

What did Abraham know? What was his divinely inspired know-how that literally "bubbled forth"? The text suggests that even Abraham was taken aback by his awesome responsibility before God. Think about it; he was God's emissary on earth for the ministry of "muchness." Within him was the power of life and death. He could effectually counter curses of barrenness, decrease, and death itself. "Be fruitful and increase," said the Lord to him, time and again (Genesis 1:22, 28; 9:1, 7). It was this personal knowledge of Almighty God that enabled the man to live excessively above life's pettiness and lowliness.

Against all hope, Abraham in hope believed and so became the father of many nations, just as it had been said to him, "So shall your offspring be." Without weakening in his faith, he faced the fact that his body was as good as dead—since he was about a hundred years old—and that Sarah's womb was also dead. Yet he did not waver through unbelief regarding the promise of God, but was strengthened in his faith and gave glory to God, being fully persuaded that God had power to do what he had promised. This is why it was credited to him as righteousness.

Romans 4:18–22 (NIV)

Then came the fateful day when God said to Abraham, "Take your son, your only son, Isaac, whom you love, and go to the region of Moriah. Sacrifice him there as a burnt offering on one of the mountains I will tell you about" (Genesis 22:2, NIV). God wanted to test and prove his servant as part of His progressive revelation.

Without hesitation, Abraham rose early the next morning and saddled his donkey. Most Godly things are initiated by our intentional "rising" unto His appointed tasks.

Now we come to a pivotal verse that sets the tone of all that follows. The Word of God says Abraham did as instructed; he went to the land of Moriah, fully trusting that God would show him the appointed place of worship. "Then on the third day, Abraham *lifted his eyes* and *saw* (i.e., *ra'ah*) the place afar off" (Genesis 22:4, NKJV, emphasis added). The NIV says, "...he looked up and saw" the place in the distance. There was something in his looking up and seeing (i.e., *ra'ah*) that sets the tone of the passage. These two elements play an essential role in God's scheme of deliverance—His Holy Symphony of Doing. Throughout Scripture, *seeing* is fundamental. "All the land that you *see*," declared the Lord, "I will give to you and your offspring forever" (Genesis 13:15, NIV). Moses *saw* the burning bush and thought, "I will go over and *see* this strange sight—why the bush does not burn up" (Exodus 3:3, NIV, emphasis mine). God later said to him, "*See*, I have made you like God to Pharaoh..." (Genesis 7:1, NIV, emphasis added). "*See*, the Lord your God has given you the land. Go up and take possession of it as the Lord, the God of your fathers, told you. Do not be afraid; do not be discouraged" (Deuteronomy 1:21, NIV). "*See*," declared the Lord, "I set before you today life and prosperity, death and destruction" (Genesis 30:15, NIV). "*See now* that I myself am He!" affirms the Lord (Genesis 32:39, NIV). The seeing concept is found throughout the Scriptures.

"My father!" exclaimed Isaac. "Look, the fire and the wood, but where is the lamb for a burnt offering?" (Genesis 22:7, NKJV). Little did the lad know that it was his father's "looking" that set the stage of his deliverance. Ultimately, it would be his salvation; Isaac's words were prophetic.

> Then on the third day, Abraham *lifted his eyes and saw* the place afar off.... So Abraham took the wood of the burnt offering and laid it on Isaac his son; and he took the fire in his hand, and a knife, and the two of them went together. But Isaac spoke to Abraham his father and said, "My father!"
>
> And he said, "Here I am, my son."
>
> Then he said, "*Look*, the fire and the wood, but where is the lamb for a burnt offering?"
>
> And Abraham said, "My son, *God will provide* [i.e., (*ra'ah*): literally, see] for Himself the lamb for a burnt offering."
>
> Then Abraham *lifted his eyes and looked* [i.e., (*ra'ah*) saw], and there behind him was a ram caught in a thicket by its horns. So Abraham went and took the ram, and offered it up for a burnt offering instead of his son. And Abraham called the name of the place, The Lord Will Provide [i.e., (*ra'ah*) see]; as it is said to this day, "In the Mount of the Lord it shall be *provided* [i.e., (*ra'ah*) seen]."
>
> Genesis 22:4–8, 13–14 (NKJV), emphasis added.

The King James Version renders verse 14 of the above passage: "Abraham called the name of the place *Jehovah-jireh*: as it is said to this day, 'In the mount of the Lord *it shall be seen*'" (emphasis mine). The sacrificial offering was revealed when Isaac's father looked up and saw it. As he had previously declared, "God Himself will *provide* (literally, *see to it*) a lamb for the burnt offering" (Genesis 22:8, AMP).

Additionally, the Biblical narrative stresses the mutual agreement of father and son. "So the two went on *together* [i.e. *yachad*, in unison]" (Genesis 22:8b, AMP, emphasis mine). The two of them stained and struggled together, in one accord and with one purpose. This too is later discussed because even as Abraham's "seeing" played an essential role in the Lord's scheme of deliverance, so too does shared agreement and common accord.

Many are the questions, logical restraints, natural hindrances, and inherent weaknesses that keep us from experiencing the fullness of God. For this reason God Himself *provides*, or literally, *sees to it* (i.e., *ra'ah*). I've come to believe that this probably became Abraham's mantra when straining against all opposition. Whenever challenged or tested, pressed or tried, he would simply utter the Lord's name, "*Jehovah-jireh*, the Lord Will See to It." Time and again, he would return to his altar and call upon that holy name. Armed with this knowingness, Abraham became and even greater emissary of divine provision. He did not know all things about his God; but such as he knew, he lived and practiced for the benefit of all humankind.

Consider Abraham! (Galatians 3:6a, NIV)

When at the site of ordained worship, I am convinced that Abraham did not generally call upon the Lord. Knowing His name, the man called to Him very specifically and in keeping with his new insight of the divine character. He praised *Jehovah-jireh*, the Lord Who Will See to It.

On that eventful day of sacrifice when Abraham built his altar to the Lord, the Word of God says that he properly arranged (i.e., ordered, esteemed) the essential elements. We lightly skip over this part of the story but I cannot emphasize enough the importance of carefully arranging the elements of our altars to properly worship and praise. Like the altars built by Abraham, our altars must also be arrayed before the Lord according to His ordained designs, His holy details, and in keeping with His purposes (see 1 Kings 18:30–33). It is never enough to haphazardly throw our altars together with negligent disregard. As one Lexical Aid put it, "The language of the passage is meant to reiterate the calculated obedience of all people."[2]

The events of the narrative unfold as if in slow motion. Abraham bound his son and laid him on the altar. Then he resolutely raised the sacrificial blade to make the fatal stab to his heart. But, at the last possible moment, God stayed his hand, saying, "Do not lay your hand on the lad, or do anything to him; *for now I know* [i.e., *yada'*] that you fear God, since you have not withheld your son, your only son, from Me (Genesis 22:12, NKJV, emphasis mine). Somehow, and in some way, the weight of *knowingness* was the key for unlocking Abraham's great destiny.

Why is *knowingness* a necessary ingredient in the above story? How does it add to it, and does it suggest that *seeing* with *knowingness* is of vital importance? Why did God declare unto him divine *knowingness*?

I stress this point because *knowingness* with know-how is another key principle of this book, *The Divine Conception*. First, Abraham "lifted his eyes and saw the place afar off" (Genesis 22:4, NKJV). Then he "lifted his eyes" again and looked to see the ram caught in a nearby thicket by its horns (v. 22). Now we have this added component—the importance of understanding (i.e. *knowingness*). Also notice that when he first lifted up his eyes and saw, the place of his sacrifice was far off. Then, when he lifted his eyes again, the ram—his sacrificial lamb—was nearby. We always begin from a place far-off and, as we move closer to God, His sacrificial lamb becomes more and more pertinent and real to us. He was there all along but is missed by many who fail to "look-up" from their mundane affairs of life.

Abraham's lifted of eyes to *see* the Lord's intended sacrifice (v. 13). *Ra'ah* (the Hebrew word at the heart of this passage) is the beginning of *knowingness* with know-how. To this day, it is said, "In the mount of the Lord it shall be seen" (v. 14, KJV). In other words, the divine principles that underscore this great event are still in operation today—their importance and relevance has not been lost.

Additionally, another element is introduced in the same passage—the role of Abraham's hearing in God's producing scheme. Genesis 22:11 explains that the angel of the Lord called out to him from heaven. "Here I am," said Abraham, hearing the voice of God!

> "Because thou hast done this thing, [with] blessing I bless thee, and multiplying I multiply thy seed as stars of the heavens, and as sand which [is] on the sea-shore; and thy seed doth possess the gate of his enemies; and blessed themselves in thy seed have all nations of the earth, because that thou hast *hearkened* to [i.e., *shama,'* heard] My voice."
>
> Genesis 22:16–18 (YLT), *Young's Literal Translation,* emphasis mine.

Abraham looked up and *saw* (i.e., *ra'ah*). He also *heard* with implied attention and obedience. Jesus said to those closest to Him, "Blessed are your eyes because they see, *and* your ears because they hear. For I tell you the truth, many prophets and righteous men longed to see what you see and did not see it, *and to hear what you hear but did not hear it*" (Matthew 13:16–17, NIV, emphasis mine).

Only after these things was Abraham blessed with blessing, and with multiplying he multiplied.

> And the messenger of Jehovah calleth unto Abraham a second time from the heavens, and saith, "By Myself I have sworn—the affirmation of Jehovah—that because thou hast done this thing, and hast not withheld thy son, thine only one—that [with] blessing I bless thee, and multiplying I multiply thy seed as stars of the heavens, and as sand which [is] on the sea-shore; and thy seed doth possess the gate of his enemies…
>
> Genesis 22:15–17 (YLT)

In summary, we've learned from Abraham's mountaintop experience the importance of "lifting up" our eyes to see. *Seeing* is critical to the divine scheme of God's provision. The principle of right seeing (i.e., *ra'ah*) is the beginning of strength. Seeing is the fountainhead of all things created (Genesis 1:4, 10, 12, 18, 21, 25 and 31) and all things within God's kingdom. Additionally, Abraham *heard* (i.e., *shama'*) the voice of God with implied comprehension

The Divine Conception

and understanding. "Now I *know* (i.e., *yada'*)," declared the Lord to Abraham, hinting that the perfect will of God comes through the avenue of *knowingness* (inspired awareness with cognition). Finally, it was necessary for Abraham to fully commit himself (i.e. explicitly come into heartfelt agreement) to God's perfect intension. Thus, he went forth, took hold of the ram (the Lord's provision), and then sacrificed it as a sign of his intimate commitment (Genesis 22:13). Requisite action must always chase holy intention. Only in this way did Abraham emerge as "a tried man." He presented himself as a living sacrifice, devoted and consecrated unto the Lord's holy scheme of provision (Romans 12:1). Only in this way was the man changed to become "heir of the world" (Romans 4:13, NIV). He had finally come into the fullness of his name and character—Abraham, the father of multitudes. With blessing, he was blessed and could bless; and with multiplication, he multiplied to bring forth swelling increase. This was his appointed destiny. Abraham was God's emissary of divine provision and vitality on earth and we are his spiritual descendants. Earlier, I quoted Ayn Rand, the well-known Russian-American novelist and philosopher. She said. "You can ignore reality, but you can't ignore the consequences of ignoring reality." Abraham "believed in *and* trusted in *and* relied on God, and it was reckoned *and* placed to his account *and* credited as righteousness as conformity to the divine will in purpose, thought, and action)" (Galatians 3:6, AMP).

"I urge you, brothers," said the apostle Paul, "in view of God's mercy, to offer your bodies as living sacrifices, holy and pleasing to God—this is your spiritual act of worship." The Apostle continued, "Do not conform any longer to the pattern of this world, *but be transformed by the renewing of your mind.* Then you will be able to test and approve what God's will is—his good, pleasing and perfect will" (Romans 12:1–2, NIV, emphasis added).

Consider Abraham!

Abraham offered himself as a living sacrifice and was thereby transformed. His mind was renewed as he participated with God. He discovered the necessity of practice as well as principle. While *right seeing* and *right hearing* are the foundation to all things *known* (i.e., *yada'*), they are not sufficient in themselves to bring about needed change. It was only as Abraham came into active agreement with those things *seen* and *heard* (i.e. his life was entangled with, and connected to, God and His revelation) that he was enlivened and transformed.

From that day forward, Abraham lived a new reality. Whereas he'd previously seen as through a glass dimly, now he saw rightly with understanding. Hard pressed for words, Abraham simply called his experience, "The Lord Will Provide." To this day, it is said, "On the mountain of the Lord, it will be provided" (Genesis 22:14, NIV). He called his God by the name *Jehovah-jireh* (i.e. the Lord Will See to It).

Those who later heard Abraham's amazing tale of divine encounter undoubtedly shook their heads in wonder. Some believed, but most did not understand. Some even considered it the fodder of fools or blamed it on the previous night's pizza. "It's nothing more than a fanciful dream," they argued.

One thing was certain, however. All who heard Abraham's tale never laughed at him; at least, not to his face. Kings attested that Abraham was indeed the Lord's prophet; a man not to be messed with (Genesis 12:20; 20:14–15). An inherent providence of productivity and vitality followed after the man and his family, wherever they went. Conversely, to curse him was to become cursed (Genesis 12:3).

Abraham knew (i.e., *yada'*) what he knew, and no one could convince him otherwise. The Hebrew *yada'* means *to ascertain by seeing*.[3] The Scriptural *yada'* is used in a variety of senses: figuratively, literally, euphemistically, and inferentially. *Yada'* is variously translated in the King James Bible as "(to be) *aware, comprehend, consider, discern, discover, be endued with, feel, perceive, to be sure of,*" and "*to understand.*"[4]

To know that you know that you know—this is blessedness. Human consciousness consists of more than mere awareness; it also consists of *self-awareness*.

> In saying that a conscious being knows something, we are saying not only that he knows it, but that he knows that he knows it, and that he knows he knows he knows it, and so on...[5]

Beyond all shadow of doubt, Abraham believed that his God would always *see to it*. This was his new reality and he lived the remainder of his days in that truth.

Were there trying times still ahead? Most assuredly! Even Jesus, the Son of God, faced many difficulties while here on earth. But one thing was certain, Abraham never lacked for adequate care, strength, and provision, because he knew and praised (i.e., extending his hand toward) the Lord Who Always Sees to It." The man was blessed beyond measure, and with multiplication, he exceedingly multiplied (Genesis 17:5–6).

Exceeding multiplication with increase was Abraham's heritage (Genesis 17:5–6). In this aspect of God's nature, Abraham flourished (Genesis 24:1). He believed in and relied on God, and it was credited to him as righteousness (as conformity to the divine will in purpose, thought, and action).

> Know *and* understand that it is [really] the people [who live] by faith who are [the true] sons of Abraham. And the Scripture, foreseeing that God would justify (declare righteous, put in right standing with Himself) the Gentiles in consequence of faith, proclaimed the Gospel [foretelling the glad tidings of a Savior long beforehand] to Abraham in the promise, saying, 'In you shall all the nations [of the earth] be blessed.' So then, those who are people of faith are blessed *and* made happy *and* favored by God [as partners in fellowship] with the believing *and* trusting Abraham.
>
> Galatians 3:7–9 (AMP)

Chapter Seven Evaluation

1. Abraham was at a loss for words when trying to explain his supernatural encounter with God. Perhaps you can identify with his experience and are also unable to adequately define your experience. In any event, that didn't hinder Abraham and neither should it deter you. Don't let other people's opinions, doubts, experiences, or skepticism cloud or kill your vision. It is yours and yours alone so be faithful to that which you know. Above all, measure your vision, revelation, dream, special insight, etc. against the one true standard—the written Word of God. God will never contradict Himself. Why is this important?

2. I am confident that Abraham continually spoke of his divine encounter. Do you? Anyone who knew Abraham undoubtedly heard his story because, for him, it was a defining moment. Does your special knowingness of God likewise define you? Does it define your praise?

3. Perhaps you recall the story of Jabez? At the time of his birth, his mother named him Jabez, saying, "I gave birth to him in pain" (1 Chronicles 4.9, NIV). At the core of his being, and the defining quality of his heart, was pain and grief. But in a God-Moment, in a twinkling of an eye, Jabez met the Lord and was given an entirely new reality of truth. Where once he was destined to follow an offensive, grievous course, God blessed him; morphing him into an entirely new creature (v. 10). If God is the same yesterday, today, and forever, will He not also do the same for you? Cry out to the Lord as did Jabez. Hold nothing back and then get ready for some big changes!

CHAPTER EIGHT

"I Have Met El-Roi"

> Hagar asked herself, "Have I really seen God and lived to tell about it?"
>
> So she called the Lord, who had spoken to her, "A God Who Sees."
>
> That is why people call the well between Kadesh and Bered "The Well of the Living One Who Sees Me."
>
> Genesis 16:13–14 (TEV)

No one really knew for sure what Abraham had experienced except, perhaps, his son, Isaac, and another unlikely soul—Hagar, the Egyptian maidservant of Sarai, Abram's wife.

Despairing in her old age and refusing to wait any longer for the Lord's promised seed, Sarai gave Hagar to her husband as a concubine. "The Lord has kept me from having children," [she moaned]. "Go, sleep with my maidservant; perhaps I can build a family through her" (Genesis 16:2, NIV). Any offspring Hagar bore to Abram would be considered Sarai's (compare Genesis 30:3–9), since Hagar was the property of her mistress.

Sadly, when the path of faith is abandoned, the way of human calculation begins. Then we set a chain of events in motion that often leads to much grief. In this case, the offspring of Abram's unholy union was Ishmael, the ancestor of the Arabs.

Much to Sarai's chagrin, when Hagar conceived, she began to look with contempt upon her mistress and despise her. "May [the responsibility for] my wrong *and* deprivation of rights be upon you!" screamed Sarai to her husband. "I gave my maid into your bosom, and when she saw that she was with child, I was contemptible *and* despised in her eyes. May the Lord be the judge between you and me" (Genesis 16:5, AMP).

What was Abram to do? He was between the proverbial rock and a hard place. "See here," he said, trying to absolve himself, "your maid is in your hands *and* power; do as you please with her" (Genesis 16:6, AMP).

Thereafter, Sarai dealt severely with Hagar, humbling and afflicting her. Life became so miserable for the servant girl that she fled from her mistress' wrath into the wilderness. "It should seem, she [Hagar] was making toward her own country; for she was in the way to Shur, which lay toward Egypt," comments Matthew Henry. "Hagar was now out of her place, and out of the way of her duty, and going further astray, when the angel found her."[1]

In most cases, God allows those of us who fitfully follow such paths to wander. Hagar was no exception and roamed deep into the wilderness of despair. Finally, when she'd had enough, she sat down despairingly in frustration and weariness. It was then that God intervened.

The angel of the Lord found Hagar near a spring in the desert; it was the spring that is beside the road to Shur. And He said, "Hagar, servant of Sarai, where have you come from, and where are you going?" (Genesis 16:7–8, NIV).

Genesis 16:8 gives hope to everyone who aimlessly wanders along life's lonely pathways. It's for all people who hopelessly exist from one day to the next with no prospect of change. "Hagar, Sarai's maid," said the Lord, "whence camest thou and whither wilt thou go?" (Genesis 16:8a, KJV).

In this regard, I love the prophetic words buried deep within a tiny Old Testament book named for its author, Hosea. God declares, "...behold, I will allure her, will bring her into the wilderness, and speak comfort to her. I will give her vineyards from there, and the Valley of Achor as a door of hope; She shall sing there, as in the days of her youth, as in the day when she came up from the land of Egypt" (Hosea 2:14–15, NKJV).

Importantly, Hagar's visitation is the first mention in Scripture of an angelic appearance. Even more profound is the fact that this was the angel of the Lord. *The Bible Knowledge Commentary* notes this angel is identified with Yahweh in Genesis 16:13, as well as in Genesis 22:11–12; 31:11, 13; 48:16; Judges 6:11,16, 22; Judges 13:22–23; and Zechariah 3:1–2. The conclusion is, "the angel of the Lord may refer to a theophany of the pre-incarnate Christ (cf. Genesis 18:1–2; 19:1; Num 22:22; Judges 2:1–4; 5:23; Zechariah 12:8)."[2]

"Hagar, Sarai's maid," said the theophanic angel to the wayward woman, "where have you come from, and where are you going?" (Genesis 16:8, NKJV). These questions forever frame our fortunes, whether good or evil. The first question demands that we come to a reckoning with our roots—our innate tendencies, our fleshly desires, and our human limitations. God's second question begs us to stop and carefully examine your feeble intentions and future plans. "Whither wilt thou go and how will you get there? Have you the strength and fortitude to make it?"

It's incredible how we often run about like rats in a maze, frantically twisting and turning in search of an exit. At such times we are victims of our passions and emotions, when all along we should stop in our tracks and say to ourselves, "Where am I going and how will I get there?"

The Bible Knowledge Commentary gives additional insight on this important passage in Genesis 16. "God gave Hagar two sure words: One was hortatory—return and submit (Genesis 16:9), and the other was promissory—she would give birth to a boy (v. 10–12). She called God the One Who Sees Me (v. 13), and to commemorate the event, she named the well at that (unknown) location *Beer Lahai Roi* ("Well of the Living One Who Sees Me"; cf. 24:62; 25:11)."[3]

These same commentators also note the use of etymologies often capture the message of Genesis:

> These are rhetorical devices that draw from the account the explanation of names. Thus the name was a mnemonic device for remembering the events and their significance. In this passage two popular etymologies form not only the climax of the section but the point of the whole unit. God Himself named the boy Ishmael, which He then explained: for the Lord has heard of your misery (16:11). Clearly He meant this primarily for Hagar, but it was also meant for Abram and Sarai.
>
> The other naming was Hagar's referring to God as "the One who sees" after her, that is, looks out for her. So in these two names is a world of theology: God hears and God sees. This spot would afterward become holy, a place where God could be found providing for and hearing the cries of His people.[4]

Genesis 16:6–16 is crucial in this study of God's producing principles because it reiterates the importance of right seeing and right hearing. When in great distress, we must never turn away from the Lord but always run toward Him. He knows exactly where we are and sees our need. He is intimately acquainted with our afflictions and sorrow and hears our cry.

Jesus once asked His followers: "Will you also go away? And do you too desire to leave Me?" (John 6:67, AMP). The Lord was challenging each one of them to carefully consider his ways; from whence he came, and what were his future goals and intentions. We all would do well to answer the Lord's question for ourselves. What path do you contemplate? Are you on the right track or are you, even now, following after Hagar on the road that leads to Shur?

You can imagine the deathly silence that undoubtedly fell as each of Christ's followers wrestled with his or her response? It is a deeply personal question that demanded a careful searching of the heart. "Will you also go away?" asked God.

Finally, it was the impetuous disciple named Simon Peter who answered. "Lord," [he said], "to whom shall we go? You have the words (the message) of eternal life. And we have learned to believe and trust, and [more] we have come *to know* [surely] that You are the Holy One of God, the Christ (the Anointed One), the Son of the living God."

John 6:68–69 (AMP), emphasis mine.

Well said, Peter! The NIV renders Simon Peter's statement, "Lord, to whom shall we go? You have the words of eternal life. We believe *and know* that you are the Holy One of God" (v. 69, emphasis added).

From his response, Peter had grasped the importance of *knowingness* for maintaining right paths. "Lord," he said, "we believe *and know* that you are the Holy One of God."

To make this discussion all the more real and tangible, allow me to ask a very personal question. Do you have a similar relationship with God that is deeply rooted in *knowingness*? *The International Standard Bible Encyclopedia* says *to know* (i.e., *ginosko*, Strong's NT:1097) is *to apprehend by the mind some fact or truth in accordance with its real nature*.[5] The Greek *ginosko* is used by the Apostle Paul in his first epistle to the Corinthians. He compares life to the image seen in a mirror which is sometimes dim and blurred, and is only an imperfect reflection of reality as in a riddle or enigma. "But then," he says, "[when perfection comes] we shall see in reality and face to face! Now I *know* [*ginosko*] in part (imperfectly)," he declares, "but then I shall *know* [*epiginosko*] and understand fully and clearly, even in the same manner as I have been fully and clearly known [*epiginosko*] and understood [by God]" (1 Corinthians 13:12, AMP, emphasis mine).

Epiginosko (*Strong's* NT:1921) has *ginosko* at its root, and the prefix, *epi*, means *to become fully acquainted with*.[6] This word means *to know accurately and completely so as to recognize*.[7] In Paul's writings, it sometimes "refers, not to a theoretical knowledge of God, but rather to obedient recognition of the will of God."[8] We "shall *know* [*epiginosko*] and understand fully and clearly, even in the same manner as I have been fully and clearly *known* [*epiginosko*] and understood [by God]" (1 Corinthians 13:12b (AMP) emphasis mine

Returning to the Lord's questions of Hagar, He asked her to consider her mortality, her limited resources, and her finite strength. Only in this way could she come to grips with her inadequate and imperfect prospects.

Even as Hagar reflected on her failings, her unremarkable past, and her roots (i.e. all that she was and from whence she'd come), she must have realized she was sadly lacking. Suddenly, she recognized that her continued flight back to Egypt was useless. It was doomed to despair.

Now her destiny hung in the balance. It waited on her answer. What would she do?

Even as she contemplated the Lord's questions (i.e. her past failings and her future prospects), she heard the divine response. The angel of the Lord said unto her, "Return to thy mistress, and submit thyself under her hands" (Genesis 16:9, KJV).

Let's be painfully honest. God's solution is not what you or I want to hear. It's abhorrent to our fleshly natures and natural inclinations (i.e. instincts) to "go back" and "submit." This was especially abhorrent to Hagar who was stubbornly "Egyptian." The maidservant's roots are repeatedly mentioned in the Scriptures to stress the strength of her past leanings and convictions.

> Now Sarai, Abram's wife, had borne him no children. *But she had an Egyptian maidservant named Hagar,*
>
> Genesis 16:1 (NIV), emphasis added.

> So after Abram had been living in Canaan ten years, Sarai his wife took her *Egyptian maidservant* Hagar and gave her to her husband to be his wife.
>
> Genesis 16:3 (NIV), emphasis added.

> But Sarah saw that the son whom *Hagar the Egyptian* had borne to Abraham was mocking,
>
> Genesis 21:9 (NIV), emphasis added.

> This is the account of Abraham's son Ishmael, whom Sarah's maidservant, *Hagar the Egyptian,* bore to Abraham.
>
> Genesis 25:12 (NIV), emphasis added.

God told Hagar the Egyptian to *go back* and submit. The Lord's admonition to "go back" is often repeated throughout the Bible whenever God is redirecting the steps of His wayward people. For example, God said to Jacob, "Go back" (Genesis 31:3, 13; 32:9, NIV). To Moses, He also said, "Go back" (Exodus 4:19, NIV). And to Elijah, who was fleeing from Jezebel, the Lord said, "Go back" (1 Kings 19:15, NIV). Additionally, the idea of going back is an essential ingredient of the prodigal son's restoration. When telling His well-known parable, Jesus said the wayward son finally came to his senses and said, "How many of my father's hired men have food to spare, and here I am starving to death! I will set out and *go back* to my father and say to him: 'Father, I have sinned against heaven and against you. I am no longer worthy to be called your son; make me like one of your hired men.' So he got up and went to his father (Luke 15:17–20, NIV, emphasis added). It was in his submissive "going back" that the young man discover the beginnings of his restoration.

The Psalmist asks, "What shall I render to the Lord for all His benefits toward me?" (Psalm 116:12a, AMP). For that matter, what will you render or turn away from? Perhaps you too should consider going back to where you first went wrong and humbly submit.

Furthermore, the Psalmist wonders, "How can I repay Him for all His bountiful dealings?" (v. 12b, AMP). Then, with sudden inspiration, the Psalmist voices his response. "I will lift up the cup of salvation and deliverance and call on the name of the Lord. I will pay my vows to the Lord, yes, in the presence of all His people" (Psalm 116:13–14, AMP).

So it was that Hagar obeyed the Lord and returned to Sarai.

"I have met *'El-Roi,* the God Who Sees," she proclaimed. "He has seen my affliction and heard my cry." But, hard pressed to explain her epiphany, Hagar could only acknowledge her experience by recalling the name of the Lord Who spoke with her. "He is *El-Roi,*" she declared. "He is my God of seeing."

Most people, when hearing Hagar's amazing tale, considered it a fabrication of her imagination or even the result of a delirium of deprivation when in the desert. Some claimed it was her way of garnering sympathy and saving face. But through it all, Hagar stubbornly clung to her beliefs, declaring. "Have I [not] even here [in the wilderness] looked upon Him Who sees me [and lived]? *Or* have I here also seen [the future purposes or designs of] Him Who sees me?" (Genesis 16:13b, AMP).

It is a comfort to know that God looks upon us and is aware of our situations! He is *El-Roi* and determines the times and exact places of our residence. As stated elsewhere in Scripture, "For in him we live and move and have our being [existence]" (Acts 17:28a, NIV). It is a blessed realization to know beyond all shadow of doubt that the Lord is always close by.

Hagar saw the future purposes and designs of God concerning her life and the life of her son, Ishmael. "*Behold* ... you shall call his name *Ishmael*," declared God, "because the Lord has heard your affliction" (Genesis 16:11, NKJV, emphasis added). The Lord's interjection, "Behold" (NKJV) or "See now" (AMP) demands our full attention. It gives emphasis to the information that immediately follows, its "here and now-ness."[9] The Lord *hears* our grief. He intelligently discerns our misery and sorrow. The name *Ishmael* emphasizes this by joining *'el* (*Strong's* OT:410), denoting "God's strength," and *shama'* (*Strong's* OT:8085) which means *to hear intelligently* (often with implied attention and obedience).

The well of Hagar's visitation was called *Beer Lahai Roi*—A Well to the Living One Who Sees Me (v. 14, AMP). The fact that it is still there (Genesis 16:14, NIV) means the abiding influence of *El-Roi* has not waned, even to this day.

Additionally, the fact that Abram didn't resist when first hearing the God-given name of his new son suggests that he believed Hagar's incredible tale. He didn't discount it as a fanciful fabrication of Hagar's imagination. It seems the two of them, Abram and Hagar, shared a common bond of *knowingness* regarding the Lord. He understood her vision; and now, for the first time, she understood his.

"God has heard!" proclaimed Abram when he dedicated his newborn son.

Chapter Eight Evaluation

1. God's question, "Whence camest thou and whither wilt thou go?" (Genesis 16:8, KJV), still applies today. The Lord is asking each of us to closely examine our life. In Hagar's case, she was running away. Additionally, the inquiry begs you and me to scrutinize our chosen path. "Wither wilt thou go?" We are divinely asked to put our struggles into proper perspective. What are your plans? Where do you wish to be one year from now? How do you see your future? Is Egypt, with all its associated baggage (i.e. past affections, affiliations, and afflictions) the answer? There is no denying the strong pull of old habits, past friendships, and previous affiliations, but do you really want to go back there? Didn't that life-style once leave you destitute and spiritually bankrupt? All these things are found along the road that leads to Shur in the wilderness. In the end, how will you fair? How will you respond, or, better yet, how have you responded thus far?

2. Can you identify with Hagar who was wandering through life's wilderness? Perhaps, even now, you are struggling and wasting away in some nameless desert of despair. It is a private hell of torment. If so, the challenge is to remember the anointed words of Genesis 16:11b. "God hears, because the Lord has heard and paid attention to your affliction" (AMP). The promise of these words is just as real today as it was back then. Do you agree?

3. After asking Hagar to carefully consider the path so rashly chosen, the Lord told her to go back and submit to her mistress. This is easier said than done because the idea of *going back* in naturally repulsive. The Hebrew word translated "go back" suggests that she needed to turn around and go back to her point of departure. It essentially denotes a reversal of direction. Likewise, the Lord puts upon us the onus of going back to where we first went wrong. The problem for Hagar and all of us is that we haven't the innate strength to

do so. For this reason, we should thank God for His spring of living water in the wilderness on the road to Shur. Like Hagar of old, we too can find refreshment in the wilderness. Perhaps it is time for you to praise Him and faithfully declare, "Even here, in the wilderness, I have looked upon Him Who sees me."

4. Read the Parable of the Prodigal Son found in Luke 15:11–24. Notice the emphasis on his submissive going-back (v. 18). If in a group setting, discuss the son's fate if he'd steadfastly refused to "go back." For that matter, what would have happened had Hagar resisted God and returned to Egypt. From her response, we learn that great reward comes to those who surrender. From these lessons we learn that it is important to go back and live the revealed will of God. We must each forsake our Egyptian roots (our fleshly-ties) and renew ourselves in God's spring of living water.

5. What is your impression regarding the Well of the Living One Who Sees Me, *Beer Lahai Roi* (Genesis 16:14)? Why do the Scriptures emphatically state that the well can still be found there today? Perhaps I go too far in my interpretation, but I am inclined to believe that it is God's expression of reliable trust upon which we can still depend. The Lord still sees and hears our complaints. He is intimately acquainted with our miseries. This realization is strength to my struggling soul. It is my comfort and encouragement in the midst of my storms (Psalm 107:29). Hagar's tale teaches us many wonderful truths. Among these profound wonders is the divine purpose as it applies to each of our lives. God has a plan for you and me, but we must stand still and see the salvation of the Lord (Exodus 14:13). Then we must live it! This is all encapsulated in the "going back" of Hagar to Sarai. If you are in a group setting, discuss the implications of this story as it applies to you.

CHAPTER NINE

Room Enough

> Then Isaac sowed in that land, and reaped in the same year a hundredfold; and the Lord blessed him. The man began to prosper, and continued prospering until he became very prosperous; for he had possessions of flocks and possessions of herds and a great number of servants. So the Philistines envied him.
>
> Genesis 26:12–14 (NKJV)

Abraham lived a long and prosperous life; being one hundred seventy-five years old when he breathed his last. The Amplified Bible says he died at a good (*towb*: ample, full) old age; an old man, satisfied and satiated (Genesis 25:8). His life testifies of God's manifest goodness. It's the same goodness (*towb*) that characterized the creation at its beginning (Genesis 1:4, 10, 12, 18, 21, 25 and 31; NIV). Indeed, Abraham was *blessed with blessing*, and *with multiplication, he multiplied*.

Then the Angel of the Lord called to Abraham a second time out of heaven, and said: "By Myself I have sworn... [with] blessing I will bless you, and multiplying I will multiply your descendants as the stars of the heaven and as the sand which *is* on the seashore; and your descendants shall possess the gate of their enemies. In your seed all the nations of the earth shall be blessed, because you have obeyed My voice."

Genesis 22:15–18 (NKJV)

With divinely apportioned capacity and capability, Abraham increased. With multiplying he multiplied according to his legacy of *knowingness* of the Lord Who provides (Genesis 22:14), and prospered accordingly.

But is it really true that Abraham's blessing was passed to his descendants? Can we rely on the promise in Galatians 3:8 that says God's pledge to Abraham has percolated down through the ages to you and me? God said, "My covenant, My promise and pledge, I will establish with Isaac" (Genesis 17:21a, AMP). Does the Scriptural narrative back this up? Did Isaac's life give evidence of God's favor? Did the man of laughter (for this is the inner meaning of his name) carry on the promise?

The beginning of Isaac's story, at least as far as this book is concerned, is recorded in the twenty-sixth chapter of Genesis. The first verse tells us "there was a famine in the land... and Isaac went to Abimelech king of the Philistines in Gerar" (Genesis 26:1, NIV).

The Lord had previously warned Isaac not to go down to Egypt. "Live [i.e., abide, continue, rest] in the land where I tell you to live" [declared the Lord]. "Stay in this land for a while [i.e., turn aside from the road to lodge and dwell for a purpose], and I will be with you and will bless you. For to you and your descendants, I will give all these lands and will confirm the oath I swore to your father Abraham. I will make your descendants as numerous as the stars in the sky and will give them all these lands, and through your offspring all nations on earth will be blessed, because Abraham obeyed me and kept my requirements, my commands, my decrees and my laws" (Genesis 26:2b-5, NIV).

"Live where I tell you to live, and stay for a while (by implication, without permanence)," said the Lord. The next verse is only five words in length but has tremendous significance. "So Isaac stayed in Gerar" (Genesis 26:6, NIV). Easier said than done because it's not always easy to *live* (i.e. abide, continue, and rest) in the land of God's intention, let alone *stay* there; that is, turn aside from the road that everyone else follows and dwell there with temperance. But Isaac obeyed the Lord and abided in the land of the Philistines. Even in desperate times, when famine and draught lay waste to our lands, we can prosper if we choose to abide in the Lord. "If you abide in Me, and My words abide in you," said Jesus, "you will ask what you desire, and it shall be done for you. By this My Father is glorified, that you bear much fruit; so you will be My disciples" (John 15:7–8, NKJV).

So it was that Isaac sowed and reaped abundantly. Others just barely scraped by, but it was not so with Isaac. He and his family prospered with exceedingly increase. They were blessed with blessing, and with multiplication they multiplied.

Isaac planted crops, and God greatly blessed him. In the same year that he sowed, he also reaped a hundredfold. He became so wealthy with flocks and herds and servants that the Philistines began to stand up and take notice. They envied him (v. 14).

Finally, the Philistines, in whose land Isaac temporarily resided, couldn't stand it any longer. They had had enough! The success and triumph of Abraham's descendants galled them.

"Move away from us," [said their king to Isaac]; "for you have become too powerful ['atsam, Strong's OT:6105] for us" (Genesis 26:16, NIV). By their own admission, the man of God was mightier than they. *'Atsam* in the Hebrew is a primitive root that means "to bind fast" or "be increased."[1]

What was Isaac's response? Did he make a stand and fight? After all, he was mightier than they were. It was his chance to permanently grab a piece of the land for himself. With one word from him, the many servants of Isaac would have gone to battle. Were they not mightier?

Put yourself in Isaac's place. Try to imagine the man's inner turmoil and frustration. The entire camp was in tumult because it goes against the grain to picked-up stakes, abandon everything, and simply move on. He and his family had invested the many years of toil and sweat. They had worked hard for all they had! Even the Lord's abundant harvests require much labor and sustained input. It was by the sweat of their brows that they had what they had!

But God's Word flatly states: "So Isaac moved away from there" (v. 17a, NIV).

Though the Holy Scriptures don't tell us, I believe Isaac held firmly to his father's mantra, "The Lord will see to it!" I personally think he often repeated this phrase, having once stood beside his father on the mountain of God's provision (Genesis 22). "The Lord will see to it!" Isaac knew this reality was true and would not swerve from it.

Some said Isaac's good fortunes were a matter of luck but he knew otherwise. His greatness was handed down by God from his father so that he blessed with blessing and multiplied with multiplication.

In contrast, the eyes of the Philistines were tightly shut to the ways and means of God. They were blind to the Lord's provision and, like a hungry man who dreams that he is eating, they awoke with cravings not satisfied. Like a thirsty man who dreams that he is drinking, they awoke and were faint; their thirst was not quenched. So shall all nations be that fight against the Lord.

> "Stop and wonder...and be confounded [reluctantly]," declares the Lord. "Blind yourselves [now, if you choose; take your pleasure] and then be blinded [at the actual occurrence]. They are drunk, but not from wine; they stagger, but not from strong drink [but from spiritual stupor]. For the Lord has poured out on you the spirit of deep sleep. And He has closed your eyes, the prophets; and your heads, the seers, He has covered *and* muffled."
>
> Isaiah 29:8–10 (AMP)

Much to the chagrin of the Philistines, Isaac sowed and abundantly reaped. He harvested a hundred times more than they, prospering where they could not. Genesis 26:13 explains he became great and gained more and more until he was very wealthy and distinguished (AMP). He lived as did his father before him, according to God's declared *goodness* (i.e., *towb*). So he conceded to Abimelech's demands; he packed-up and moved on fully reliant on his God—*Jehovah-jireh* (The Lord Will Provide). He'd been to the mountain of seeing with his father and had also met *The Lord Who Will See to It.* He knew what he knew and that was enough.

Without doubt, tempers flared and disagreements arose within the camp. Hot-tempered men considered the move to be a sign of weakness and surrender. Besides, they'd worked hard in that harsh and unforgiving land. Additionally, they didn't share Isaac's vision of God. They'd heard his stories but the tales were foreign and unreal to their own experience. Hence, they grumbled and complained.

The family and servants of Isaac dragged their feet but eventually gave in because they could not deny God's favor. Somehow, and against all odds, Isaac succeeded where others failed. The Philistines would also plant and gather, but Isaac's harvest was always greater. When Isaac would say, "We shall *see!*" they knew God would indeed *see* and provide. As his father knew and praised, so too did Isaac. "I will sing to the Lord, because He has dealt bountifully with me" (Psalm 13:6, NKJV).

Isaac didn't say so much as one angry word when he "departed *from there* and pitched his tent in the Valley of Gerar and dwelt there" (Genesis 26:17, NKJV, emphasis added). The maxim "from there" is a recurring theme throughout this chapter (Genesis 26:17, 22 and 23, NIV) and testifies that life with God is characterized by such crossings from here to there. To realize the Lord's fullness of grace we cannot stand still! Like Isaac, we must continually forge ahead and make new paths were none are found. "So Isaac moved away *from there* and encamped in the Valley of Gerar *and settled there*" (Genesis 26:17, NIV, emphasis mine).

Each time Isaac moved, he flourished in his new home. The record of Isaac's "from there" experiences also details his reclamation of his father's old wells. "Isaac dug again the wells of water which had been dug in the days of Abraham his father, for the Philistines had stopped them after the death of Abraham; and he gave them the names by which his father had called them" (Genesis 26:18,

AMP). Isaac called the wells of water by the same names as did his father. Thereby, he upheld his prerogative to them and re-establish his claim. Never underestimate the importance of names and the naming of names. Speak over your situations the Word of God.

Not by coincidence, Isaac's servants dug and discovered a valuable subterranean resource of water. *The Living Bible* describes it as "a gushing underground spring" (Genesis 26:19, TLB). It was literally flushed with a life-giving flow. In that arid land, where water was its lifeblood, Isaac possessed the key to success and prosperity. Hence, Isaac's heritage surged with life-giving flow. Indeed, he was blessed with the same divine capacity and capability as his father. With multiplication he multiplied; with increase, he increased!

Once again, as is often the case when we flesh-out our destiny of inspired knowingness and know-how, conflict arose. Others envied Isaac's success and his divinely-appointed bounty. Consequently, the herdsmen of Gerar quarreled with Isaac's herdsmen over the wells. "The water is ours," they argued (v. 20), and, this time, even Isaac's patience wore thin. The names he gave the wells reflect his frustration.

> He named the well *Esek* [contention], because they quarreled with him. Then [his servants] dug another well, and they quarreled over that also; so he named it *Sitnah* [enmity].
>
> Genesis 26:20b-21 (AMP), emphasis mine.

Should he stand and fight? This is always our temptation. It is what those around Isaac advised. The water was rightfully theirs and, in truth, Isaac would have prevailed if he'd stubbornly dug-in his heels and resisted. But then he would be just like them—the quarrelsome, loud-mouthed Philistines. What was the Lord's will?

Even though Isaac was only temporarily dwelling in the Philistine land (Genesis 26:3), it was his anointing that revealed the life-giving flow of water. Ultimately, he realized it was not about him; it was all about God and God's providence. "I know that everything God does will endure forever," said Solomon; "nothing can be added to it and nothing taken from it. God does it so that men will revere him" (Ecclesiastes 3:14, NIV).

That which lay beneath the Philistine's soil was unseen by them because they lacked eyes to behold it. Moses later declared, "The hidden things belong to Jehovah our God; but the revealed ones are ours and our children's for ever..." (Deuteronomy 29:29a, Darby).

What should Isaac do? What would you have done under similar circumstances? I love how the Psalmist frames our answer:

> "Let me understand the teaching of Your precepts; then I will meditate on Your wonders," [sings the psalmist]. "My soul is weary with sorrow; strengthen me according to Your word. Keep me from deceitful ways; be gracious to me through Your law. I have chosen the way of truth; I have set my heart on Your laws. I hold fast to Your statutes, O Lord; do not let me be put to shame. I run in the path of your commands, for you have set my heart free."
>
> Psalm 119:27–32 (NIV)

As before, Isaac once again abandoned his wells. He even abandoned the well that "gushed" with life-giving flow. I can only imagine the turmoil and dissension that arose within the ranks of his servants. They had to slink off like dogs with heads hung low and with tails tucked between their legs. The Philistines cheered. How humiliating!

As in previous times, Isaac and those with him moved on. For a third time Isaac's servants dug for water. This was really getting old! I am confident you can readily identify with such enduring trials.

It is said that three times is a charm. When used in Scripture, the number three suggests a beginning, middle and end. Familiar trios are heaven, earth, and sea; morning, noon, and night; and right, middle, and left. It is "therefore regarded as symbolic of a complete and ordered whole."[2]

Thus, when Isaac's servants dug for water a third time, there was no dispute over it. Isaac had sufficiently removed himself from his continuing source of contention—the Philistines. This is another lesson that is well learned.

So it was that the patriarch rejoiced in his victory. The well was not one of his father's making but was entirely new and of his own doing. It testifies of his ongoing revelation when walking with God. Hence, he named it *Rehoboth* which, by definition, refers to an *open space*. "Now the Lord has given us room and we will flourish in the land," he proclaimed (Genesis 26:22, NIV). The New King James Version says Isaac declared, "For now the Lord has made room for us, and we shall be fruitful in the land."

Rehoboth signifies God's intended, wide-open places that are broad, and spacious. To live wide and free is bliss, but to have the Lord's *room enough* is divine. "He brought me out into a spacious place; he rescued me because He delighted in me," praised David when delivered from the hand of Saul (Psalm 18:19, NIV). "I will be glad and rejoice in Your mercy," sang David, "for You have considered my trouble; You have known my soul in adversities, and have not shut me up into the hand of the enemy; You have set my feet in a wide place" (Psalm 31:7-8, NKJV).

The root of the name *Rehoboth* is *rachab* (*Strong's* OT:7337), referring to that which is *broad* or *roomy*. It was used by the prophet Isaiah when he declared: "He [the Lord] will give the rain for your seed with which you sow the ground, and bread of the increase of the earth; It will be fat and plentiful. In that day your cattle will feed in *large* [i.e., *rachab*] pastures" (Isaiah 30:23, NKJV, emphasis mine). Isaiah also announced: "Then thou shalt see, and flow together, and thine heart shall fear, and be *enlarged* [i.e., *rachab*]; because the abundance of the sea shall be converted unto thee, the forces of the Gentiles shall come unto thee" (Isaiah 60:5, KJV, emphasis mine).

Notably, the name *Jesus* is the Greek form of the name *Joshua* or *Jeshua*, a contraction of *Jehoshua* (*the help of Jehovah* or *savior*).[3] In turn, the Hebrew root of Joshua's name is *yasha'* (*Strong's* OT:3467), which means *to be open, wide, or free* and, by inference, *to be safe*.[4] Hence, the Lord's name connotes the object of His mission—to save (Matthew 1:21).[5] Jesus came to enlarge our lives; to make our world, wide and free. "The Spirit of the Lord is on Me," He announced, "because He has anointed Me to preach good news to the poor. He has sent Me to proclaim freedom for the prisoners and recovery of sight for the blind, to release the oppressed, to proclaim the year of the Lord's favor" (Luke 4:18–19, NIV).

As previously discussed, we must never shy away from invoking the name of Jesus because it is an assertion of our ascended-freedom. When bound or restricted, call upon the Lord's name, *Jesus*. When the devil tries to put you in a box, one that tightly confines you and affords little room to move and breath, evoke the name that is above all names. Like Isaac, proclaim God's *broadness* and declare His *room enough* over your various situations!

> "And everyone who calls on the name of the Lord will be saved [healed, preserved, made to be well]," [declares Peter]…"Repent and be baptized, every one of you, in the name of Jesus Christ for the forgiveness of your sins. And you will receive the gift of the Holy Spirit. The promise is for you and your children and for all who are far off—for all whom the Lord our God will call."
>
> Acts 2:21, 38–39 (NIV)

Peter's bold declaration is taken from the Old Testament where the prophet Joel proclaimed, "And it shall come to pass that whoever calls on the name of the Lord shall be saved" (Joel 2:32, NKJV). *Saved* in this passage is *yasha'* (the root of Jesus's name). It means to be *open*, *wide*, or *free*. Thus, in this proclamation is God's principle of *room enough*.

Room enough to live a wide-open life!

Room enough to be free!

Room enough to live unbounded by restrictions!

One day, when on their way to the temple, Peter and John were passing through the city gate named Beautiful. There was a crippled man there begging for help (Acts 3:2). He was the antithesis of all that Jesus's name engenders—he was encumbered, constrained, and restricted.

When the poor fellow saw Peter and John, he immediately begged for mercy. Looking straight at the man, Peter said, "Look at us!" Don't miss the importance of "looking" in this story.

> Now Peter and John were going up to the temple at the hour of prayer, the ninth hour (three o'clock in the afternoon).
>
> [When] a certain man, crippled from his birth, was being carried along, who was laid each day at that gate of the temple [which is] called Beautiful, so that he might beg for charitable gifts from those who entered the temple.
>
> So when he *saw* Peter and John about to go into the temple, he asked them to give him a gift. *And Peter directed his gaze intently at him*, and so did John, and said, "Look at us!" *And [the man] paid attention to them*, expecting that he was going to get something from them.
>
> But Peter said, "Silver and gold (money) I do not have; but what I do have [an *ascension-awareness*], that I give to you: in [the use of] the name of Jesus Christ of Nazareth, walk!"
>
> Acts 3:1–6 (AMP), emphasis mine.

The passage first directs our attention to the man. It notes that he *saw* (*eido*, Strong's NT:1492) Peter and John. *Eido* is a primary verb expressing the idea of *seeing* with knowledge.[6] In other words, the man perceived that Peter and John offered hope of help. What he got, however, went far beyond anything he could have dreamt possible.

He saw Peter and John, but Peter also saw him. Fastened his eyes on the man, Peter steadfastly gazed, underscoring the significance of his focused attention. This is a recurrent theme thoughout this passage and underscores our need of focused intention when seeking God's deliverance. "Peter looked (*atenizo*) straight at him, as did John" (Acts3:4, NIV). The Greek *atenizo* (Strong's NT:816) stresses

Peter's concentrated awareness and deliberate intent. In like manner, we must always begin the process of our salvation or deliverance by *fixing our eyes* (i.e., *atenizo*), not upon the problem, but on their solution. A mere cursory glance heavenward isn't nearly enough to cure our various ills and complaints. We must determine to give God our all-in-all; by and through our focused, deliberate intention.

"Look at us!" said Peter. Peter demanded th man's rapt attention. Perhaps the crippled man's eyes were downcast from self-loathing. Maybe he had looked away, not daring to look directly into Peter's eyes. When beaten down, we often divert our eyes downward, finding it difficult to gaze at anything but our own pitiful plight. But Peter insisted that the man turn his eyes toward him. *Atenizo* is the beginning of all things amazing and wonderful! Remember this point as we probe deeper into God's orchestrated plan of salvation—*The Divine Conception*.

To emphasize the important principle of focused attention with implicit connection, recall the story of Stephen's epiphany (i.e. his sudden, intuitive perception of the Lord, Jesus Christ). At the time, a council of religious leaders was steadfastly examining (i.e., *atenizo*) him. "All who were sitting in the Sanhedrin looked intently at Stephen, and they saw that his face was like the face of an angel" (Acts 6:15, NIV). But they were unable to resist his wisdom and the spirit by which he spoke (v. 10). The story begins with their steadfast gaze but ends with the statement that Stephen, being full of the Holy Spirit, looked-up steadfastly (i.e. with *atenizo*) into heaven and saw the glory of God and Jesus standing on the right hand of God. "Look!" he exclaimed, "I see the heavens opened, and the Son of man standing at God's right hand!" (Acts 7:56, AMP).

Returning to the miraculous healing at the Beautiful Gate of Jerusalem, Peter fixed his gaze intently upon the crippled man and said to him, "Look [i.e., *blepo*] at us!" (Acts 3:4). *The Hebrew Greek Key Word Study Bible* notes that *blepo* is often used figuratively regarding recognition of truth or mental perception (Mark 8:18; Luke 8:10; and Romans 11:8, 10).[7] Peter knew that the key to this man's salvation (i.e., *yasha'*—his ability to live wide and free) was in his looking with focused intent so as to recognize the truth.

"Silver or gold I do not have," Peter continued, "but what I have I give you. In the name of Jesus Christ of Nazareth, walk!" (Acts 3:6, NIV). Then, taking the man by his right hand, Peter helped him up. There is no word of the man's objection. He didn't argue, saying that his legs were too weak. He did not chide Peter because of his past sins or his current depravity. None of these things were important to him, as long as his focus remained on the apostle. With crippled legs and all, the beggar reached out his right hand toward God. *Just as he was*, the man held nothing back. Importantly, the right hand is biblically significant because it symbolizes one's strength. It is the left hand that rocks the cradle, and it is the right that swings the sword. With all the strength he could muster, the disabled man reached forth his right hand toward God. In essence, he gave God his all!

Metaphorically, the right hand is the hand of power. This imagery is employed in Psalm 110:1 where the Lord says, "Sit at My right hand until I make your enemies a footstool for your feet" (NIV). It also is used of Jesus' royal status in Acts 2:33 and, as noted in one commentary, "is used as a sign of fellowship."[8] When defending his credentials as God's apostle to the Gentiles, Paul stated that James, Peter and John had given him and Barnabas "the right hand of fellowship" when they recognized the grace given to him (Galatians 2:9, NIV).

So it was that the man who was crippled extended his right hand to God and with help from Peter, he stood. Immediately, his feet and ankles were strengthened (i.e., established). He leapt forth! If you will let Him, God will elevate you above your incapacitation. You will not just stand but you will leap forth with newfound vitality and strength.

How do these two stories (i.e. the accounts of Isaac's well and that of the rejuvenated man) apply to you and me? First, we must always recognize the principle of God's *room enough*. When Isaac finally came into its full apprehension, he declared, "For now the Lord has made room for us, *and we shall be fruitful in the land*" (Genesis 26:22, AMP, emphasis mine). His well was named *Rehoboth* which means *wide-open spaces*. "Now God has given us plenty of space to spread out in the land," declared the patriarch (Genesis 26:22, *The Message*).⁹

Everything God does is to provide *room enough* (literally, plenty of space) for you and me to spread out and be fruitful.

The Scriptures offer one additional insight into the Lord's *room enough*. After his proclamation of God's *room enough*, Isaac went up to his special place at Beersheba (v. 23). Why Beersheba? Because it was at Beersheba that the Philistine king had previously met Abraham and reluctantly recognized the blessing and surpassing greatness of God. He said, "God is with you in everything you do. Now swear to me here before God that you will not deal falsely with me or my children or my descendants. Show to me and the country where you are living as an alien the same kindness I have shown to you." (Genesis 21:22–23, NIV).

We must each reach a place in our spiritual walk and Christian experience where we recognize God's abiding presence and influence. This was essential to Hagar in her wilderness revival. It was vital to Abraham at Beersheba. And it was greatly appreciated by Isaac after facing so much turmoil over his wells. It should also our *Beersheba Declaration*—the unqualified acknowledgement of God's presence and blessing. Thus, when Abraham called on the name of the Lord at Beersheba, he gave to God a new name according to his unfolding realization and fresh insight. After the treaty had been made with Abimelech, he called upon the Eternal God, *El 'Olam*, Who is always there (Genesis 21:32–33, NIV). Although *'olam* often refers to indefinite continuance into the very distant future, it sometimes refers to the past.¹⁰ Abraham's impression of his God now included His abiding presence wherever he went. Thus, this chapter in the history of God's people ends with one last remark: "And Abraham stayed in the land of the Philistines for a long time" (Genesis 21:34, NIV). It seems his *Beersheba Declaration* was an essential statement of realization for his continued well-being and endurance. The awareness of *Jehovah-jireh* (The Lord Will Provide) and *El 'Olam* (The Lord Who Is Always There) was critical to Abraham's abiding knowingness and blessing. In this knowledge, the man turned the world upside down.

Following Isaac's *Rehoboth* experience—his dawning comprehension of God's *room enough*—the patriarch returned to Beersheba, the place of his spiritual roots. The Lord met him there and said, "I am the God of your father Abraham. Do not be afraid, for I am with you; I will bless you and will increase the number of your descendants for the sake of my servant Abraham" (Genesis 26:24, NIV).

We quickly skip over the next verse, seeing little importance there. But pause for a moment and consider the deeper meaning of verse 25. In a very matter-of-fact way, this passage says, "Isaac built an altar there and called on the name of the Lord. There he [also] pitched his tent, and there his servants dug a well" (NIV). Isaac was like his father in this regard. "Isaac was identified by his tent and altar."[11] I believe Isaac's altar was dedicated to the character of God expressly revealed there. You may recall it was at Beersheba that Abraham planted a tamarisk tree and called on the name of the Lord, the Eternal God (*El 'Olam*—The Lord Who is Always There). Like his fathers before him, Isaac purposely praised in accord with his unique knowingness (Genesis 4:26, 12:8, 13:4, 21:33, 26:26). While the Scriptures are silent regarding the name of God that was evoked, it makes sense that Isaac praised according to his previous night's revelation. "I am the God of your father Abraham," said the Lord to him. "Do not be afraid, for I am with you; I will bless you and will increase the number of your descendants for the sake of my servant Abraham" (Genesis 26:24, NIV). If we are to follow the patriarch's model of praise, we must always raise our hands in recognition of Him we know.

The second truth found in verse 26 concerns Isaac's tent. He pitched it at Beersheba, signaling his intent to abide in the presence of *El 'Olam* (The Lord Who is Always There). He was determined to continue in God's *room enough* at Beersheba. "Do not be afraid," assured the Lord. "I will bless you and will increase the number of your descendants..." (Genesis 26:24, NIV). God's "fear not" is what Isaac needed most. It was the Eternal God's personal affirmation of divine comfort and protection. Isaac would need this reassurance in light of coming events because the Philistines were never far behind.

> Meanwhile, Abimelech had come to him from Gerar, with Ahuzzath his personal adviser and Phicol the commander of his forces.
>
> Genesis 26:26 (NIV)

The opening word from this passage speaks volumes to me. The New International Version of the Bible says, "*Meanwhile*, Abimelech had come to him from Gerar, with Ahuzzath his personal adviser and Phicol the commander of his forces" (Genesis 26:26, emphasis mine). To me, the word *meanwhile* loosely suggests that something unseen was brewing behind the scenes that would challenge Isaac's *room enough* (his *Rehoboth* experience). If he was going to hold on to it, Isaac would have to be vigilant and shrewd; he had to *abide* (pitch our tent) in the place where God resides.

Accompanying Abimelech was Phicol, the commander of all the Philistine forces. Unsaid, but undoubtedly true, there was also a large entourage and many troops.

But Isaac refused to be intimidated. "Why have you come to me, since you were hostile to me and sent me away?" said Isaac boldly with much backbone. Armed with the knowledge of the Lord's "fear not," Isaac didn't cower or back down.

Without a doubt, this galled Abimelech because he hated to admit that he and his country needed this enigmatic man of God. His accompanying blessing of increase and multiplication was dearly missed. Isaac was much favored by heaven and the God of his father, Abraham. .

"We saw clearly that the Lord was with you," said the king, grudgingly. "There ought to be a sworn agreement between us—between us and you. Let us make a treaty with you that you will do us no harm, just as we did not molest you but always treated you well and sent you away in peace. *And now you are blessed by the Lord*" (Genesis 26:26–29, NIV, emphasis added).

The Philistine' leaders had come to realize that God was on the side of Isaac. The unseen hand of the Lord's protective presence couldn't be denied. The New American Commentary notes that "the acknowledgment of Isaac as 'blessed by the Lord' (v. 29; cp.

24:31)...by Abimelech illustrates the necessary response of the nations to experience the blessing God has offered by Abraham's descendants (12:2)."[12]

"Truly, providence smiles upon you," Abimelech reluctantly admitted. Even as he uttered these words, and as if in confirmation, Isaac's servants brought glad tidings—a new source of water had been discovered.

Indeed, Isaac was the favorite of heaven, as was his father before him. It is truly said: "The secret things belong to the Lord our God, but the things revealed belong to us and to our children forever" (Deuteronomy 29:29, NIV).

Chapter Nine Evaluation

1. Read the amazing story of Isaac's *Rehoboth*—his wondrous tale of God's "room enough" (Genesis 26). Have you ever been so tightly hemmed in that you could hardly move or breathe? You were squeezed and claustrophobic? If within a discussion group, discuss your emotions and how you felt. Were you relieved when finally freed? Also take time to write the Lord's mission statement found in Luke 4:18–19. It is yours to claim, if you will!

2. Even though Isaac was temporarily residing within the land of the Philistines, he thrived. He had a special anointing to find hidden resources of fresh water that were unknown to the native inhabitants. A treasure of life-giving flow lay beneath the Philistines' feet but they knew it not! Have you ever had a similar situation when God wondrously opened your eyes to an unseen treasure? We often struggle and toil while all along God's well of refreshing is within easy reach or just around the corner. A good example of this is Hagar's second encounter with the Lord. One day, after her son was weaned, Sarah saw Ishmael mocking. "Get rid of that slave woman and her son, for that slave woman's son will never share in the inheritance with my son Isaac" (Genesis 21:10, NIV). To keep family peace, Abraham sent them packing. They went on their way and wandered in the desert of Beersheba until their water was gone. Hagar left the boy in the shade of a scant desert shrub and went off. "I cannot watch the boy die," she sobbed (v. 16, NIV). From out of nowhere came a voice saying, "What is the matter, Hagar? Do not be afraid; God has heard the boy crying as he lies there. Lift the boy up and take him by the hand..." (v(v). 17–18, NIV). Then God opened her eyes and she saw a well of water. It was there all along but she didn't see it. So she went and filled the skin with water and gave the boy a drink. Read this story in Genesis 21, paying particular attention to the interplay of seeing and hearing throughout the narrative.

3. The enemy of our souls continually seeks to restrain us or keep us tightly confined with few options. Whether it is by sickness or disease, financial strain or debt, family issues or marital squabbles, the devil seeks tries to imprison us in a tight box with little room to breathe. When in such situations, I encourage you to learn from Isaac at Beersheba or Paul and Silas in prison. Paul and Silas had every reason to be distraught, having been severely flogged and imprisoned for declaring the Lord's *room enough* (Acts 16:23). But despite their horrid circumstances, having been thrown into the innermost prison, they sang songs. It was a different tune than most people sing when in similar circumstances. They sang an unchained melody and others stopped to listen and took notice. Though they were down and out, they did not give in to intimidation or fear. They sang as did David when also afflicted: "Yea, though I walk through the valley of the shadow of death, I will fear no evil: for Thou art with me; Thy rod and Thy staff they comfort me" (Psalm 23:4, KJV).

4. This chapter's challenge is to rattle the cages of restraint that confine us. God has a plan by which prison doors are flung open. He has reserved a *Rehohoth Experience* (His *room enough*) for each of us. If within a study group, discuss the implications of Jesus' name. "And it shall come to pass that whoever calls on the name of the Lord shall be saved," said Joel (Joel 2:32, NKJV). "You shall call His name *Jesus*, for He will save His people from their sins" (Matthew 1:21b, NKJV, emphasis mine). The name *Jesus* is derived from the Hebrew name *Joshua*, which itself is from *Jehovah yasha,*' meaning *God—to be open, wide, or free*. What does the name *Jesus* mean to you? Should you merely pray, "In Your name we pray"? Is it sufficient to end your prayers with a simple "Amen"? More importantly and now that you know the inner meaning of our Lord's name, will you pray differently?

5. End this chapter by declaring the name of *Jesus* over your troubles. Your various afflictions and troubles are, in many

respects, your "Philistines" to resist. The story of Isaac's *Rehoboth* concludes with the ruler of the Philistines grudgingly having to admit a great truth. When he was asked by Isaac, "Why have you come to me, since you were hostile to me and sent me away?" Abimelech reluctantly said, "We saw that the Lord was certainly with you... You are now the blessed *or* favored of the Lord!" (Genesis 26:28–29, AMP).

Part Two

Activating God's Anointing

CHAPTER ONE

God's Holy Symphony of Doing

> When the Lord saw that Leah was unloved, He opened her womb...
>
> Genesis 29:31 (NKJV)

Her name was Leah, and she was unloved. She was an unhappy, bitter woman who lived in the ever-present shadow of her lovelier, younger sister, Rachel. Rachel was the pretty one, "beautiful and well favoured" (Genesis 29:17b, KJV).

Leah was...

You complete the above sentence because her story is often a prelude of our own... it's your story to tell. In many ways, you and I are Leah. Most of us have grown-up or lived in the shadow of another. In many respects, we are the "less favored" one who is always at the bottom, only an unfortunate afterthought. Even worse, some of us are an ugly inconvenience, seemingly always in the way. Heaven help us!

Have you ever experienced the pain of being second-best in most things? I believe the Scriptures say it all when it was written, "And Jacob loved Rachel" (Genesis 29:18a, AMP). What about Leah? Who loved her? If you fill in the blanks you'll discover many hurts and scars that run deep. Put yourself in her place and try to imagine her suffering. It is encapsulated in the white spaces between the lines. Leah struggled for meaning and significance, for her place under the sun; but no matter what she did, she was the one with "the weak and dull looking" eyes. "Weak eyes"—that's how the Scriptures put it! And then there was Rachel; she was "beautiful and attractive" (v. 17, AMP).

Then, to make matters worse, the young man of her dreams, Jacob, went to her father and said: "I'll work for you seven years in return for your younger daughter Rachel" (Genesis 29:16–18 (NIV). Poor Leah! Scorned in life and love.

Jacob was the son of Isaac and possessed the same supernatural proclivity toward productive abundance as did his father and his father's father. The land was blessed wherever Abraham and Isaac dwelt. Now, the same could be said of Jacob—good fortune and multiplied increase followed him wherever he went. Jacob was as much the favorite of heaven as was Rachel in the eyes of him who loved her. Rachel was Jacob's heartthrob.

Laban was a shrewd man and knew a good bargain. Jacob would be his for seven long years, to labor in his fields and shepherd his flocks. All the while, the land would prosper under his care (v. 20).

For seven painful years, Leah had to watch the two lovebirds frolic in each other's devotion. She quietly remained behind the scenes, trying to ignore their games and affection. All the while she desperately hurt inside. Her heart ached for Jacob but, to him, she was like a sister.

Finally, the long-awaited time came for the two young lovers to be joined in holy matrimony. Amid great celebration, friends and relatives gathered to eat, drink, and witness the union of the two great families. Wine flowed, and there was much laughter and mirth. All were merry, and when it was time, Jacob was wed in the dim shadows of early evening.

Strangely, Leah was absent, or so it was supposed. Sadly, she was not missed.

The next morning, Jacob woke to discover a horrid deception had been perpetrated upon him. He turned to see his young bride and found that it was not his beloved Rachel lying next to him. It was Leah... he'd been tricked!

"What have you done?" raged Jacob. "Did I not work for you for seven years that I might have Rachel?" he said to Laban, his father-in-law. "Why have you deceived and cheated me? Why have I been thrown down like this?" (v. 25).

Laban cringed before the irate young man but did not relent. He smugly answered, "It is not our custom to give the younger daughter in marriage before the older. Wait until the bridal week is over and I will give you Rachel as well. But you must work for me another seven years in exchange."

Jacob was furious but had no choice. He stormed from Laban's tent, vowing to someday get even. It is always a bitter pill when one reaps what he sows for Jacob was himself a deceiver and the inner meaning of his name means "a supplanter."

As for Leah, she had the man of her dreams, but Jacob wanted nothing to do with her. He blamed her for the part she played in the deception. Her situation became even more deplorable than ever. And lest we forget Rachel, she was devastated. Forevermore, she would be known as Jacob's second wife. Leah had stolen her husband, her rights, and her rightful place within the family. Such was the competition between the women, one that would continue throughout the remainder of their lives.

When Jacob finished Leah's bridal week, he took Rachel as his wife. The Bible minimally states, "and he loved Rachel more than Leah" (v. 30b, NIV). Poor Leah! She was a miserable, embittered and naturally disadvantaged woman trapped in a hopeless situation.

So it was that the Lord *saw* (i.e., *ra'ah*) Leah and that she was unloved. Therefore, He orchestrated a divine conception—His plan of salvation. With inestimable compassion, God looked upon Leah and saw her with the same measuring eye that upholds creation (Genesis 1:4, 10, 12, 18, 21, 25, and 31). He opened her womb and Leah conceived a child; the first of twelve sons granted to His servant, Israel. In His glance was fruitfulness.

When her son was born, Leah named him *Reuben*. She declared, "It is because the Lord has seen my misery. Surely my husband will love me now" (Genesis 29:32, NIV). Her reference was to Jehovah, the self-existent and eternal God, which is the Jewish national name of the Lord. But also, she Leah referenced the seeing principle of God. It was a prophetic utterance in keeping with her son's fate. *Reuben* was Leah's son of seeing; the first oracle within God's kingdom of Israel. This gracious dispensation first began when the Lord *saw* [*ra'ah* (*Strong's* OT:7200)] Leah's loathsome dilemma (Genesis 29:31a). *Seeing* was, and still is, the beginning of God's goodness and vitality. The Lord's *seeing* sets the stage of divine deliverance. It was, and still is, the foundation of His Producing Principles. For example, the story of Abraham on Mount Moriah begins when he first *looked up* (i.e., *ra'ah*) and *saw* (i.e., *ra'ah*) the place where he was to worship (Genesis 22:4, NIV). Then he *looked up* again and *saw* a ram caught by its horns in a thicket (v. 13, NIV). Appropriately, Abraham called the name of that place "The Lord Will Provide" which literally means "Jehovah Will See to It." The divine principles revealed on Moriah's slope still applied and were now being carried out through God's servant, Leah. It was the same "seeing attitude" that underscored Hagar's salvation experience in the wilderness. It was only as she looked up to *see* that God provided a way of escape.

The tale of Jacob's two wives is heaven's contrast between fertility and barrenness, productivity and lack, vitality and flawed weakness. The story of Leah and Rachel is God's sketch of blessing and productivity verses lack and barrenness. Leah's tale unravels the mystery of God's Producing Principle—His scheme of divine blessing for all men.

"Lord, make my husband love me," pleaded Leah. She was desperate for her husband's affection. "Give him an heir through me!" she prayed.

In that day, the highest sanctions of religion and devotion were heaped upon the fruitful woman. Fruitfulness was considered God's special blessing (Exodus 23:26; Deuteronomy 7:14; Psalm 113:9) and a complete family was emblematic of beauty (Song of Solomon 4:2; 6:6).

So when the Lord granted a child to Leah, she must have heaved a great sigh of relief. She believed she would no longer be overwhelmed by contempt. She would at last have a place within the family of God. She would bring forth the firstborn son of Israel.

Thus, she named him Reuben and said, "It is because the Lord has *seen* [i.e., *ra'ah*] my misery. Surely my husband will love me now" (Genesis 29:32, NIV, emphasis added). The Amplified Version of this same passage better stresses the *seeing* element of Leah's tale. "See, a son!" [she declared]. "[It is] because the Lord has *seen* my humiliation and affliction; now my husband will love me" (emphasis mine).

The root of Reuben's name is the imperative of *ra'ah* (*Strong's* OT:7200) which generally refers to the supremacy of true and right sight. Reuben, Jacob's firstborn son, was the beginning of Israel's strength. As in the story of creation (Genesis 1:4, 10, 12, 18, 21, 25, and 31), *seeing* plays a primal role. Even as God *saw* the darkness that initially hovered over His creation (Genesis 1:1–2), He also *saw* with discerning eyes the deplorable condition of Leah.

"It is because the Lord has seen my misery. Surely my husband will love me now," Leah declared (Genesis 29:32b, NIV). Little did she know at the time that Reuben was only the beginning of blessing. More is needed within God's kingdom to produce measurable change (i.e. to set the captive free). Hence, her situation didn't change as she anticipated. Even after the birth of Reuben, Leah remained unloved. She was still without favor and honor within her own household. What more is necessary to procure blessing? Obviously, something was lacking...but what?

This was Leah's quandary and is ours as well. What must we do to procure the fullness of God's vitality? What is needed to change our destiny from despair and ugliness to joy and beauty? The "weak eyes" that so aptly described Leah's legacy are obstinate and resilient. They don't easily relinquish their hold upon us.

From Leah's story, one thing is certain: true and right sight is the beginning of blessedness within God's kingdom, but it is not the final word. Additional revelation is needed which the Apostle Paul compared to looking into a mirror that only gives a dim (blurred) reflection of reality as in a riddle or enigma. "But then [when perfection comes]," he declares, "we shall see in reality and face to face! Now I know in part (imperfectly), but then I shall know and understand fully and clearly, even in the same manner as I have been fully and clearly known and understood [by God]" (1 Corinthians 13:12b, AMP).

While Reuben is worthy of a double portion, this being his birthright as Israel's firstborn son (Deuteronomy 21:17), the ability to rightly see is insufficient, in and of itself, to bring forth heaven's full bounty and great joy. Reuben was not the sole oracle of God's blessings. In fact, he is the first of four sons born to Leah, each of which proclaim divine truths that build upon one another.

"Lord, I am still unloved!" Leah complained. "Reuben, my precious *son of seeing*, is the beginning of miracles, but more is needed. My husband still does not love me, and I am without honor within my own household. What more must I do to break the chains of my present bondage?"

So it was that Leah *conceived* (*harah*, Strong's OT:2029) again (v. 33). The use of the Hebrew *harah* is interesting because of its implications. *The Theological Wordbook of the Old Testament* says of *harah*:

> [*Harah* is] generally is used to state the results of sexual intercourse. In this respect there is often a connection with some phase of the redemptive program of God, that is, the conceptions of which the OT speaks concern children who were to play an important part in redemptive history.
>
> The successive births of Cain, Abel, and Seth set out for us the hope of personal redemption. All did not go in the way of Cain, and the message of grace was preserved until and through Noah. The selective, monergistic power of God is demonstrated in the conception of Isaac (Genesis 21:2), demonstrating that the power of God alone is able to bring about his redemptive purposes, for both Abraham and Sarah were too old to have children. Men must trust solely in God's power, not in their own desperate attempts.

Rebekah was barren, and Isaac prayed for her to conceive (Genesis 25:21). Isaac presumably expected children early in his marriage, almost as a matter of course, for he lived under God's promise that Abraham would become the father of many nations (Genesis 17:4). But only when he resorted to God in prayer was Rebekah granted conception, emphasizing again that the creation of the holy line is in God's hands.

In Jacob's case the same principles hold true. First, there is no doubt about the identity of the inheritors of the land of promise. Second, the people who carry the oracles of God are clearly defined. Third, it is clear that through the faith delivered to Abraham, the true people of God are to be known in all time.

The creative power of God is finally manifested in the birth of the Messiah, for he was to be begotten of God the Spirit in the womb of the virgin (Isaiah 7:14), thus completing God's long work of redemption. The birth of the virgin's son, in light of the context, stands as a rebuke to the ideas of Ahaz to secure safety for Israel, and the divine character of the son proclaims that peace and safety will come only as God himself rules the earth.[1]

Leah conceived again and this time, when she gave birth to a son, she proclaimed, "Because the Lord *heard* [i.e., *shama'* (*Strong's* OT:8085)] that I am not loved, He gave me this one too." So she named him *Simeon* (Genesis 29:33, NIV, emphasis added). *Young's Literal Translation* says she conceived again, and bore a son, saying, "Because Jehovah hath heard that I [am] the hated one, He also giveth to me even this [one]" (YLT).

The root of Simeon's name is *shama'* (*Strong's* OT:8085) and generally refers to hearing, especially intelligent hearing, often with the implication of attention or obedience.[2] *Vine's Expository Dictionary* on *shama'* (*Strong's* OT:8085) notes that "hearing" can be both intellectual and spiritual:

Spiritually, one may "hear" God's Word (Num 24:4), or "learn" it from God. Conversely, God told Abraham that He had "heard" his prayer and would act accordingly (Genesis 17:20). In this context, to "hear" means not only to hear what is said, but to agree with its intention or petition (cf. Genesis 16:11). In the case of hearing and hearkening to a higher authority, *shama'* can mean to "obey"... [Additionally,] to have a "hearing heart" is to have "discernment" or "understanding."[3]

Leah hoped she was now worthy of her husband's affection, since God's creative power was made manifest through her. Without a doubt, she had personal revelation of God. Her sons were living witnesses of this fact, being oracles of God's great deliverance. Reuben was the Lord's progeny of seeing and Simeon was His son of hearing. "The hearing ear and the seeing eye, the Lord has made them both" (Proverbs 20:12, NKJV).

It would seem that right seeing and right hearing would have lifted Leah from the doldrums of her desperate circumstances. However, this was not the case because Rachel remained Jacob's favorite wife and Leah was still without honor within her family—the household of God. It seems more was required. God's benevolent scheme of deliverance was not yet fully realized and brought to fruition.

Consequently, for a third time Leah conceived. This time she was convinced of her husband's affection. She prophesied, "Now at last my husband will become attached to me, because I have borne him three sons" (Genesis 29:34, NIV). She named her third son *Levi*, because he is God's oracle of *attachment*. *Levi* is the Lord's third statement within His Divine Conception—the way of salvation.

Through her three sons, Leah leapt into a new awareness of divine possibility. It was an ascension awareness that can only be described as God's higher calling. With eyes wide open (as represented by Reuben), and with ears unstopped so as to hear with right understanding (the implications of Simeon), God's next revelation required that Leah come into close affinity (i.e. joined as a companion) with those things seen and heard. It was necessary for her to be in absolute agreement with her special knowingness.

This is the implicit revelation of God through Leah's third-born son, *Levi*.

But, as before, Leah reckoned faultily. Her statement, "Now at last *my husband* will become attached to me" (v. 34b, NIV, emphasis added) infers her expectation was that Jacob would change. The KJV quotes her as saying, "Now this time will *my husband* be joined unto me." The Amplified Bible quotes her as saying, "Now this time will my husband be a companion to me." Leah still didn't realize that God's revelation was for her, not her husband, and that change would only come as *she* participated with the Lord.

While *change* seems simple enough on the surface, oftentimes people haven't a clue where to begin. It is sometimes difficult to reconcile what God says to our situations and predicaments. For example, Leah was by nature a bitter, complaining woman of low self-esteem. She'd grown up under the heavy burden of her lovelier sister. She had "weak eyes" while her sister, Rachel, was "lovely in form, and beautiful" (Genesis 29:17, NIV). Consequently, Leah had trouble reconciling her life situation to God's perception of her. It was much easier to believe that God's revelation was for her husband than for herself. But it was her duty to become *a companion* to those things specially seen and heard (i.e., her unique awareness). This is the divine intent behind Israel's third son, *Levi*. "Put off the old man with his deeds," says Paul. "Put on the new man who is renewed *in knowledge* to the image of Him who created [you]" (Colossians 3:9–10, NKJV, emphasis mine).

With Leah as our witness, we learn to overcome our natural inclinations and dispositions, the innate bonds that restrain us. Leah was frustrated by Jacob's slowness of response to *her* vision when, in truth, it was her dullness that was the stumbling block. It was always about her, not her husband!

The Scriptures warn that those who live according to the flesh are controlled by its unholy desires. Such people set their minds on and pursue those things that gratify the flesh. As the Scriptures say, "the mind of the flesh [which is sense and reason without the Holy Spirit] is death [death that comprises all the miseries arising from sin, both here and hereafter]. But the mind of the [Holy] Spirit is life and [soul] peace [both now and forever]" (Romans 8:6, AMP).

The writer of Romans explains that the mind of the flesh, with its carnal thoughts and purposes, is hostile to God because it does not submit itself to God's Law. "Those who are living the life of the flesh [catering to the appetites and impulses of their carnal nature] cannot please *or* satisfy God, *or* be acceptable to Him" (v. 8, AMP). Right-mindedness is essential to divine life and peace. This was what Leah had to learn!

"There are two distinct and contrasting ways of living," notes *The New American Standard Commentary*. "One

> [Of these two dissimilar ways of living,] one is to follow the dictates of one's lower nature. Those who choose to live according to their sinful nature set their mind and heart on what that nature desires. 'Their thoughts are shaped by the lower nature' (Weymouth). People's decisions about how they intend to live determines how they think about things. Moral choice precedes and determines intellectual orientation. People do not think themselves into the way they act but act themselves into the way they think. Ethical decision, more often than misguided reason, lies at the heart of error.
>
> The other way to live is to place oneself under the control of the Spirit. In this case people focus their interests on the things of the Spirit. In Galatians 5, Paul contrasted the acts of the sinful nature with the fruit of the Spirit (v(v). 19–23); sexual immorality, fits of rage, and selfish ambition (to name but three of the fifteen) are set over against such qualities as love, kindness, and self-control.[4]

When Leah's third son was born, she did not reference the Lord. Neither did she do so in her fourth declaration of truth. In previous conceptions, Leah had rightly proclaimed, "the Lord has seen" and "the Lord has heard." In such matters, it is entirely God's prerogative. However, with the birth of her third son, awareness crept into Leah's soul and she began to recognize humankind's role in the scheme of God's divine conception. But when she said, "Now at last *my husband* will become attached to me!" she was wrong. In the language of the Bible, the name *Levi* is an expression of affiliation and attachment that *we* must declare and live. The root of the name *Levi* is *lavah* (*Strong's* OT:3867) meaning *to twine, to unite,* or *to remain*.[5] Levi is God's inclination of *affiliation* (i.e., connectedness by close association). Coupled with *right seeing* and *hearing* (i.e., knowingness), affiliation is the trigger of new beginnings, natural and supernatural, mortal and immortal.

Through Levi's birth Leah was shown the necessity of affiliation and agreement. Her *knowingness* was uniquely hers and did not necessarily hold sway over her husband or his resolve. Jacob's spirit was his own and, while Leah could influence him, it was his choice as to how he would live and prosper. What he chose to hold dear or despise was his prerogative!

"People lack abundance," said Jesus, "because, though seeing, they do not see; and though hearing, they do not hear or understand" (Matthew 13:13). In this passage, Jesus was speaking of kingdom principles as they relate to increase and vitality. Importantly, He also referenced the necessity of heart affiliation—the Levitic Principle as revealed to Leah. "For this people's heart has become calloused," Jesus said (v. 14, NIV). Then, Jesus concluded by alluding to the fourth ingredient of success—the Judaic Principle of kingdom increase. "You will be ever hearing but never understanding; you will be ever seeing but never perceiving; for this people's heart has become calloused; they hardly hear with their ears, and they have closed their eyes. Otherwise they might see with their eyes, hear with their ears, understand with their hearts *and turn,* and I would heal them" (Matthew 13:14–15, NIV, emphasis mine).

When our hearts are calloused and hardened (the Principle of Levi); our ears become dull and heavy, and our eyes are tightly shut to divine intention. Conversely, when our hearts are properly engaged, we see and hear and can effectually *turn* (be converted). The Greek *epistrepho* (*Strong's* NT:1994) rendered *turn* in Matthew 13:15 is God's concluding principle of consecration and deliverance. The preposition *epi* in *epistrepho* refers to the *superimposition* (*of time, place, order, etc.*), thus affecting the relation of distribution. *Strepho* means *strengthening from the base* so as to be turned quite around or reversed.[6] Leah's responsibility was to superimpose God's power over her current situations by taking it to heart and then turning in active regard.

Thus, to finish His hallowed work in and through Leah, God gave her one last statement of truth. As before, it came through the conception and birth of a son—the fourth-born son of Israel. So it was that Leah conceived again and bore a son. This time she said, "Now *I* will praise the Lord." Therefore she called his name Judah (Genesis 29:35, NKJV, emphasis mine).

Through praise, Leah began to vigorously enjoy her deliverance. She did not reference the Lord or her husband in this conception, her fourth, because praise was hers to appropriate. Praise is our God-ordained response to things divinely revealed. Little did Leah know that this would be her last revelation of truth (her last conception) for some time to come. With this last conception of truth, the Word of God succinctly states: "Then [for a time] she ceased bearing" (v. 35b, AMP). The Lord's work in and through Leah was now complete and nothing more was needed for her deliverance and healing. She could now effectually turn from her awful plight.

Leah's final declaration suggests that she hadn't previously committed herself to her inspired awareness. Vigorous connectedness—the Levitic and Judaic principles of supernatural increase—is God's final key of deliverance and salvation. Lively entanglement was Leah's concluding affirmation of divine success. Thus, she extended her hands toward God and called her fourth son *Judah* (*Strong's* OT:3063). The name *Judah* has at its root the word *yadah*, which refers to the holding out of one's hand. Physically, it is used with regard to throwing a stone and especially has reference to revered worship with extended hands. As she held out her hand to the Lord, Leah was transformed from the unloved to the blessed. Worship is to praise God with open hands and in knowingness of Who He is.

To be sure, it was at first difficult for Leah to see herself as anything but an ugly inconvenience. But with resolve and perseverance, Leah stubbornly claimed her rightful place within the family of God and opened her hands to the Lord's full bounty. Thus, she discovered the secret of fullness within the holy community, and her reality slowly and deliberately began to change. Leah lived her new reality in accordance with the divine prospect of *becoming* and *being* (*'asah*). *Right seeing* (Reuben) and *right hearing* (Simeon) were coupled with *willful affiliation* (Levi) and *active participation* (Judah). This is God's holy symphony of doing, His producing principle. It is God's parenthetical statement in and through the life of Leah.

Nothing more remained to be done. Heaven's fullness was now Leah's. In the beginning, she was a desperate, miserable person who was unwanted and unloved. In the end, Leah was blessed, a mother, and beloved wife in Israel. Leah was shown divine principles by which God's children can live. Her sons are oracles of these divine mercies. "You will know the truth, and the truth will set you free," declares the Lord (John 8:32, NIV).

With all things having been accomplished, nothing more remained to be done. Thus, the Word of God summarily states, "Then she [Leah] stopped having children" (v. 35b, NIV). God's dispensation toward the woman, as least for a time, was over.

But there is one more truth regarding God's kingdom not yet discussed. It concerns the order of Leah's conceptions. Their arrangement (i.e., birth order) is succinct and very specific. The principle of seeing, under the banner of Reuben, is of prime importance. "In righteousness I will see your face. When I awake, I will be satisfied with seeing your likeness," declared the psalmist (Psalm 17:15). Conversely, the Lord declares, "You shall have night without vision, and you shall have darkness without divination" (Micah 3:6a, NKJV). Seeing with the eyes of God is where we first begin.

Following on the heels of right seeing is right hearing; the Simeonic Principle of Hearing (i.e., right comprehension with implied obedience). What is gained if you or I do not understand what is seen? "Make the heart of this people dull, and their ears heavy, and shut their eyes; Lest they see with their eyes, and *hear with their ears, and understand* with their heart, and return and be healed" (Isaiah 6:10, NKJV, emphasis added). We must each pray for understanding as to what God has shown us.

Heart affiliation comes next in God's holy scheme of deliverance. Whole-hearted affection and affiliation is represented by Israel's third progeny, Levi. "In them is fulfilled the prophecy of Isaiah," asserted Jesus. "You will be ever hearing but never understanding; you will be ever seeing but never perceiving. *For this people's heart has become calloused*" (Matthew 13:14–15a, NIV, emphasis mine). In other words, we must take to heart our unique, God-given perspective and insight and make it our own. We must live it, day by day, and no matter what! Otherwise it will wither and die.

The recipe for success is still not complete, however, because one more ingredient is needed. To bring into fruition God's fullness, we must appropriately *turn* and actively champion our cause (i.e. our unique insight, divine perspective, etc.). "They hardly hear with their ears, and they have closed their eyes," declared Jesus. "Otherwise they might see with their eyes, hear with their ears, understand with their hearts and *turn*, and I would heal them." (Matthew 13:15, NIV, emphasis mine). "Turning" (i.e., the practice of Judah) is God's requisite activity that completes His sacred formula of deliverance and success. How many churches are unsuccessfully employed in the Lord's business for lack of vision? How many fail to hear His voice. How many more churches fail for lack of heartfelt commitment to the Lord's cause? Finally, how many churches fall short for lack of workers who champion His cause?

A man born blind was once healed by Jesus and the religious establishment ruggedly questioned the miracle. They wanted to know how he received his sight. Don't we all!

"He put clay on my eyes, and I washed, and I see," the man answered (John 9:15, NKJV). But the Pharisees did not believe him and wanted to know the means by which he saw. This is, in fact, this book's theme—how to receive and avail ourselves of the Lord's healing; His full bounty (Matthew 13:15).

The man stubbornly didn't budge, clinging to what he knew. "One thing I do know," [he declared]. "I was blind but now I see!" (John 9:25, NIV).

Then they said to him again, "What did He do to you? How did He open your eyes?" These are both valid questions; their answers are at the heart of the Lord's Producing Principle and this book, *The Divine Conception*. How can we be made whole? How does God do it?

Sadly, the hearts of the Pharisees were calloused and their hearing was dull. Hence, they refused to believe and accept the man's testimony. "I have told you already and you did not listen," [said the man]. "Why do you want to hear it again? Do you want to become his disciples, too?" (v. 27, NIV).

The man had now overstepped his bounds and the religious leaders were furious. They hurled insults at him and said, "You are this fellow's disciple! We are disciples of Moses! We know that God spoke to Moses, but as for this fellow, we don't even know where he comes from."

The man answered, "Now that is remarkable! You don't know where he comes from, yet he opened my eyes. We know that God does not listen to sinners. He listens to the godly man who does His will. Nobody has ever heard of opening the eyes of a man born blind. If this man were not from God, he could do nothing."

To this they replied, "You were steeped in sin at birth; how dare you lecture us!" And they threw him out (v. 34, NIV).

Jesus heard of the man's plight and went looking for him. We are often rejected when our testimony contradicts what people want to hear.

"Do you believe in the Son of God?" said Jesus to him.

"Tell me so that I may believe in him."

Jesus said, "You have now *seen* Him; in fact, He is the One speaking with you" (v. 37, NIV). Again notice the stress of the passage on the man's *seeing* and *hearing*. He had seen and heard but now more was required to finish the work.

"Lord, I believe," and he worshiped Him. In other words, the man "turned."

Christ summarily concludes: "For judgment I have come into this world, so that the blind will see and those who see will become blind" (John 9:39, NIV). The Amplified quotes Jesus as saying, "I came ... to make the sightless see and to make those who see become blind." Sadly, many come near to Jesus but only give Him lip-service. Their hearts are far from Him.

Our responsibility is to learn from Leah what it takes to walk in the fullness of God. In the beginning, she was a desperate, miserable person who was unwanted and unloved. In the end, Leah was blessed, a mother, and beloved wife in Israel. Leah was shown divine principles by which God's children can live. Her sons are oracles of these divine mercies. "You will know the truth, and the truth will set you free," declares the Lord (John 8:32, NIV).

Chapter One Evaluation

1. We must always be careful not to lock ourselves into unfortunate circumstances and predicaments through erroneous or inferior conceptions. Learning from Leah, dare to challenge your circumstances. Read the well-known story of Israel's demise in Numbers 13. Do you similarly suffer from small mindedness? They declared, "We [are] like grasshoppers *in our own sight*, and so we [are] in their sight" (Numbers 13:33, NKJV, emphasis mine). From then on, this was their reality; it was a self-fulfilling prophecy. They should have *seen* themselves differently. Perhaps you too have a self-limiting perception? Think about it. Do you suffer under the exceeding weight of small-mindedness?

2. The Hebrew verb *ra'ah* (*Strong's* OT:7200) appears in the Bible about 1,300 times and basically connotes seeing with one's eyes. Importantly, other meanings include perception or conscious awareness, as to realize. According to the *Brown-Driver-Briggs Hebrew and English Lexicon*, *ra'ah* may also refer to miraculous power so as to rightly see. "O Lord, open his eyes so he may *see*," prayed Elijah (2 Kings 6:17, 20, emphasis added). This same miraculous power of vision is denied of idols (Deuteronomy 4:28; Psalm 115:5; 135:16) and is used figuratively of spiritual vision (Deuteronomy 29:4; 1 Samuel 14:27; Isaiah 6:10; 29:18; 42:18; Jeremiah 5:21; Psalm 40:13; 69:24; Proverbs 20:12, and Ezekiel 12:2). One meaning of *ra'ah* is to see absolutely, as when receiving revelation (Isaiah 30:10).[7] Extended meanings of *ra'ah* refer to perceiving or ascertaining something apart from seeing with one's eyes. For example, Hagar saw that she had conceived (Genesis 16:4). In Genesis 26:28, *ra'ah* is used to represent mental recognition that something is true: "We saw clearly that the Lord was with you" (NIV). The challenge here is to understand the importance of *seeing* in the Holy Scriptures. Take time and search your Bible's concordance for other references regarding the importance of seeing.

3. An interesting case study regarding true and right sight (i.e., *ra'ah*) is its preeminence in the life of the prophet Ezekiel. The meaning of Ezekiel's name is literally *God Strengthens*. He opens his Old Testament book with the statement, "In the thirtieth year, in the fourth month on the fifth day, while I was among the exiles by the Kebar River, the heavens were opened, and I *saw* (*ra'ah*) visions of God" (Ezekiel 1:1, emphasis added VERSION). The phrase "and I saw visions of God" sets the tone of Ezekiel's entire life. Thereafter, the Hebrew *ra'ah* is used over thirty times by the prophet to describe his prophetic utterance (1:15; 2:9; 8:2, 5, 7, 10; 10:1, 9; and 44:4). Numerous times, the prophet says, "I looked, and I saw" (NIV). Do you "look" so as to "see"? Read the above references and discern the importance of "seeing" as it applies to you.

4. Why is *seeing* so important? Begin by reviewing what is known about Reuben, Israel's firstborn son. The Scriptures are clear about the firstborn's rights of inheritance (Deuteronomy 21:17). Why is this important and what are the implications with regard to the operation of Kingdom Principles?

5. Our last question deals with the principle of seeing. How does one go about *seeing* since this is entirely within God's prerogative? Hint: read Mark 4:24–25. Now read the entire passage. What are the implications of this passage with regard to *seeing*. How can you apply this to your own life?

CHAPTER TWO

Reclaiming Your Roots: The Experience Of Supernatural Muchness

> "I have learned by experience that the Lord has blessed me for your sake."
>
> Genesis 30:27b (NKJV)

Peter and six other disciples had been fishing all night. With Simon Peter in the lead, they'd abandoned their divine prerogative in favor of the mundane. But despite their knowledge of fish and fishing, for several of them were fishermen by trade, the disciples were unsuccessful and had little increase for their night's efforts. It seems they'd forgotten the Lord's previous admonition that apart from Him, and when cut off from their vital union with Him, they could do nothing (John 15:5b). Hence, Jesus decided to remind them.

The tale begins with the saying, "After these things..." (John 21:1a, KJV, NKJV, NASU). As previously noted, the phrase "after these things" signals a turn of events. Jesus was raised from the dead and had shown Himself to the disciples; but, with Simon Peter in the lead, they had abandoned their high calling and went fishing. Morning had already broken when Jesus came and called to them.

"Children, have you any food?" the Lord hollered to them (John 21:5, NKJV). The Lord's question chimed loud and clear from across the void. In truth, it still rings true today for most of us who toil for a pittance. The Bible's "after these things" and Christ's inquiry signal the possibility of change. Something was in the works that would invigorate the disciple's trifling efforts.

Without a doubt, Jesus knew the answer to His question for He'd been watching from afar. I believe His intent was to make His disciples contemplate their folly, their inherent insufficiency apart from Him. From time to time, we all need to be awakened from the ordinary unto the supernatural abundance of God.

"Throw your net on the other side of the boat and you will find some," Jesus instructed the wayward few. His instructions were simplistic and nonsensical—what difference would a few feet make?

"It's absurd!" the disciples almost certainly reasoned. "It makes little sense to switch from one side of the boat to the other. Besides," they probably argued, "who is this stranger? What gives him the right to meddle in our affairs? Doesn't he know that we are experienced fishermen? What does he know about us, let alone our situation? Why doesn't he mind his own business?"

This too is our challenge. Will we listen and obey the Lord, or will we stubbornly persist in folly? The solution is to fish from the "other side" of the boat. But this seems too easy. In fact, it is ridiculously simple and assuredly absurd! But what's the harm in trying?

The disciple's musings are typical of most people, especially those who are self-assured and confident of their own strength or knowledge. The Lord's question, "Children, have you any food?" begs an answer. Don't underestimate the Lord's simple stratagem of success. It's easily within reach and simply accessed by switching to the *right side* of your boat (i.e., wherever you find yourself). The sad reality of John 21:3 is that all too many people are busy all day long with nothing but empty nets to show for it.

In truth, I've wrestled with my share of empty nets. Haven't you? Moreover, I've also turned a deaf ear to heaven's solution, relying instead on presumed wisdom and experience. In times past, I've argued against the knowledge of God because it seemed too simplistic, ill conceived, or irrational. Heaven forgive me because I too have reasoned away my divine bounty.

God's question rings loud in my ears for, as I fumble my way through life, God is constantly reminding me that His solutions are easily within reach if only I will properly cast my net. As in Hagar's case, there is a well of refreshing but I must open my eyes to see it (Genesis 21:19).

> Then Jesus said to them, "Children, have you any food?"
>
> They answered Him, "No."
>
> And He said to them, "Cast the net on the right side of the boat, and you will find some." So they cast, and now they were not able to draw it in because of the multitude of fish.
>
> John 21:5–6 (NKJV)

To their credit, the disciples didn't argue with the stranger who stood upon the distant shore. Having previously experienced the *muchness* of Christ, they understood the reality of heaven's bounty (i.e., harvests that are supernaturally gotten). Abundant supply often comes by unconventional means when God is involved (Matthew 14:18–21; 15:33–38). If only more people would cast forth their nets from God's side of reality's boat (i.e., the right side). On one side is deficiency and lack; on the other side is sufficiency and strength. Which will you choose? Which side have you chosen thus far? Lord, bless our empty nets!

At the Lord's command, the net was lifted from one side of the boat and let down on the other. This time, however, the net was miraculously filled to overflowing. It was an astonishing catch: one hundred fifty-three fishes in all.

Then Scripture make a small, seemingly insignificant insertion. It is a truth often overlooked and concerns the nets we employ.

> It was full of large fish, 153, but even with so many, *the net was not torn.*
>
> John 21:11b (NIV), emphasis added.

The net was not torn even though there were so many fish. Perhaps I make too much of it, but I believe this testifies of right and wrong ways to pull in heaven's harvest. Having deployed our nets, many of us have suffered loss because of torn nets. We've all seen God's harvest squandered. Even now, we have little to show for our labor and are sadly disappointed. Believe me when I say I've experienced the disappointment of torn nets.

The brief inclusion of the words "and although there were so many, the net was not broken" (NKJV) suggests that God's symphony of doing must be orchestrated so as to complement the natural order of things. In keeping with the Lord's Producing Principle, we begin by rightly seeing and hearing and then are required to pull in the nets through heartfelt agreement and lively pursuit. We must cast our nets from the right side of reality and then know how to pull them in when full.

As previously discussed, Leah was shown God's ways and means—His Producing Principle. But His orchestrated plan must be strictly followed. First, there is the Reubenic Principle of Right Seeing. Reuben was Israel's son of seeing and he is worthy of a double-portion. Reuben is followed by God's Simeonic Principle for Simeon was the second-born son of Israel. According to his mother's declaration, he is the Lord's oracle of hearing with comprehension. Levi was Israel's third-born son and testifies of association with agreement. Finally, Judah emphasizes the importance of praise (i.e., the opening of one's hand toward God). This Divine Conception was carefully crafted and conceived by God to produce abundant harvests and full nets; in this case, 153 large fish. Perhaps, if you're experiencing torn nets, you may want to go back and revisit the oracles of God's holy family, Israel.

Things must be done smartly and in proper order; otherwise, they may end up cancelling each other out. Bruce Lipton describes such things in terms of harmonic resonance. "If you drop a pebble into a pond," he writes, "the 'energy' carried in that falling pebble (due to the force of gravity pulling on its mass) is transmitted to the water.

> The ripples generated by the pebble are actually energy waves passing through the water. If more than one pebble is thrown into the water at the same time, the spreading ripples (energy waves) from each source can interfere with each other, forming composite waves where two or more ripples converge. That interference can be either constructive (energy amplifying) or destructive (energy deflating)...Where ripples overlap, the combined power of the interacting waves is doubled, a phenomenon referred to as constructive interference, or *harmonic resonance*. When the dropping of the pebbles is not coordinated, their energy waves are out of sync. As one wave is going up, the other is going down. At the point of convergence, these out-of-sync energy waves cancel each other...This phenomenon of canceling energy waves is called destructive interference.[1]

It was the disciple whom Jesus loved that first recognized the hand of God in the miraculous catch of fish (John 21). "It is the Lord!" exclaimed John (v. 7, NKJV). With dawning recognition, all the men's eyes were suddenly opened. However, it was only Simon Peter who seized the moment and thrust himself away from that which separated him from God. He impetuously cast himself from the boat to swim to Jesus. Symbolically, he would not be deterred any longer from his God-ordained duty.

First, however, Simon Peter did something very unusual for a man about to take a dip. Before he dove into the water, he donned his heavy outer cloak. It seems that Simon Peter was acutely aware of his nakedness. Such is often the case when our eyes are freshly opened and our folly is fully exposed. The sudden presence of God is very sobering. As in the story of Adam and Eve, the eyes of both of them were opened and they realized they were naked. To cover their nakedness they sewed fig leaves together and made coverings for themselves (Genesis 3:7).

Meanwhile, the other disciples busied themselves towing their brimming net to the shore. The Lord waited for them but was not idle. Upon that distant shore, He carefully laid a bed of burning coals. As the men struggled with nets that did not tear, heaven's repast was being prepared. At the Lord's invitation, the disciples reclined at God's table and participated in the goodly provision (John 21:12a). "Bring some of the fish which you have just caught," said the Lord to His disciples.

To be sure, Jesus could have had all the fish He wanted. They could already have been on the spit and sizzling hot. Instead, Jesus lit the fire and prepared the coals, but He expected the men to supply some of their catch. Why is this? Perhaps it's because we are created in God's image and likeness to complement (i.e. harmonize with) His work (Genesis 1:27-28). To heaven's supply we must add the work of our hands to create a satisfying meal.

> And God raised us up with Christ and seated us with Him in the heavenly realms in Christ Jesus, in order that in the coming ages He might show the incomparable riches of His grace, expressed in His kindness to us in Christ Jesus. For it is by grace you have been saved, through faith—and this not from yourselves, it is the gift of God—not by works, so that no one can boast. *For we are God's workmanship, created in Christ Jesus to do good works*, which God prepared in advance for us to do.
>
> Ephesians 2:6–10 (NIV), emphasis added.

None of the disciples dared ask, "Who are you?" for they *knew*. They perceived it was the Lord; even as you and I must discern Him and His handiwork. This too is accomplished through the Reubenic and Simeonic Principles of right seeing and hearing. Additionally, the passage specifically states: "This was now the third time Jesus appeared to His disciples after He was raised from the dead" (John 21:14, NIV). The number *three* signals that God's thought was now complete. *The International Standard Bible Encyclopedia* says, "The number three ... [is] the number in which beginning, middle, and end are most distinctly marked, and [is] regarded as symbolic of a complete and ordered whole."[2]

"Simon son of John," said Jesus, "do you truly love Me more than these?" (John 21:15, NIV). The "these" of Christ's inquiry concerned all of Simon Peter's natural appetites and inclinations; the things that naturally tugged at his heart to cause him to stumble and stray from God's path. They included his companions and the lure of the sea (i.e. his preoccupation with boats, nets, fish, and fishing). What distractions irresistibly beckon to you? What tugs at your heartstrings and reek havoc with your affections? Do you love them more than Jesus? I encourage you to do a spiritual check-up and remember the Lord's third producing principle as revealed to Leah—the Levitic Principle of wholehearted affection with affiliation.

Christ challenged Simon Peter to reconsider his ways. He'd strayed from that which was uniquely his ... the special revelation of Christ (Matthew 16:16). It was this that distinguished him and made Peter the rock upon which Jesus would build His church and overcome the powers of Satan. In that instance, Simon Peter proclaimed Christ as the Son of the living God. In response, Jesus said, "Blessed are you, Simon son of Jonah [the natural man with wavering tendencies], for this was not revealed to you by man, but by my Father in heaven. And I tell you that you are Peter [a new creation], and on this rock I will build my church, and the gates of Hades will not overcome it. I will give you [the spirit man who was newly christened Peter] the keys of the kingdom of heaven; whatever you bind on earth will be bound in heaven, and whatever you loose on earth will be loosed in heaven" (Matthew 16:17–20a, NIV).

It's the interplay of names in this exchange that engages our attention. Simon Peter first recognized the Lord's divinity. I believe he characterizes all of us who know the ways of God but also struggle against our natural inclinations and carnality. Hence, Jesus blessed Simon, the son of Jonah [the natural man], and gave to him a new appellation, Peter (the rocklike man who was solid and dependable).

Returning to the narrative of Peter's reclamation in John 21, notice that it was first Simon Peter, the terribly conflicted man, who said to his fellow disciples, "I am going fishing." Again, it was Simon Peter who donned his heavy cloak and plunged into the water to meet Jesus (the inference is that he recognized his nakedness). Also, it was Simon Peter who left Jesus' side and went to help drag the heavy net to shore (v. 11). Simon Peter couldn't resist the temptation of the catch and wanted to see what there was.

For all these reasons, Jesus addressed this naturally conflicted man. After they'd eaten breakfast, Jesus said, "*Simon*, son of Jonah, do you love Me more than these?" (John 21:15a, NKJV, emphasis added).

"Yes, Lord," said the man. "You know that I love You."

"Feed My lambs," Jesus replied.

Jesus turned His attention to Simon Peter but first addressed Simon, the son of Jonah. I believe Jesus recognized the inherent conflict within the man because of his two natures. Thus, He began by speaking to the carnal man who was weak and vacillating by nature; *Simon*, the son of Jonah. The Amplified Version expands on Christ's inquiry. "Simon, son of John, do you love Me more than these [others do—with reasoning, intentional, spiritual devotion, as one loves the Father]?"

I also love how the Amplified Bible expands on Simon's response. "Yes, Lord," [the man said], "You know that I love You [that I have deep, instinctive, personal affection for You, as for a close friend].

Then Jesus said to Simon, "Feed My sheep." But in the Lord's admonition is an implied predicament that was beyond Simon's limited ability to solve. In and of himself, he was incapable of feeding (i.e., tending to and nurturing) Christ's sheep! His natural inclinations were too strong and, when tempted, he would go fishing.

The narrative suggests that Christ's question stung the man to the core. But who was hurt; Simon, Simon Peter, or Peter (the unwavering, rocklike man who possessed divine insight regarding Jesus)?

John gives Jesus' response. Again He said to him, "*Simon*, son of Jonah, do you love Me?" (v. 16a, NKJV, emphasis mine).

As before, Simon said to Him, "Yes, Lord; You know that I love You." The Amplified Bible renders his response; "You know that I love You [that I have a deep, instinctive, personal affection for You, as for a close friend]" (v. 16a, AMP).

Once again Jesus said to him (Simon), "Shepherd (tend) My sheep" (v. 16b, AMP). But, as before, the Lord's admonition was beyond the man's natural, limited resources to perform.

Within this humble story I see a great conflict between Simon Peter's two natures. On the one hand he was *Simon* (the carnal man); on the other hand he was *Peter* (the spiritual "rocklike" man). Simon Peter is the union of these two unctions. He was a conflicted creature with two natures struggling within, one against the other. Thus, it was Simon Peter (the desperately conflicted man) who violated the third precept of God's Producing Principle, the Levitic Principle named for Israel's third son, Levi. Levi is the oracle of wholehearted affiliation and affection within God's kingdom; something completely beyond the narrow limits of Simon Peter's reach. His natural affections and inclinations struggled against his Godly nature and, in this case, won out. Thus, Simon returned to his old lifestyle epitomized by his predilection to fish and fishing. So it was that Jesus twice called to the man by his natural name, Simon.

Now we come to the pivotal passage of this story. Jesus said to him a third time, "Simon, son of Jonah, do you love Me?" (v. 17a, NKJV). As before, the Amplified Bible expands on His remark saying; "Simon, son of John, do you love Me [with a deep, instinctive, personal affection for Me, as for a close friend]?"

This time the Scriptures point out that *Peter* was deeply grieved. Saddened and hurt that Jesus should ask him a third time, Peter replied, "Lord, You know everything; You know that I love You [that I have a deep, instinctive, personal affection for You, as for a close friend]" (v. 17, AMP).

Jesus said to him, "Feed My sheep." In the context of the passage, I believe Christ's third admonition was addressed to him who responded *Peter* (the rocklike man whose testimony and actions were unwavering and solid).

Much is lost in the translation from the original Greek to the English. It seems to me that Simon's initial response was most likely instinctual and reflexive. With little thought, he blurted out, "You know (*eido*, *Strong's* NT1492) that I love you" (v. 15b, NKJV, emphasis added). When Simon was again confronted, the errant man said, "Yes, Lord; You know (*eido*) that I love you" (v. 16b, NKJV, emphasis added). But in the third exchange between him and Jesus, the Lord said to him, "Simon, son of Jonah, do you love Me?" This time, *Peter* responded, saying, "Lord, You know all things; You *know* that I love You" (v. 17b, NKJV). Previously, Simon had spoken up concerning *knowingness* (*eido*). In his last response, however, *Peter* spoke up and used a different verb to express *knowingness*. He used the verb *ginosko* (*Strong's* NT:1097).

In the King James Version of the Bible, the Greek *eido* (*Strong's* NT:1492) is variously translated as *be aware, behold, perceive,* and *consider*.³ But Peter's assertion, "You know (i.e., *ginosko*) that I love You," adds another dimension to the narrative because it emphasizes relationship or association. It seems that *Peter* finally understood the Lord's persistent inquiries. *Vine's Dictionary* notes that the verb *ginosko* often indicates a *relationship* between the person's "knowing" and the object known.⁴ Likewise, *The Theological Dictionary of the New Testament* says *ginosko* (*Strong's* NT:1097) denotes close acquaintance with something, relating "to the knowledge acquired in experiences both good and bad"⁵ This dictionary adds, "To this understanding of knowledge there corresponds the understanding of what constitutes reality."⁶ Peter's use of *ginosko* emphasizes his deep, instinctive, personal affection; like that of a close friend.

With Peter's declaration, Christ appeared to be satisfied. But then Peter turned and looked back. Seeing the disciple whom Jesus loved following close behind, Peter said, "But Lord, what about this man?" (John 21:21, NKJV).

Christ's response is very instructive. He said to Peter, the man whose affections were now wholly restored, "If I will that he remains till I come, what is that to you? You follow Me" (v. 22, NKJV). In other words, what John did was John's business. Peter's responsibility was to remain focused and intent on his own high calling. Each of us has a unique message and purpose within God's kingdom. We would do well to remember this and stay focused. What was John's was for him to know and do (*'asah*); what was said and taught to

Peter was for him to fulfill. John later wrote, "But as for you, the anointing (the sacred appointment, the unction) which you received from Him abides [permanently] in you; [so] then you have no need that anyone should instruct you. But just as His anointing teaches you concerning everything and is true and is no falsehood, so you must abide in (live in, never depart from) Him [being rooted in Him, knit to Him], just as [His anointing] has taught you [to do]" (1 John 2:27, AMP).

God's *charisma* (i.e. His special endowment of the Holy Spirit that is our unction and strength) is an intensely personal thing that must always be our center "doing" (*'asah*). In Paul's words, we must "continue to work out our salvation with fear and trembling [with self-distrust and diligent], for it is God Who works in [us] to will and to act according to His good purpose" (Philippians 2:12b-13, NIV). We are admonished to bring to fruition the demands of our salvation; remembering that it is God Who effectually works in us to energize and create in us the power and desire, both to will and to work for His good pleasure and satisfaction.

Lest there be any confusion regarding the Lord's abiding *charisma* (our unction from God to "do"), consider Jacob's temptation prior to his return to Bethel and his altar. God's will for him was to *provide* (i.e. *'asah*) for his household. But Satan resisted as was to be expected. Thus, when Jacob said to his father-in-law, "Send me on my way so I can go back to my own homeland." Laban responded, "If I have learned by divination that the Lord has blessed me because of you. Name your wages, and I will pay them" (Genesis 30:25, 27–28; NIV).

But Jacob resolutely refused to be distracted. So he said to Laban, "The little you had before I came has increased greatly, and the Lord has blessed you wherever I have been. But now, when may I *do* [*'asah*] something for my own household?" (Genesis 30:30, NIV, emphasis mine).

But crafty Laban wasn't about to let Jacob go because he relished the Lord's continuing blessing. "Name your wages and I will pay them," he persisted with feigned affection, knowing all along he never planned to let his son-in-law go.

But being forewarned by God, Jacob wasn't fooled. He knew it was a trap to forever keep him subservient and impoverished.

"What shall I give you?" Laban asked.

"You shall not give me anything," Jacob wisely retorted. He knew his father-in-law never gave anything without attached strings. But then, like Peter who looked back, Jacob hesitated and looked back. "You shall do this one thing for me," he began (Genesis 30:31a, NIV). In a moment of weakness, he pressed his advantage.

"What shall I give you?" Laban pleaded.

"If you will do this one thing for me, I will go on tending your flocks and watching over them. Let me go through all your flocks today and remove from them every speckled or spotted sheep, every dark-colored lamb and every spotted or speckled goat. They will be my wages" (v(v). 31–32, NIV).

Knowing Laban's inherent distrust, Jacob added a caveat to sweeten the deal.

"And my honesty will testify for me in the future, whenever you check on the wages you have paid me. Any goat in my possession that is not speckled or spotted, or any lamb that is not dark-colored, will be considered stolen" (v. 33).

"Agreed," Laban readily said. "Let it be as you have said."

Laban was ecstatic, believing the bargain was wholly in his favor because the vast majority of the flock was either white or black. Additionally, before Jacob could cull the flock, Laban went out and removed all the goats that were speckled or spotted, as well as all the black sheep. He placed them in the care of his own sons because the combined fortunes of Laban and his sons were forged in opposition to Jacob and his household. The flock was then pastured three days' journey away so that Jacob would never find them. With so small a beginning, Laban thought he could forever hold sway over Jacob and his burgeoning family. This is always Satan's scheme: to deny God's people the ability to provide (i.e., *'asah*, accomplish or advance) for themselves.

Laban thought he had tricked Jacob but failed to consider his son-in-law's divinely enabled proclivity for abundance and multiplied increase. He didn't fully reckon on Jacob's God or the ability of Jacob through his God to *provide* (*'asah*) for his household (Genesis 30:30). *'Asah* is the same word used with great frequency in the Genesis account of creation: God *made* (*'asah*) the expanse (Genesis 1:7), and the plants and trees that *make* (*'asah*) seed after their various kinds (v. 11). He also *made* (*'asah*) the day and the night (v. 16) and the animals after their kind (v. 25). Of humankind, however, it is written that "God *created* (*bara*) man in His own image, in the image of God He *created* (*bara*) him" (v. 27, NIV).

The *Theological Wordbook of the Old Testament* on *'asah* says:

> The significant interchange between the words *bara*, create, and *'asah* is of great interest. The word *bara* carries the thought of the initiation of the object involved. It always connotes what only God can do and frequently emphasizes the absolute newness of the object created. The word *'asah* is much broader in scope, connoting primarily the fashioning of the object with little concern for special nuances.[8]

There was never any doubt in Jacob's mind that he could *provide* (*'asah*) for his household according to the Lord's revealed will. Furthermore, he possessed God's capacity and capability to do so. Past experience had proven this. In the language of John 21, he had the uncanny knack for casting his net "on the right side of the boat" (v. 6, NIV, AMP, NKJV). Hence, and according to his God-given ability to fashion and advance (*'asah*), Jacob grew exceedingly prosperous. Even though the combined fortunes of Laban and his sons were forged in opposition to him and his household, Jacob's flocks increased in size and he became very rich with maidservants and menservants, camels and donkeys. Behind his back, however, Laban and his sons grumbled, accusing Jacob of robbing them.

At long last, Jacob finally decided it was time for him to leave and return home to his native land. When he first arrived in Padan Aram twenty years before, all Jacob had was his staff. Now he had a large family and had increased exceedingly. Additionally, God had given to him an awareness of His continuing presence. "Go back to the land of your fathers and to your relatives, *and I will be with you*," said God to Jacob (Genesis 31:3, NIV, emphasis mine).

"I have had a dream," Jacob told his household when it was time to pack-up and leave. Recalling his vision, he said, "I looked up and

I saw that the rams which mated with the she-goats were streaked, speckled, and spotted. And the Angel of God came to me and said, 'Jacob.' And I said, 'Here am I.' And He said, 'Look up and see, all the rams which mate with the flock are streaked, speckled, and mottled; for I have seen all that Laban does to you. I am the God of Bethel, where you anointed the pillar and where you vowed a vow to Me. Now arise, get out from this land and return to your native land.' (Genesis 31:10–13, AMP).

So I looked up and saw..." said Jacob (Genesis 31:10a, AMP). "Then, to reinforce my dawning awareness, the Angel of God called me by name" (v. 11). He knew me as I was.

With eyes wide open (for the Lord would not have told me to look up and see without granting sufficient power to do so), I was then reminded of my prior vision—my earlier *eureka-moment*. 'I am the God of Bethel, where you anointed the pillar and where you vowed a vow to Me,' said God (Genesis 31:13a, AMP). Then I knew that I'd delayed too long in following Him. As the years have passed and as I busied myself with all my daily chores, I've become remiss in my spiritual duties. Therefore, the Lord has stirred me again. 'Now arise, get out from this land and return to your native land,' He said to me" (Genesis 31:13b, AMP).

From this passage I glean that I too have a responsibility before God. He expects me to remember and revive my vision of Him. His challenge is that I recall my spiritual roots (i.e., from whence I have come) and determine where I am going. I am called to remember my special awareness (i.e. who and what I am in Him) and, in this manner, arise. Life's busyness, with it many diversions and distractions, have held sway over me too long. Like Jacob, it is now time for me to "arise" from my spiritual stupor and move on with God unto my Bethel, the place of my altar.

"How did the Lord tell Jacob that it was time to leave?" wonders Warren Wiersbe in his commentary on *Freedom–Reclaiming Your Roots*.[9] He answers: "The same way He leads His people today: through the inner witness in the heart, the outward circumstances of life, and the truth of His Word." Wiersbe explains:

Six years before, God had put the desire in Jacob's heart to return to his own country (30:25), and that desire had never left him. While not every longing in the human heart is necessarily the voice of God (Jeremiah 17:9), and we must carefully exercise discernment, the Lord often begins to speak to us in that way.

Along with the desire within us, God also directs us as He did Jacob through the circumstances around us (Genesis 31:1–2). Toward the end of those six critical years, Jacob noticed that his in-laws weren't as friendly toward him as before, largely because of the increase in his wealth. Circumstances aren't always the finger of God pointing out His way (Acts 27:1–15), but they can be significant indicators of God's will. When God wants to move us, He occasionally makes us uncomfortable and "stirs up its nest" (Deuteronomy 32:11).

The third and most important way God leads us is through His Word. God had already spoken to Jacob in a dream (Genesis 31:10–13), but Jacob remained in Padan Aram to acquire his wealth. Then God said to him, "Go back to the land of your fathers and to your relatives, and I will be with you" (v. 3). As the story of Jacob unfolds, you will discover that God spoke to him at every important crisis in his life: leaving home (28:12–15), returning home (31:1–13), meeting Esau (32:24 ff), visiting Bethel (35:1 ff), and moving to Egypt (46:1–4). God leads us in the paths of righteousness if we're willing to follow (Psalm 23:3).[10]

This chapter's conclusion is encapsulated in the wise counsel offered by Jacob's wives, Leah and Rachel. When they heard their husband's vision and how he was confronted with God's calling, they encouraged him, saying: "Whatever God has said to you, do it," (Genesis 31:16b, NKJV). The New International Version renders their wise advice: "So *do* (*'asah*) whatever God has told you" (emphasis mine).

No better counsel can be given: Revive your vision of God and remember what He has called you to do; recall your spiritual roots (i.e., where you came from and where you are going); renew your previous vows when He first called you; and respond properly. It is time to put aside the diversions and hindrances that have too long held sway over our lives!

Chapter Two Evaluation

1. Laban knew that Jacob possessed an uncanny ability. "I have learned by divination that the Lord has blessed me because of you," he said (Genesis 30:27b, NIV). But then he did the opposite of what was right. Out of voracity, he tempted the young man to lay aside his vision. "Name your wages, and I will pay them," he declared. While those around us often resent God's presence and influence, they are reluctant to let us go. They deny God but covet His blessings. They grudgingly admit they need God's people but often enticed us to lay aside our divine vision. Have you been similarly beguiled? Perhaps, even now, you have put your dreams and heavenly visions on hold? "What shall I give you to stay?" begs the flesh. Analyze your own circumstances. Are you stuck in Paddan Aram (Genesis 28:2, 5, 6, 7; 31:18) and more importantly, do you plan to finally "arise" unto the Lord's calling?

2. In His Parable of the Sower (Matthew 13), Jesus spoke of everyday concerns that tend to divert God's people from their intended paths and divine heritage. He warned that such distractions, as well as the deceit of riches, can choke God's Word and make it unproductive (v. 22). Laban's alluring statement still tugs at our souls today: "Say then what your payment is to be and I will give it" (Genesis 30:28, Bible in Basic English, BBE). What has caused you to quit your dreams? What controls you?

3. Jacob yearned to advance the cause and wellbeing of his household. God puts this desire in all our hearts because it is His desire that we prosper. Thus, Jacob said to his father-in-law, "When shall I also *provide* (*'asah*: do, accomplish) for my own house?" (Genesis 30:30, NKJV, emphasis added). God's desire is that we have great success so as to accomplish and provide blessings. So what's stopping you? Isn't it time to stop what you are doing, examine your life, and begin to

advance the cause of Christ for you and your household? What's holding you back?

4. At the beginning of this book, we considered a question posed by God to Hagar. Like many of us, she was aimlessly wandering through life with no particular place to go and with very little in her hand to share. What were His questions of Hagar (Genesis 16:8) and do they still apply today? What has God given you to do? His overwhelming desire is that you prosper and succeed (*'asad*).

CHAPTER THREE

Ability with God and Men

[The Man] asked him, "What is your name?" And [in shock of realization, whispering] he said, "Jacob [supplanter, schemer, trickster, swindler]!"

And He said, "Your name shall be called no more Jacob [supplanter], but Israel [contender with God]; for you have contended and have power with God and with men and have prevailed."

Genesis 32:27–28 (AMP)

G enesis 32 stresses Jacob's "shock of realization" when he finally took a good, long look at himself (v. 27, AMP). His reaction is posed for our admonition because it is time for each of us to carefully consider our ways. As said to Hagar, "Where have you come from and where are you going? (Genesis 16:8, NIV).

In the spotlight of everything we've discussed, the Lord of hosts is asking you and me to carefully consider our ways. We are to set our minds on what has befallen us. He declares: You have sown much, but you have reaped little; you eat, but you do not have enough; you drink, but you do not have your fill; you clothe yourselves, but no one is warm; and he who earns wages has earned them to put them in a bag with holes in it. Thus says the Lord of hosts: 'Consider your ways (your previous and present conduct) *and* how you have fared.'" (Haggai 1:5–7, AMP).

Jacob had finally come to the end of himself. He was running for his life to escape the evil clutches of his father-in-law. With Laban in hot pursuit and with his brother, Esau, laying in wait before him, Jacob was utterly and completely spent. He was between the proverbial rock and a hard place.

Finally, because he had the advantage of speed, Laban overtook the fugitives in Gilead's hill country.

"What have you done?" shrieked Laban in rage. "You've deceived me, and you've carried off my daughters like captives in war. Why did you run off secretly and deceive me?...You have done a foolish thing" (Genesis 31:26–28, NIV).

Laban's question is well put and is also ours to answer. We must all come to a conviction and reckoning with ourselves. As God said, "Consider your ways!" (Haggai 1:7, NKJV).

It had been six long years since God had given Jacob the impetus to leave Paddam Aram. Now Jacob was running in fear of his life having forgotten the Lord's pledge to be with him and watch over him (Genesis 28:15a). Also, God had promised to bring him back to native land of Beersheba. "I will not leave you until I have done what I have promised you," said the Lord (Genesis 28:15b, NIV).

But Jacob had delayed and put off his holy prerogative. Says Warren Wiersbe, "It is not enough to know and do the will of God; we must also do His will in the way He wants it done, the way that will glorify Him the most."[1]

"You've deceived me," Laban shrieked, accusing his son-in-law of carrying off his daughters and stealing from him. But for all his blustering, Laban was helpless to harm Jacob because the Lord had previously warned him to be careful. God had come to Laban in a dream and said, "Be careful not to say anything to Jacob, either good or bad" (Genesis 31:24, NIV).

So when Laban spoke to his son-in-law, he heeded the Lord's warning and was at a loss as to what to do. "It is in my power to do you harm," declared Laban, "but the God of your father spoke to me last night, saying, 'Be careful that you speak to Jacob neither good nor bad.'"

Greatly emboldened, Jacob seized the moment. Realizing the hand of God's protection was with him, he declared: "Thus I have been in your house twenty years; I served you fourteen years for your two daughters, and six years for your flock, and you have changed my wages ten times. Unless the God of my father, the God of Abraham and the *Fear* of Isaac, had been with me, surely now you would have sent me away empty-handed. God has seen my affliction and the labor of my hands, and rebuked *you* last night" (v(v). 41–42, NKJV, emphasis added). The Amplified Version says, "And if the God of my father, the God of Abraham and *the Dread [lest he should fall] and Fear [lest he offend] of Isaac*, had not been with me, surely you would have sent me away now empty handed. God has seen my affliction and humiliation and the [wearying] labor of my hands and rebuked you last night" (v. 42, emphasis mine).

What a tremendous declaration! O that we would all be so emboldened as fellow heirs with Jacob. It is our heritage in God.

In Jacob's declaration is a new name of the Lord not yet discussed. It goes back to the time when Isaac was sojourning in the land of the Philistines. Isaac had numerous conflicts with the indigenous people but, no matter what his opposition, he always prevailed. Finally, the Philistines grudgingly attributed his success to God—*The Dread of Isaac*. Apparently, this same *Dread* also guarded Jacob lest he should fall; and the *Fear* was with him lest he be offended. God will not allow His children to be sent away *empty handed* (i.e., *reyqam*). As Jacob declared, He sees our affliction and humiliation and the wearying labor of our hands; and He stands in opposition to barrenness and ineffectuality (i.e., that which brings to naught). *Emptiness* (*reyqam*) is not in keeping with our destiny in God. *The Theological Wordbook of the Old Testament* on this adverb notes that its initial usage is found in the above passage when Jacob said, "Surely now you would have sent me away *emptily*" (31:42). This adverb is used in the sense of "not fulfilled" or "unsuccessful" (2 Samuel 1:22).[2]

Laban could not deny that his son-in-law possessed a remarkable ability of supernatural success and *full hands*. "God has seen (i.e., *ra'ah*) my affliction and the labor of my hands," declared Jacob (Genesis 31:42b, NKJV).

Abraham, Isaac and Jacob had a unique connection with the Lord. He made their hardship less cumbersome. *Rehoboth* (i.e., *enlargement*) was Isaac's expression of it—his special relationship with God. He declared the name Rehoboth, saying, "Now the Lord has given us room and we will flourish in the land" (Genesis 26:22, NIV). Neither could Laban deny it, having himself experienced *the Dread* (lest Jacob should fall) and *the Fear* (lest he be offended). Indeed, God *saw* (i.e., *ra'ah*) Jacob's affliction and humiliation. "Be careful that you speak to Jacob neither good nor bad," God had warned the man (31:29b, NKJV). The implied threat was an overwhelming divine intervention.

Laban was forced to admit defeat, but as Warren Wiersbe put it, "…the old deceiver put on a brave front just the same and tried to make everybody think he was a peacemaker."[3] Thus, Laban claimed he only wanted to send them away with joy and gladness; and that he wanted to kiss his grandchildren and daughters good-bye. "So come now," he said, "let us make a covenant or league, you and I, and let it be for a witness between you and me" (Gen. 31:27-28, 44, AMP).

Jacob then took a stone and set it up as a pillar of remembrance. So too did his relatives join with him to pile stones into a heap. The mound of stones commemorated the pact of peace between the two families. The heap of stones served as a "watchtower" (i.e., *Mizpah*) or boundary marker that neither Jacob nor Laban should cross. Their agreement was not a declaration of peace but only a truce that could be broken if either party violated the terms. Sadly, Laban never saw Jacob's God as a gracious Lord Who had brought them together for mutual benefit and wellbeing. "Mizpah was a monument to suspicion and fear, not to love and trust."[4]

Having finally gotten clear of Laban, Jacob pursued his journey homewards toward Canaan (a journey symbolic of our heavenward march). Along the way an army of ministering spirits met him so that where he pitched his tents, they also pitched theirs around him. Matthew Henry comments that they had invisibly attended to him all along, but now they appeared to him because he had a greater danger before him, his brother Esau. "When God designs his people for extraordinary trials, He prepares them by extraordinary comforts."⁵ Jacob gave a name to the place, calling it *Mahanaim* (two armies). They appeared to him in two hosts; one in the front to protect him from Esau and the other in the rear to protect him from Laban. They were a complete guard to encompass him round about with the favor of God.

Then Jacob received a terrifying report: Esau was on his way to meet him with four hundred armed and dangerous men (Genesis 32:6). Greatly afraid, Jacob divided his household into two groups lest Esau should attack. Then he prayed, "O God of my father Abraham and God of my father Isaac, the Lord Who said to me, 'Return to your country and to your people and I will do you good.'... Deliver me, I pray You, from the hand of my brother, from the hand of Esau; for I fear him, lest he come and smite [us all], the mothers with the children" (Genesis 32:9–10, AMP).

Jacob lodged there but in the dark of night he arose and took his two wives, his two women servants, and his eleven sons and passed over the ford of the Jabbok. He sent them across the brook and he was left alone.

Suddenly, when the night was darkest, a lone man stole into his meager campsite and attacked him. They wrestled, one with the other, and Jacob resisted valiantly. They fought throughout the night until daybreak and still, neither had claimed the advantage. Finally, as the sun was coming up, the man saw that he did not prevail against Jacob so he touched the hollow of his thigh and Jacob's thigh was put out of joint.

"Let Me go," said the man, "for day is breaking" (v. 26a, AMP).

"I will not let You go unless You declare a blessing upon me," Jacob persisted.

"What is your name?" the man asked him.

And [in shock of realization, whispering] he said, "Jacob [supplanter, schemer, trickster, swindler]!" (v. 27, AMP)

"Your name shall be called no more Jacob [supplanter], but Israel [contender with God]; for you have contended *and* have power with God and with men and have prevailed."

Realizing he had contended with God, Jacob asked an important question that is this book's basis. "Tell me, I pray You," he said, "what [in contrast] is Your name?" (v. 29a, AMP).

When struggling against the Lord, Jacob suddenly saw himself for what he was—a struggling, conniving schemer who had wrestled his whole life through. With dawning comprehension, the man realized how flawed and depraved he truly was. But more importantly, he realized how tired he was of it. He desperately wanted to change and begin again. But how?

Jacob's quandary is this book's impetus. How does a person escape the heritage of his upbringing? How does one transform his innermost being into something he is not? This was the same dilemma faced by Hagar in the wilderness when God asked her where she had come from and where she was going. Leah, the unwanted woman with weak eyes, struggled with the same issue when fighting for a place within her own household. And it was Abraham who struggled to find a suitable sacrifice on Moriah's height. Then and now, as in the case of Jacob, we all need to know, "Who and what (in contrast to all that we are) is God? It is this contrast that we so desperately want and need. Does God have anything in contrast to my despicable plight?

Such realizations are the fountainhead of transformation. They are the salt which, when thrown into the deep waters of our soul, often begin God's purging of the heart. Bruce Lipton, in his book *The Biology of Belief*, describes his own instant of transformation. Struggling to describe his experience, he called it his "eureka moment," and frames it in the language of his profession.

> It resembled the dynamics of super-saturated solutions in chemistry. These solutions, which look like plain water, are fully saturated with a dissolved substance. They are so saturated that just one more drop of the solute causes a dramatic reaction in which all the dissolved materials instantly coalesce into a giant crystal.[6]

In a moment, a brief instant in the grand scheme of eternity, Jacob's heart was suddenly opened. In that "aha!" moment, he comprehended his deeply flawed nature. He was a schemer and a swindler who fought his whole life through. Something had to change because, in himself, he realized he couldn't go on. His frustration is described in the Amplified Bible as "affliction and humiliation and the [wearying] labor of his hands" (Genesis 31:42, AMP).

Jacob was undone! His innate abilities, his emotions, his passions, and his inclinations had all betrayed him in the end. He had nothing left upon which to rely. The words, "So Jacob was left alone" (Genesis 32:24a, NIV) say it all and frame his wretchedness. It is his epitaph that declares he'd given it his best but had failed in the end. Jacob was utterly and entirely spent; physically, emotionally, and spiritually.

"Woe is me! for I am undone," said the prophet Isaiah at such a time (Isaiah 6:5a, KJV). "Woe unto us! Who shall deliver us?" (1 Samuel 4:8a, KJV).

The Biblical Illustrator refers to the man's unease and dread as "the soul's agony."

> So is everyone in similar experiences. In times of agony, friendly sympathy seems distant and ineffectual. We are even impatient with well-meant words of kindness. Then comes a sense of powerlessness. The afflicted one has done all he can, and now can only wait. At this juncture he begins to ask himself as to the cause of his misery. Why is he thus situated? Perhaps, like Jacob, he recognizes his sorrows as the lineal descendants of some former sin; or more likely, he now perceives, as never before, the general fact of his sinfulness, his imperfections as a Christian, and his failure to enjoy religious privileges.[7]

It is at such disquieting times that God often speaks. Solitude is often "the audience chamber of God."[8] Bruce Lipton refers to such precipitous times as "Aha!" moments[9] when our storm-tossed hearts are stirred by consciousness of God.

When we're alone, we can't escape into other people's hearts and minds and be distracted; we have to live with ourselves and face ourselves. Twenty years before, Jacob had met the Lord when he was alone at Bethel; and now God graciously came to him again in his hour of need (v(v). 28, 30; Hosea 12:2–6).

God meets us at whatever level He finds us in order to lift us to where He wants us to be. To Abraham the pilgrim, God came as a traveler (Genesis 18); and to Joshua the general, He came as a soldier (Josh 5:13–15). Jacob had spent most of his adult life wrestling with people—Esau, Isaac, Laban, and even his wives—so God came to him as a wrestler. "With the pure You will show Yourself pure; and with the devious You will show Yourself shrewd" (Psalm 18:26, NKJV).[10]

The Scriptures are replete with stories of such men and women who were awakened from restive states to rise and "get up" again. For example, after the Lord had rained down fire and brimstone upon Sodom and Gomorrah, Abraham *got up* early to survey the scheme of destruction (Genesis 19:27, NIV). Similarly, when God called to Moses from within the burning bush, Moses hid his face but God said to him: "So now, *go*! I am sending you to Pharaoh" (Exodus 3:10a NIV). When Joshua was distraught because of Israel's defeat at Ai, God said to him, "Stand up! What are you doing down on your face?... Go, consecrate the people" (Joshua 7:10, 13a; NIV). Once, when Elijah was in a fit of depression, the Lord touched and fed him. "What are you doing here, Elijah?" said God. "Go out and stand on the mountain in the presence of the Lord, for the Lord is about to pass by" (1 Kings 19:9, 11; NIV). And finally, when Saul's eye's were abruptly opened, the Scriptures say he *got up* and was baptized (Acts 9:18, NIV). Appropriately, when the light of heaven first flashed around him, Saul asked, "Who are you, Lord?" (Acts 9:5, NIV). In light of this discussion, "Who is Jesus to you?" Saul's question is like Jacob's when he asked, "Tell me, I pray You, what [in contrast] is Your name?" (Genesis 32:29a, AMP).

Importantly, the Lord didn't chastise Saul for his prior resistance. Neither did He censure Jacob who capably wrestled against Him. But God did blind Saul for three days, signaling the man's dramatic change. The number three distinctly marks beginning, middle, and end and is regarded as symbolic of a complete and ordered whole. The Bible contains many familiar trios, such as heaven, earth, and sea; and morning, noon and night.

In Damascus there was a disciple named Ananias. The Lord called to him in a vision and told him to go to a particular house and ask for a man from Tarsus named Saul. "In a vision he has seen a man named Ananias come and place his hands on him to restore his sight," said the Lord (Acts 9:11, NIV).

It is impossible to read the story of Saul's eureka moment and not notice the role of seeing and vision in the man's spiritual revitalization. Our challenge is to recall Leah's revelation through her son, Reuben. To rightly see is the beginning of God's orchestrated plan of salvation. Thus, when Hagar was revived, she declared, "You are the God who sees me" (Genesis 16:13a, NIV). Similarly, Abraham looked up to see his ordained sacrifice.

With dawning comprehension, Jacob suddenly realized how flawed he was. But he also realized how tired he was of it and how he needed to be changed and renewed. But how? How does a person escape the heritage of his upbringing? How are we transformed into something we are not?

What Saul did next exemplifies what must be done after such "aha" moments. The Scriptures say that something like scales fell from Saul's eyes. Seeing again, he got up (arose) and was baptized; that is, he re-consecrated himself (as if reborn). After strengthening himself with food, he then set out on a new course as God's chosen instrument to carry the name of Jesus to the Gentiles. Consequently, he grew more and more powerful and baffled the Jews living in Damascus by proving that Jesus is the Christ (Acts 9:22). The Amplified Version says he "increased all the more in strength."

When later writing of his divine encounter, Paul describes it as "a light from heaven surpassing the brightness of the sun, flashing about me and those who were traveling with me" (Acts 26:13, AMP). He also recalled how Jesus told him to get up and stand on his feet.

"I am sending you to open the eyes of the people that they may turn from darkness to light and from the power of Satan to God, so that they may thus receive forgiveness and release from their sins" (Acts 26:18, AMP). Who better to open the eyes of those in darkness than one who was himself once blind?

After Jacob's encounter with God, he called the name of the place *Peniel*. "It is because I *saw* [*ra'ah*] God face to face, and yet my life was spared," he declared (Genesis 32:30, NIV). He was broken and transformed, divinely inspired and supernaturally increased with strength.

"From Jacob's standpoint," notes *The New American Commentary*, "what was most remarkable was that he had made demands on the divine combatant and had lived.... his life was in jeopardy at any time the 'man' wished to take it. The passive voice of the Hebrew verb, 'was spared' (*niph.*, *wattinnasel*), suggests that Jacob ... lived only because God's grace preserved him."[11] Additionally, from the vantage of *Peniel*, Jacob lifted his eyes and looked to see Esau and his four hundred men (Genesis 33:1). The two men spied each other from across a lifetime of insight and Esau undoubtedly had to look twice because he saw a man of his father's likeness. In his spirit he knew that to fight with Jacob was to content with the *Dread* of Isaac. While the Scriptures are silent in this regard, I believe Esau cringed at the thought; recalling how Abimelech had cowered before Isaac, the divinely-empowered man. Now, standing before him, was Jacob who exuded the same godliness. This man could ably contend with men and win!

Thus, God's affirmation was confirmed. Truly, his name was Israel for in his fight with God and with men he had overcome. Concerning this, Warren Wiersbe writes that "receiving a new name signifies making a new beginning ([Genesis]17:4–5, 15; Numbers 13:16; John 1:40–42), and this was Jacob's opportunity to make a fresh start in life. The new name God gave him was 'Israel,' from a Hebrew word that means 'to struggle'; but scholars aren't agreed on what the name signifies. Some translate it 'one who wrestles with God' or 'God strives' or 'let God rule.'"[12]

"You have striven with God and with men and have prevailed [*yakol, overcome*]," declared the Lord (Genesis 32:28, NASU). *Yakol* is used in Scripture to reference the control of oneself (Genesis 45:1) or his circumstances (Exodus 2:3). In another example, the Egyptian magicians couldn't stand (i.e., *yakol*) before Moses because of his supernatural ability (Exodus 9:11).

As *Israel*, the man who was once named Jacob could stand with restraint and implied ability. Matthew Henry concludes, "Wrestling believers may obtain glorious victories, and yet come off with broken bones; for *when they are weak then are they strong*, weak in themselves, but strong in Christ, (2 Corinthians 12:10)."[13]

Instead of running at him with sword in hand, Esau ran to meet his brother and embraced him; he threw his arms around his neck and kissed him. Jacob had finally emerged from his period of testing; he was a tried man who limped. But his limp was a mark of power and not weakness. His strength was now in his limp, for it was a constant reminder that God had conquered him and that he could likewise conquer. *Barnes Notes* says:

> Jacob, true to his character, struggles while life remains with this new combatant. [God] touched the socket of his thigh, so that it was wrenched out of joint. The thigh is the pillar of a man's strength, and its joint with the hip the seat of physical force for the wrestler. Let the thighbone be thrown out of joint, and the man is utterly disabled. Jacob now finds that this mysterious wrestler has wrested from him, by one touch, all his might, and he can no longer stand alone. Without any support whatever from himself, he hangs upon the conqueror, and in that condition learns by experience the practice of sole reliance on one mightier than himself. This is the turning point in this strange drama. Henceforth Jacob now feels himself strong, not in himself, but in the Lord, and in the power of his might.[14]

Throughout his entire life, Jacob had wrestled; contending both with God and man. As an infant, Jacob had struggled against his brother in his mother's womb. As a young man, he fought for every modicum of comfort and favor within his father's household.

Nothing changed when he lived in Haran with his Uncle Laban. Now he ran for his life from his father-in-law's entire household. By nature, Jacob was a wrestler. But as *Israel* (one who prevailed with God and men), he was entirely able to wrestle with overcoming strength and ability. As C. S. Robinson notes: "When once a believer is truly in Christ, his standing with God is entirely changed. Every barrier is broken down. God's displeasure is over, and man's enmity is ended. Not only in state but in character is the true believer a new man. If he be in Christ, he will grow assuredly to resemble Christ. The new creation of a believer in Christ extends even to his experience, as well as to his state and character [his] confidence, [his] freedom, [and his] contentment."[15]

Were Jacob's struggles finally over? Now that every barrier was broken down, was he finally able to enter into God's rest (i.e. his homeland)? From your own experience, did your conflicts end after giving your heart and life to Jesus? Did Paul's struggles end after meeting Christ on the road to Damascus? What about Simon's after coming into the full realization of Jesus?

Perhaps this is why the Scriptures say that it was Jacob, not *Israel*, who looked up to see Esau coming with his four hundred men. Even as God's *Israel*, Jacob's struggles did not end. But with God at his side, he needn't fear because of assured victory. As God's *Israel*, the man could successfully wrestle and win! When the Lord rules our lives, He puts His power within our hands to effectually contend.

As a Christian, do you still struggle with your old nature, who and what you are in the flesh; your carnality? Perhaps you are like the apostle Paul who said, "O wretched man that I am! Who will deliver me from this body of death?" (Romans 7:24, NKJV).

> So I find it to be a law (rule of action of my being) that when I want to do what is right *and* good, evil is ever present with me *and* I am subject to its insistent demands.
>
> For I endorse *and* delight in the Law of God in my inmost self [with my new nature]. [*Ps* 1:2.]

> But I discern in my bodily members [in the sensitive appetites and wills of the flesh] a different law (rule of action) at war against the law of my mind (my reason) and making me a prisoner to the law of sin that dwells in my bodily organs [in the sensitive appetites and wills of the flesh].
>
> O unhappy *and* pitiable *and* wretched man that I am! Who will release *and* deliver me from [the shackles of] this body of death?
>
> Romans 7:21–24, AMP

When Abraham received his new name, he was never again called in the Scriptures by his former name. He was no longer called Abram; he was entirely changed once and for all. Jacob, on the other hand, is called by both names, interchangeably. He is called by the one name and then by the other. For example, God named him *Israel* and said to him, "be fruitful and increase in number" (Genesis 35:11, NIV), but it was Jacob who then set up a stone pillar at the place where God had talked to him (v. 14). Likewise, when Rachel died and was buried, it was Jacob who marked her grave but it was Israel who moved on from there. Also, when the time came to bless his sons, Jacob called them together but their father *Israel* prophesied over them (Genesis 49:1–2).

Both names, Jacob and Israel, have spiritual significance because they recognize the man's two natures. In like manner, we each have two names by which we live and act. We have our name given at birth and we have our new name written down in glory. Each name has a corresponding nature. "He who has an ear, let him hear what the Spirit says to the churches," [said Christ]. "To him who overcomes, I will give some of the hidden manna. I will also give him a white stone with a new name written on it, known only to him who receives it" (Revelation 2:17, NIV).

Chapter Three Evaluation

1. Why is it important to understand the dual nature of the man named Jacob whom God called Israel? There is no denying that two natures struggle within each of us, one against the other. Perhaps this is why the story of Simon Peter is an important part of Christ's Gospel. He was Simon by birth; bendable like a reed and often unstable in character. One moment he was laughing and the next moment he was petulant and ready to fight. Jesus recognized Simon's inherent weakness and consequently said to him: "You are Simon the son of Jonah [but] you shall be called *Cephas* [meaning *rock*]" (John 1:42, NKJV, emphasis mine). Whereas Simon was characteristically wavering and unsteady (i.e., changeable by nature), Peter was durable with the nuance of permanence and stability. He had to be rock-like (i.e., *petros*) in character to carry the torch of Christ's revelation to the world. He is also called *Simon Peter* in the Scriptures (Matthew 16:16; Luke 5:8; John 6:68, 13:6, 13:9, 13:24, 13:36; 18:10, 18:15, etc.) suggestive of the constant conflict between his two natures. What is our remedy for this dilemma? How do we overcome the carnality within us?

2. Have you ever had an "Aha!" moment when heaven's light suddenly illuminated your soul? Genesis 32 stresses Jacob's "shock of realization" (v. 27, AMP) when he suddenly saw himself for what he was. Have you ever had a similar "shock of realization"? Most importantly, it was also at that instant of intuitive recognition that Jacob made up his mind that things had to change. In this regard, have you finally come to our senses as did the prodigal son in Christ's parable (Luke 15:17). Recall your own special "Aha" moment. If within a group session, share your inspiration (your sudden realization).

3. J. Brewster said, "Power with God is the right application of the knowledge of God in Christ at the right time, in the

use of right means to accomplish the right end."¹⁶ Jacob's realization and sudden transformation came at a most opportune time. What was his situation and what was the outcome? But J. Brewster also makes the point that God's power is perfected in our lives when rightly applied at the right time. Once again, recall your own transformational moment. What was your state of mind just prior to that special moment when heaven reached down to touch your soul? In Jacob's case, he'd run his course and had come up short. With Laban and his sons in hot pursuit, and with his brother, Esau, riding with four hundred mighty men to cut him off, Jacob was between a rock and a hard place. Also recall Hagar's awakening in the wilderness of Beersheba when she hung her head and sobbed (Genesis 21:16). She was in the lowest of low places; emotionally and physically drained. It is for such times that God waits because you are finally open to His gentle, quiet stirring. Once again read the story of Jacob in Genesis 32. Perhaps it's finally time for you to stop wrestling, give up, and let God complete His work in you? God's desire is that you are "mature and complete in Him, not lacking anything (James 1:4, NIV).

4. Following his enabling as God's *Israel*, Jacob stumbled forth with new vigor and hope. From that day forward, he never walked in the same old way; his limp was a constant reminder that he was a divinely-enabled man with uncanny ability to multiply with supernatural increase (Genesis 35:11). This chapter's challenge is to remember who and what you are in Christ. Peter reminds us in his second epistle to the Church that God's grace and peace are ours in abundance through the knowledge of God and of Jesus Christ (2 Peter 1:2). "His divine power has given us everything we need for life and godliness through our knowledge of him who called us by His own glory and goodness. Through these He has given us His very great and precious promises, so that through them you may participate in the divine nature and escape the corruption in the world caused by evil desires"

(v(v). 3–4, NIV). Peter is speaking from personal experience. He had knowledge with essential know-how as to the divine nature of Christ. But he was also a man of many failings. Who better than Peter to say to the fledgling Church: "Of a truth I perceive that God is no respecter of persons" (Acts 10:34, KJV). The Amplified Version renders this same passage: "Most certainly *and* thoroughly I now perceive *and* understand that God shows no partiality *and* is no respecter of persons, but in every nation he who venerates *and* has a reverential fear for God, treating Him with worshipful obedience and living uprightly, is acceptable to Him *and* sure of being received and welcomed [by Him]" (Acts 10:34–35, AMP). Never call yourself anything less than does God!

5. "What is power with God?" asks J. Brewster in his commentary on Genesis 32:28.[17] Do you have an answer? According to the apostle Peter, God's favor and perfect well-being, as well as all spiritual prosperity and freedom from fears and agitating passions, are multiplied to us through the personal and correct knowledge of God and of Jesus our Lord (2 Peter 1:2). Brewster believes that inspired knowledge (i.e., the Holy Scriptures, visions and divine insights from God) forms the basis of all power with God. Do you agree and, if so, what is your personal knowledge of God and Christ that has set you free?

CHAPTER FOUR

What Would You Do If You Knew You Could Not Fail?

> Grace and peace be yours in abundance through the knowledge of God and of Jesus our Lord.
>
> His divine power has given us everything we need for life and godliness through our knowledge of him who called us by his own glory and goodness. Through these he has given us his very great and precious promises, so that through them you may participate in the divine nature and escape the corruption in the world caused by evil desires.
>
> 2 Peter 1:2–4 (NIV)

What are you and I to do after we've finally realized the fullness of God's grace and peace through knowledge of Him? According to Peter, we are to "participate in the divine nature and escape the corruption in the world" (2 Peter 1:4, NIV). Was this true of Jacob? After he had by wrestling prevailed with God to win a blessing, and after God had bestowed upon him all things necessary to a life of godliness, did he partake of God's divine nature?

What next befell the patriarch is a dire warning to us all. After telling Laban of his desire to return to his own place and country (Genesis 30:25), and after the Lord had spoken to him of returning to the land of his fathers and to his people (Genesis 31:3), Jacob turned aside and went to Shechem where he camped within sight of that enclosed city. This was despite the fact that God had said to him, "I am the God of Bethel, where you anointed the pillar and where you vowed a vow to Me. Now arise, get out from this land and return to your native land" (v. 13, AMP).

There was no doubt as to the Lord's will. Jacob didn't immediately return to Bethel to praise the Lord according to that revelation. For reasons left unsaid, he went to Shechem and pitched his tent there. Jacob also set up an altar where he called on the name of *El-Elohe-Israel*, "God, the God of Israel." After all he'd experienced, Jacob still worshipped God generally; he did not praise the Lord specifically according to his special knowingness of Him.

On the surface, the account of Jacob's actions seems innocent enough. But why did he stop short of Bethel to reside at Shechem? Furthermore, why didn't he call upon the God of Bethel? Was it because he felt that his revelation was for that time and place only? You may recall Jacob's declaration at Bethel. He said, "Surely the Lord is in *this place*, and I was not aware of it. *How awesome is this place*! This is none other than the house of God; *this is the gate of heaven*" (Genesis 28:16–17, NIV, emphasis mine). I believe Jacob never realized that his revelation of the Lord at Bethel was meant to be an ongoing, continuing experience. The ministering angels descending from heaven and ascending again unto God were his assured promise of continuing peace and goodness. *Bethel* was not just a physical local; it was also a place in his heart and soul where God abides—Jacob's *gate of heaven*.

You may recall God's explicit instructions to Jacob were for him to return to his native land and worship there. "I am the God of Bethel, where you anointed the pillar and where you vowed a vow to Me," said the Lord. "Now arise, get out from this land and return to your native land" (Genesis 31:13, AMP). What was he doing in Shechem?

I believe a clue to Jacob's errant behavior is found in Genesis 33:18. After Jacob came from Paddan Aram, the Word of God tells us that "he arrived *safely* at the city of Shechem in Canaan and camped within sight of the city" (NIV, emphasis added). The Amplified Bible says, "... he arrived *safely and in peace* at the town of Shechem, in the land of Canaan, and pitched his tents before the [enclosed] town" (AMP, emphasis added). Despite God's surety of divine protection and abiding peace, Jacob failed to put his entire trust in the Lord. Instead, he relied on the surety of Shechem's walls. It seems he had set aside the principles revealed through his firstborn sons; Reuben (the son of seeing), Simeon (the son of hearing), Levi (Israel's son of wholehearted attachment), and Judah (the son of Israel whose hand is lifted-up in requisite action). Consequently, Jacob lodged at Shechem.

In this respect, Jacob is like most of us who follow the Lord. We are "ever seeing but never perceiving, and ever hearing but never understanding" (Mark 4:12, NIV). Consequently, he lived outside the Lord's perfect will and, thereby, unwittingly placed himself and his family in grave danger.

At Shechem, Jacob's daughter was kidnapped by a man of that country. He savagely brutalized her; defiling, raping, and disgracing her (Genesis 34:2). Fearing to openly confront the Shechemites, however, Jacob heard of it but held his peace. In this we again see the consequence of his misplaced trust. But it was not so with Jacob's sons for they were filled with grief and fury. Shechem had done *a disgraceful thing* in Israel..."a thing that should not be done" (Genesis 34:7, NIV, emphasis added). The fact that the actions are declared "disgraceful" depicts their activities as purposely ignorant of wisdom's instructions (Proverbs 5:23).[1] Consequently, Simeon (Israel's son whose heritage it was to discern and truly understand) and his brother Levi (the son of Israel whose lot it was to rightly join with God in affiliation) decided to take matters into their own hands. It was not in their natures to do otherwise.

But they abused one of God most sacred rites in the process of their revenge. Simeon and Levi demanded that the Shechemites be circumcised in obedience to the laws of God. Circumcision is the Lord's sign of divine protection. But the sons of Israel defiled this sacred rite and turned it to the detriment of Shechem. This does not absolve the Shechemites guilt, however, because they took that which was sacred and defiled it by (1) submitting to the sacred rite, not at God's behest, but at their leaders' request, and (2) they saw it as a way to steal the riches of Israel. The point made here is that nothing secures us better than faith and religious conviction; but nothing exposes us more than belief only pretended to.

On the third day following the circumcision, when all the men of the city were still convalescing, Simeon and Levi joined forces and took their revenge. They boldly entered the city and killed all the males. They also killed Hamor and Shechem, his son, and took Dinah from Shechem's house. The rest of Jacob's sons then plundered the town, took Shechem's flocks, their herds, their donkeys, and anything else in the town and in the field, and all their wealth and all their little ones and their wives. They made spoil of everything.

"You have brought trouble on me by making me a stench to the Canaanites and Perizzites, the people living in this land," raged Jacob, chastising Simeon and Levi for their duplicity. "We are few in number, and if they join forces against me and attack me, I and my household will be destroyed" (Genesis 34:30, NIV).

Why was Jacob so enraged by his son's revenge of their sister? At the heart of this story is the Lord's response to the whole sorted affair. Early in his relationship with God, Jacob made a vow, saying, "If God will be with me and will watch over me on this journey... so that I return safely to my father's house, then the Lord will be my God" (Genesis 28:20–21, NIV). God reinforced this holy awareness when He spoke to Jacob. "I am the God of Bethel, where you anointed a pillar and where you made a vow to Me," He declared (Genesis 31:13a, NIV). But despite these things, Jacob went against all that he knew and chose, instead, to dwell in the false security of Shechem's walls. Furthermore, he worshipped *El-Elohe-Israel*, "God, the God of Israel" and not the God of Bethel Whom he knew.

Jacob should never have stopped short in Shechem. He was out of God's will and even worshipped imprecisely. Thus, God chided Jacob, repeating again, "Go up to Bethel and settle there, and build an altar there to God, who appeared to you when you were fleeing from your brother Esau" (Genesis 35:1, NIV).

Bethel was Jacob's "house of God" (Genesis 28:17). It is in Bethel, the house of God, that we should desire to dwell (Psalm 27:4). "That should be our home," declares Matthew Henry, "not our inn."[2] By reminding Jacob, not of his vow, but of its occasion (when he had fled from his brother, Esau), the Lord was challenging the man to remember the divine pledge of protection.

From this story we learn that faith has two sides: belief and trust. Reuben and Simeon, Israel's firstborn sons are the foundation of God's kingdom on earth. To rightly believe, we must have eyes that see (the legacy of Reuben) and must hear with ears that understand (the Simeonic Principle). Additionally, we must trust with wholehearted agreement (Levi's legacy) and turn accordingly (the Judaic Principle of Praise whereby we open our hand unto the Lord). There are the two sides of faith that lead to forgiveness and mighty deliverance (Mark 4:12). To accept the Lord is belief, but to come into wholehearted agreement and affiliation and then rightly turn is trust!

What good is a divine perception (i.e., a vision, a holy insight, an inspired word from God) if there is no understanding and then requisite turning (Mark 4:12)? Jacob learned this lesson the hard way. He sought out the comfort and security of Shechem but, in the process, turned his back on the God of Bethel, his Protector. The events of Shechem were a wake-up call that forced him to once again reckon on his divine knowingness.

Incidentally, it was Simeon (who is reminiscent of hearing with understanding) and Levi (the oracle of fidelity with an uncompromising heart) who took up Israel's cause. We should ask why Reuben and Judah were detached from the incident. Is the lesson of Shechem a warning to all of us on the hazards of unhearing ears or taking God's word for granted? It seems the two principles for which Simeon and Levi are oracles are central to the story. Jacob didn't rely on God's oath and paid a very high price.

How many of us are like Jacob in this regard? Even now, we are going through Shechem, or something akin to it, for lack of hearing God's word and/or adequately taking it to heart. We too quickly are distracted by the high walls and glitter of the city. From whence comes my salvation? Said Eliphaz to Job: "But now trouble comes to you, and you are discouraged; it strikes you, and you are dismayed. Should not your piety be your confidence and your blameless ways your hope?" (Job 4:5–6, NIV). You should once again consider that which you know (your special awareness of the Lord) and live accordingly in absolute agreement. This is your piety before God.

What has God previously shared with you? What do you know that you know? Has it become your way of life? Is your special revelation of truth, your sudden insight, or our divine awareness (your "Aha!" moment) become your life's centerpiece? If not, learn from Jacob at Shechem. From his experience we learn valuable lessons, perhaps one of the most important concerns Jacob's God, *El-Elohe-Israel*. By neglecting God, The God of Bethel, the narrative suggests that Jacob was not worshipping specific, according to His divine awareness. The Shechemites had their gods and only gave lip-service to the holy rites of Israel's God. It seems that Jacob was also guilty of the same thing. Never let your praise be neglectful of the Lord your God. You know Him specifically and you must build your altar accordingly.

Genesis 31–35 outlines Jacob's return to Bethel, the sacred place of his altar and where he and his household were meant to dwell. "Arise, go up to Bethel and *dwell there* [i.e., *yashab*]," said God. "And make there an altar to God Who appeared to you [in a distinct manifestation] when you fled from the presence of Esau your brother" (Genesis 35:1, AMP, emphasis added).

For several years Jacob had lingered elsewhere with disastrous results. The consequence of his disobedience became his *Shechem*. But now God reminded Jacob of his past insecurity when fleeing Esau and urged him to remember His divine care. When Jacob was fleeing from his brother, God gave him a special assurance of peace. "Behold [i.e., *see*]," said God to Jacob at Bethel, "I am with you and will keep (watch over you with care, take notice of) you wherever you may go, and I will bring you back to this land; for I will not leave you until I have done all of which I have told you" (Genesis 28:15, AMP). In response, Jacob declared that if God would be with him and keep him so that he might return again to his father's house in peace, then the Lord would be his God. He also set up a stone pillar as a witness of his visitation and sacred promise. "This stone which I have set up as a pillar (monument)," [he declared], "shall be God's house [a sacred place to me], and of all [the increase of possessions] that You give me I will give the tenth to You" (v. 22, AMP).

Bethel was Jacob's sacred place where he was meant to dwell (i.e., *yashab*). *Yashab* (*Strong's* OT:3427) means *to sit down* (specifically as *judge, in ambush, in quiet*); by implication, *to dwell, to remain; causatively, to settle,* or *to marry*."[3] *Yashab* is translated as *abide* in Genesis 22:5 (KJV). *Vine's Dictionary* notes that the verb may also carry the meaning *begin to reign* (Deuteronomy 17:18; cf. 1 Kings 1:13,17,24). It could also mean *to sit in the gate* (*hold court* or *to decide a case*) as in Ruth 4:1–2 and 1 Kings 22:10. "Sit thou [*yashab*] at my right hand" (Psalm 110:1, KJV) means *to assume a ruling position as a deputy*.[4] Thus, the Lord's command was for Jacob to return to Bethel, the place of his altar and dwell (begin to reign) there.

"Many of the problems in the Christian life and in local churches," says Warren Wiersbe, "result from incomplete obedience. We know what the Lord wants us to do, we start to do it, and then we stop. When we don't continue to obey God and accomplish His will, even what we've done starts to die."[5] To the church in Sardis, Jesus said, "Wake up! Strengthen what remains and is about to die, for I have not found your deeds complete in the sight of my God. Remember, therefore, what you have received and heard; obey it, and repent. But if you do not wake up, I will come like a thief, and you will not know at what time I will come to you" (Revelation 3:2–3, NIV).

Bethel is a spiritual representation of our fresh awakening unto the Lord's provision. Hence, Jacob said to his household, "Get rid of the foreign gods you have with you, and purify yourselves and change your clothes. Then come, let us arise and go up to Bethel, where I will build an altar to God, Who answered me in the day of my distress and Who had been with me wherever I have gone" (Genesis 35:2–3, NIV). In his remarks we see several essential rudiments of revival: (1) First, he put aside the foreign gods (i.e., his spiritual baggage) that had been picked-up along the way. We each have a sacred duty in this regard; (2) Then, Jacob demanded purification (i.e., sanctification of heart); (3) Thirdly, a change of clothes was required, signifying their regal calling; (4) Then Jacob said to those with him, "arise" (AMP, NKJV). It is only as we "go up" (NIV, KJV) or "arise" from our depravity that we are blessed; (5) Fifthly, Jacob did not stop until he had arrived at his destination, his Bethel where he was specially revived; (6) At Bethel, God required that Jacob worship rightly. This began with his carefully reconstructed altar that was firmly founded in the Lord; (7) Lastly, Jacob's altar-experience (his praise) was to be centered around that which God had previously revealed. Jacob had previously vowed that he would make the revealed Lord of Bethel *his* God (Genesis 28:21). *El Bethel* was his source of potency, provision, and strength. Thus, Jacob said, "I will make there an altar to God Who answered me in the day of my distress and was with me wherever I went" (Genesis 35:3b, AMP). Jacob's praise was very specific according to his particular awareness of God. Is yours?

Our altars should never be haphazardly built. Elijah confirmed this on Carmel's heights when he repaired the Lord's altar. "Come here to me," he said to God's people because his message is for us all (1 Kings 18:30a, NIV). After they had come to him, Elijah rebuilt the altar of the Lord, which was in ruins. He carefully laid twelve stones, one for each of the tribes descended from Jacob. They were circumspectly placed in the name of the Lord because each stone has great significance within the kingdom of God. This was attested to by the falling of His holy fire upon the sacrifice, the wood, and *the stones* (1 Kings 18:38, NIV).

Also notice Jacob's attention to the seemingly petty detail of his household's clothing. He required a change of garments because this is an outward sign of a contrite heart and God's calling. Hence, when the prodigal son returned home, his father said, "Quick! Bring the best robe and put it on him" (Luke 15:22, NIV). In another of Christ's parables, a king gave a grand wedding feast. But when the king came in to see the guests, he noticed a man there who was not wearing wedding clothes. "Friend," he asked, "how did you get in here without wedding clothes?" (Matthew 22:12, NIV). The man was speechless; he had no excuse for his carelessness. "Tie him hand and foot, and throw him outside, into the darkness," said the king to the attendants. "For many are invited, but few are chosen" (v. 14, NIV).

From Christ's remark, our garments telegraph the heart's intention and God's regal invitation.

"Many Christians are suffering from spiritual declension," observes F. B. Meyer:

> They hardly realize it, it has crept on them so quietly; but they have drifted far away from their Bethel and Peniel. Gray hairs are on a man before he knows. Summer fruit is beginning to rot within long before its surface is pitted with specks. The leaf's connection with the branch is severed, even when it looks green. The devil is too shrewd to make Judases at a stroke; he wins us from the side of Christ by hairbreadths.[6]

The text also reveals several truths regarding Jacob's family idols:

> Idols are the inevitable symptom of incipient decay. Go at autumn into the woods and see how the members of the fungus tribes are scattered plentifully throughout the unfrequented glades. All through the long scorching summer days their germs were present in the soil; but they were kept from germinating by the dryness of the air and the heat of the sun. However, there is now nothing to prevent it; nay, the dank damp of decay is the very food of their life. Where the shade is deepest and the soil most impregnated with the products of corruption, they love to pitch their tents. Wherever, therefore, you find these fungus growths, you may be sure that there is corruption and decay. Similarly, whenever there has set in upon the spiritual life the autumn of decay, you will be sure to find a fungus—growth of idols the sorrowful symptoms that the bright summer time has passed, or is passing away from the soul.[7]

From these discussions we learn that our spiritual revitalization requires much more of us than simply traipsing toward Bethel (the place of our spiritual renewal). We must also attend to our spiritual purification and sanctification by putting away our foreign gods and by exchanging our filthy rags for robes of white. Likewise, the altars upon which we worship must never be haphazardly built, but must be constructed in keeping with the Lord's orchestrated plan of salvation. Thus, Jacob said; "I will make there an altar to God Who answered me in the day of my distress and was with me wherever I went" (Genesis 35:3, AMP). Never neglect the Lord's abiding influence.

Matthew Henry shed's additional insight on this:

> God reminds Jacob of his vow at Beth-el, and sends him thither to perform it (v. 1). Jacob had said in the day of his distress, "If I come again in peace, this stone shall be God's house" (ch. 28:22). God had performed his part of the bargain...but it should seem, he had forgotten his vow, or at least had too long deferred the performance of it. Seven or eight years it was now since he came to Canaan; he had purchased ground there, and had built an altar in remembrance of God's last appearance to him when he called him Israel (ch. 33:19, 20); but still Beth-el is forgotten.[8]

Time often saps our senses of the Lord's mercies and our hallowed impressions. When at peace and ease, we often lose our moral compass and our circumspection birthed by affliction and consecrated in anguish. Then, through neglect, our altars fall into disrepair as we forget to lift holy hands in praise unto the Lord.

Hence, the neglectful family of Israel purged itself of all its foreign gods and spiritual baggage. They gave their amulets for the warding off evil spirits to Jacob because they were no longer needed. He buried them at Shechem (all the sordid business of their past); and was, once and for all, rid of them. These things no longer had a place within the Lord's Israel, the family of God's people.

It was only *after* these things (once Jacob and his household had broken with their past and made up their minds to go to Bethel) that a great dread from God fell on the towns round about them. No one pursued them as *the terror of the Lord* went before Israel. When

God's people are doing God's will in God's way, we can depend on His provision and continuing care. Hence, God fulfilled His promise to bring them safely back to Bethel.

There are two sides of faith, belief and trust, and Jacob was finally on the right track to apprehend both. At Bethel, he kept his part of the bargain and made an altar there to God (the Lord Who appeared to him in a distinct manifestation when he fled from his brother's wrath). Jacob also led his entire household in worship and gave a new name to an old place. Where once he simply called it *Bethel*, "the house of God" (Genesis 28:19), now he expanded the name of the place to *El-Bethel*, "God, the God of Bethel" (Genesis 35:7).

Something great was astir within the man's soul as he realized that it wasn't *the place* that was holy; it was *the God of the place* that made all the difference. From then on, Israel carried with him his cognizance of *El-Bethel* (God, the God of Bethel), the God of his fathers. In that special moment of dawning realization (Jacob's eureka-moment), I believe the man became fully aware of his God-endowed nature, *Israel*. It was also at that moment that God also gave him a new name upon which to rely. Israel knew *El Bethel* (God, the God of Bethel), but the Lord also declared to him, "I am *God Almighty [El-Shaddai]*. Be fruitful and multiply; a nation and a company of nations shall come from you and kings shall be born of your stock" (Genesis 35:11, AMP, emphasis added). Revelation is often progressive as we proceed upward with God from one spiritual plateau to the next. See my first book, *The Chronicles of Elijah*, for development of this spiritual principle.

The revelation of God's essence that would bring to pass all that *El-Bethel* promised is encapsulated in the name *El-Shaddai*, God Almighty. Israel's promise was, to some degree, an enlargement of that given to Isaac and to Abraham. "I will confirm my covenant between me and you and will greatly increase your numbers," said God to Abraham (Genesis 17:2, NIV). To Isaac, He declared, "I am the God of your father Abraham. Do not be afraid, for I am with you; I will bless you and will increase the number of your descendants for the sake of my servant Abraham" (Genesis 26:24, NIV). But to Israel, God said, "*I am God Almighty*; be fruitful and increase in number. A nation and a community of nations will come from you, and kings will come from your body" (Genesis 35:11, NIV, emphasis mine). God added a certain freshness and vastness to His promises now that Jacob had fully turned and drawn near to Him.

Why are we distraught and undone? What is the cause of our turmoil and the insipid chaos that underlies everything we do? Perhaps it's our lack of seeing with clear perception and our propensity to hear without understanding.

> "You will be ever hearing but never understanding; you will be ever seeing but never perceiving," [declared Jesus]. "For this people's heart has become calloused; they hardly hear with their ears, and they have closed their eyes. Otherwise they might see with their eyes, hear with their ears, understand with their hearts and turn, and I would heal them.
>
> Matthew 13:14–15 (NIV)

When Jacob finally returned to Bethel to make his altar, he talked with God and God with him. The fact that God acknowledged the man (v. 9) underscores the importance of specific and directed praise. We must always raise our open hands unto Him Who directs our paths (the basic meaning of praise). Jacob also set up a stone pillar at the place where God had talked with him and poured out a drink offering on it to signal his intention to be similarly poured out in keeping with his dawning awareness of God. Finally, he poured oil on the memorial in recognition of the holy principles for which it stood. He called the place where God talked with him Bethel. Implicitly, his worship was no longer imprecise or unfocused. Israel praised God very specifically and in keeping with his special awareness. He worshipped *El-Bethel* (God, the God of Bethel).

Do you worship God in a general sense, or do you praise pointedly and according to your specific knowledge of Him? I challenge you to remember the Lord's admonition found in Matthew's thirteenth chapter. Large crowds had gathered around the Lord and begged to hear wisdom from heaven that would improve their lot in life.

He spoke to them of heaven's increase; one hundred, sixty or thirty times more than is sown. But He spoke in parables; simple allegories that many of the people didn't understand.

"Why do you speak to the people in parables?" asked His disciples (Matthew 13:10, NIV).

Then Jesus shared a great secret. He replied, "Whoever has will be given more, and he will have an abundance. Whoever does not have, even what he has will be taken from him. This is why I speak to them in parables: Though seeing, they do not see; though hearing, they do not hear or understand. In them is fulfilled the prophecy of Isaiah: 'You will be ever hearing but never understanding; you will be ever seeing but never perceiving. For this people's heart has become calloused; they hardly hear with their ears, and they have closed their eyes. Otherwise they might see with their eyes, hear with their ears, understand with their hearts and turn, and I would heal them.'" (v.(v) 12–15, NIV).

Why do I linger on this point? Of what use it is? Our praise must also be like Israel's poignant according to our unique perspective and understanding of the Lord. Only in this way can you "turn" (be converted) and be healed (made whole).

I've noticed that many Christians no longer pray in Jesus' name. Perhaps they don't wish to offend someone so they lackadaisically say, "In Your name we pray." If you are not prepared to name the name that is above all name, save your breath. Most assuredly, you should always pray in the name of Jesus. You should also pointedly praise Him with the deep conviction of personal relationship. Hence, Israel praised God; the Lord Who appeared to him when he was fleeing from Esau. With dawning comprehension he also came to appreciate *the Fear*, the Lord who heaped dread upon those who would do him harm. Additionally, and with a budding awareness of *El Shaddai* (*the All-Sufficient Lord*), Israel's view of God was stretched to new heights of increase and productivity. "I am God Almighty," said God; "be fruitful and increase..." (Genesis 35:11a, NIV). Israel knew beyond all shadow of doubt that nothing was too hard for him. He was God's prince and in this blessed assuredness was an accompanying capacity and capability to accomplish God's intention.

So it was that Israel built a new altar and worshipped *El Bethel*—God, the God of Bethel. The Living Bible says that when they arrived at Luz (also called Bethel) in Canaan, Jacob erected an altar there and named it "The altar to the God who met me here at Bethel" because it was there at Bethel that God appeared to him when he was fleeing from Esau (Genesis 35:6–7). The fact that God acknowledged the man (v. 9) underscores the importance of specific and directed praise. We must always raise our open hands toward He Who is directly revealed to us.

On that fateful day, Israel came to know in a very real way that he would have children with an estate and an estate with children. Israel would flourish (i.e., *parah*, *grow up*) with increase (i.e., *rabah*, *harvested abundance*). Such special times of communion with the Lord are often short and transient. But, brief as they may be, they forever last against the backdrop of our gloomy days made brighter by the light of God's salvation. Jacob was a new man, as if born again. Even from his deathbed, he affirmed its reality. As Israel, he rallied his strength and sat up on his bed. "God Almighty appeared to me at Luz in the land of Canaan, and there he blessed me," declared Jacob. "He said to me, 'I am going to make you fruitful and will increase your numbers. I will make you a community of peoples, and I will give this land as an everlasting possession to your descendants after you.' And so it was!" (Genesis 48:3–4).

Chapter Four Evaluation

1. Jacob stopped short of Bethel, God's appointed place for him and his family (Genesis 31:1–3). In light of Jacob's delinquency and the high cost of his infidelity, evaluate your own spiritual place of residence. Do you and perhaps your family with you linger short God's full and perfect will? Do you lack like the crowd spoken of by Matthew—though seeing, they didn't see, and though hearing, they didn't hear with understanding (Matthew 13:15)? Perhaps it's time for you to reconsider your own "Bethel" experience when God met you in a very real and profound way.

2. Warren Wiersbe observes that the good news of the gospel is that we don't have to stay the way we are. "No matter how many times we've failed the Lord, we can go home again if we truly repent and obey. It happened to Abraham (13:1–4), Isaac (26:17), David (2 Sam 12), Jonah (Jonah 3:1–3), and Peter (John 21:15–19); and … to Jacob."[9] The challenge of this chapter is to remind us of our special altar and its special relevance. Commune there with God because it is rightly placed in our lives for a purpose. Are you and your family positioned around it or is it sadly neglected?

3. When Jacob first returned to Beersheba, he carved out a place for himself among the Canaanites at Shechem. He lived among them within sight of the city's walls (Genesis 33:18). There, he also built an altar, where he called upon *El Elohe Israel—God, the God of Israel* (v. 20). It seems that Jacob had forgotten his previous vows or, at least for a time, put them on hold. Consider your own spiritual practices. Do you honor the Lord, or have you compromised your standing?

4. In many respects, the story of Jacob's Shechem reminds me of the New Testament story of Mary and Martha (Luke 10:38–42). While Mary sat at the Lord's feet listening to Him, Martha was busy in the kitchen rattling the pots and pans. Martha reminds me of Jacob in Shechem. "Lord,"

Martha complained, "don't you care that my sister has left me to do all the work?" From the Lord's answer, we see that it was Martha who was negligent, not Mary. "Martha, Martha," He said, "you are worried and upset about many things, but only one thing is needed. Mary has chosen what is better." Jesus' response begs you and me to consider what is really important. Have you likewise become *distracted* (i.e., *perispao*; drawn away, over-occupied) by life's many things? "Only one thing is needed," Jesus reminded Martha. "She neglected a religious opportunity," says *The Essex Congregational Remembrancer*[10]; not out of necessity but by choice. Nonetheless, it irritated her that her sister didn't think or act like her. She measured her sister's conduct by her own. This too is a sad failing of many "religious" folk. The story of Mary and Martha warns against the evil of earthly-mindedness. "Influenced in such a way, the heart is in danger of being entangled so as not only to be kept from attending to what is better, but to think it strange that others should differ from ourselves. We sustain a serious loss without being sensible of it." [11] Perhaps it is time to pause and consider our own hearts and minds.

5. True power with God comes when we rightly rejoice in Him. Christ knows your deeds (read Revelation 3:1–3). Do you, like the saints of Sardis, have a reputation of being alive, but are really dead? "Wake up!" declares the Lord. "Strengthen what remains *and is about to die!*" Christ has empowered us unto deeds that are complete (i.e., crammed full with satisfaction, diffuse with influence, made perfect). Remember, therefore, what you have received and heard; obey it and repent (turn). "But if you don't wake up," warns the Lord, "I will come like a thief, and you will not know at what time I will come to you."

6. Perhaps one of the greatest challenges of this chapter concerns our various hidden idols (Genesis 35:2). Jacob had allowed "foreign" (i.e., strange) influences (gods, spiritual

tokens, etc.) to slowly creep into his household. Even as he rid himself of his foreign gods, so too should you and I dig about in the secret closets of our hearts. See what is hidden there. As E. Craig warns, "God will not suffer His people to sink habitually into this state of spiritual sloth."[12]

7. Jacob's revelation and subsequent anointing made him God's *Israel*. W. Roberts in *The Biblical Illustrator* notes the way in which all Jacob's later experiences tended to confirm in him the character of God's *Israel*. "[First], it is a glorious thing for a man, by means of a Divine discipline of life, to be made acquainted with the characteristics of his own nature. [Secondly], it is a glorious thing to have life enriched with manifold experiences. [Thirdly], it is a glorious thing to be made conscious of moral improvement and advantage. [Finally], it is a glorious thing to be brought into intimate fellowship and communion with God.[13] By divine culture, Jacob's life thus transformed from the character of a "supplanter" into that of an "Israel." Is your life similarly enriched? Having been enlightened as to who and what you are by God's Holy Word, are you living in intimate fellowship and communion with God?

8. The fact that God acknowledged Jacob's praise at Bethel (Genesis 35:9) underscores the importance of specific and directed praise. We must always be sure to lift open hands unto the Lord Who is directly revealed. The Lord appeared to Jacob according to the name *El Bethel—God, the God of Bethel*. He then confirmed to Jacob the dawning awareness his own God-given name and character—*Israel*. As God's prince, Jacob was bolstered against the fear of the Canaanites. He was also given promises that were ratified by the name *El-Shaddai*, God Almighty. It would be *the All-Sufficient Lord* Who would make good the promises. The various names of God reflect His person, His presence, and His character. The name *El-Shaddai* signifies the personal presence of God that is sufficient for every task. In

itself, it does not reflect the entirety of God. However, it was the name made special to Jacob upon which he could rely. Beyond all shadow of doubt, the man could count on *El-Shaddai* to deal with the troublesome Canaanites. By what name do you know God? By what name and character and essence has He made Himself *real* to you? Upon this you can rely!

9. *The International Standard Bible Encyclopedia* on the names of God addresses that which is called *The Gift of Revelation*. "The revelation of the Name of God stands in the centre of the biblical witness to revelation" (Brunner, p. 119). God Himself is known where His name is made known. The initiative of revelation thus lies clearly with God. The gift of knowledge of His name is an act of grace. It is appropriate, therefore, that the places where He makes His name known are places for worshiping response to His grace. Those who know God's grace, through knowing His name, are thereby led into a relationship of trust and confidence in Him (e.g., Psalm 9:10 [MT Psalm 9:11]; 91:14). When the priest invoked God's blessing of grace and peace, he 'put [God's] name upon the people' (Numbers 6:23–27); the revealed character of God guaranteed the blessing."[14]

CHAPTER FIVE

The Heritage of Israel

> And *Jacob* called for his sons and said, "Gather yourselves together [around me], that I may tell you what shall befall you in the latter or last days.
>
> Gather yourselves together and hear, you sons of Jacob; and hearken to *Israel* your father."
>
> Genesis 49:1–2 (AMP), emphasis added.

No one dared pursue Jacob and his sons after departing Shechem because the terror of God was upon them. Jacob and his household were protected by God as they journeyed to Bethel, the place of Jacob's sacred altar. "When God's people are doing God's will in God's way, they can depend on God's provision and protection" (Isaiah 41:10,14; 44:2,8; 43:1–5).[1]

Up until that time, Jacob's beloved Rachel had born him only one son. His name was Joseph which means *adding*. Joseph was Israel's son who heralded the Lord's continuing blessings. "God has taken away my disgrace," declared Rachel when he was born. "May the Lord add to me another son" (Genesis 30:23–24, NIV).

Now, on the cusp of Jacob's Bethel experience, a final son was added to God's household. He was the Lord's concluding statement in the saga of God's unfolding scheme of human deliverance. Consequently, his birth came at a high price and Rachel's labor was especially difficult. In fact, her struggle was so intense that she knew she would die. God's holy conceptions are not easily brought to fruition. It was as if all hell on earth waged war against the woman who agonized in the pains of birth. Genesis 35:17 summarizes her struggle, saying, "And as she was having great difficulty in childbirth, the midwife said to her, 'Don't be afraid, for you have another son'" (NIV).

Ben-oni ("son of my sorrow") was the name given to Israel's last-born son as Rachel breathed her last. However, his father renamed him *Benjamin*, which means "son of the right hand." No son of *Israel* would have such a sorrowful fate. This is especially true when we consider that this is God's final declaration in His divine conception. It will never end in sorrow but with an emphatic statement of power and strength.

God's orchestrated plan of salvation as revealed through *Israel's* twelve sons was now fully refined. With this last conception, the household of *Israel* was complete (crammed to satisfaction). *Benjamin*, the son of Israel's right hand, proclaims the destiny of all people who live in God's perfect will. We are in the strong right hand of God. As the Psalmist sings: "You give me Your shield of victory, and Your right hand sustains me; You stoop down to make me great. You broaden the path beneath me, so that my ankles do not turn" (Psalm 18:35, NIV). It is a fitting testimony for one who lived so close to God, Israel. Like Isaac who died "an old man, satisfied *and* satiated with days" (Genesis 35:29, AMP), Israel lived a very full and prosperous life.

"Gather together, that I may tell you what shall befall you in the last days," said Jacob, when he was a very old man. "Gather together and hear, you sons of Jacob, and listen to Israel your father" (Genesis 49:1, NKJV). Importantly, it was Jacob who called his sons together, but it was Israel who spoke prophetically over them. "Assemble, ye sons of Jacob, but listen to your father Israel. Hearken, *to hear* (i.e., *shama'*) the prophetic utterance, what will happen in days to come (Genesis 49:1b, NIV, emphasis added).

The dying patriarch first spoke to Reuben because he was the oldest, the firstborn of Israel's sons. "Reuben," declared Israel, "thou art my firstborn, my might, the beginning of my strength, the excellency of dignity, and the excellency of power" (Genesis 49:3, KJV). Reuben was and forever shall be the beginning of procreative strength. In him was invested the vigor of Israel, both in that realm and this. Reuben is the embodiment of God's foremost creative principle—the excellence of seeing. "He was superior (*excelling, yeter*, cf. *beyond measure*, Isaiah 56:12 [NRSV]) to his brothers in esteem as the firstborn. The term *honor* (i.e., *exaltation*) is also used of God's majesty (e.g., Job 31:23)."[2] As Israel's eldest son, Reuben deserved honor and respect, and all significant rights, as the firstborn (Deuteronomy 21:16). Thus, he had to be acknowledged (i.e., *nakar, recognized with respect*), and to him belonged a double share of all that his father had (v. 17a). As firstborn, Reuben is the first sign of Israel's strength (v. 17b). He is, at least in principle, the beginning of his father's potency—the embodiment of God's first conception within Israel. Reuben is the oracle of God's seeing principle.

But Reuben had greatly sinned and had abused his power. Thus, he defamed his father's bed (Genesis 35:22). "Reuben, you are my firstborn, my might, the first sign of my strength, excelling in honor, excelling in power," [declared Israel]. "Turbulent as the waters, you will no longer excel, for you went up onto your father's bed, onto my couch and defiled it" (Genesis 49:3–4, NIV).

Importantly, Israel's reference to his couch of procreation implicates Reuben's role in the overall creative process. The Hebrew *pachaz*, translated *turbulent* (NIV) or *unstable* (NKJV), connotes unhinged ability (that which is sullied or tainted). The implications of this have recently come to light through studies in Quantum Mechanics (the science of the very small). Quanta are tiny packets of energy (light and matter) that sometime behave erratically. If unfocused or out of sync, as in the case of Reuben's sin, quanta become *turbulent* or *unstable*. They may even cancel themselves out. Conversely, these tiny packets of energy which are the substance of seeing, when synchronized and sharply focused, have awesome potential. They become highly energetic—in the words of the Bible, "excelling in honor and power." The laser is just one example of this. Lasers are highly focused beams of light that are in sync. Of importance to this discussion is the fact that these tiny packet of matter or energy behave like particles or waves, depending on how they are seen or observed. John Wheeler, a pioneer in quantum theory, referred to this principle as *genesis by observership*. This concept will also be discussed in the next section of this book.

"Gather yourselves together, and hear, ye sons of Jacob; and hearken unto Israel," declares the Lord (Genesis 49:2a, KJV). The fundamental principles of Israel are ordained by God and are too important to ignore. We must therefore "hearken" (i.e., *shama'*) unto them lest we defile the couch of God—His bed of procreation. It is our responsibility to understand the importance of true and right sight in the Lord's creative scheme. Reuben, as Israel's firstborn son, has awesome potential and his influence must be clearly understood if we are to work within God's creative scheme. Reuben is the first sign of his father's strength (Deuteronomy 21:17). Consequently, when God was creating the heavens and the earth, we are told seven times that God saw (Genesis 1:4, 10, 12, 18, 21, 25, and 31).

"Give me your attention," declared Jacob. "Assemble yourselves so as to correctly understand (i.e., *shama'*) and carefully consider the sayings of *Israel* (the prince of God). "Unstable and boiling over like water, you shall not excel and have the preeminence [of the firstborn]," said Israel to Reuben (Genesis 49:4, AMP). The Hebrew word *pachaz*, translated "unstable" (AMP) or "uncontrolled" (NASU), has connotations of dissolution or irresolution. In essence, the role of seeing (observation with perception) in the creative process would become imprecise. Jesus spoke of this in Matthew 13 when elaborating on kingdom principles of increase and vitality. When He was asked about kingdom productivity that leads to supernatural increases (a hundred, sixty, or thirty times what is sown), He said, "He who has ears, let him hear" (Matthew 13:9, NIV).

> "The knowledge of the secrets of the kingdom of heaven has been given to you, but not to them," [He declared]. "Whoever has will be given more, and he will have an

abundance. Whoever does not have, even what he has will be taken from him. This is why I speak to them in parables:

'Though seeing, they do not see; though hearing, they do not hear or understand.'"

Matthew 13:11–13 (NIV)

Israel prophesied that Reuben's influence within the affairs of man would fall into disgrace. His preeminence within the family of man (Jacob) and the spiritual community of God (Israel), at least for a time, would wane. Reuben's excellency (i.e. his rights and privileges) would fall to another, Joseph and his sons (1 Chronicles 5:1).

Reuben was not alone in his abuse of power, however. Simeon and Levi vindictively had joined forces against the people of Shechem (Genesis 34:25–29). Consequently, Israel viewed them as fellow culprits in sin.

> "Simeon and Levi are brothers [equally headstrong, deceitful, vindictive, and cruel]," declared their father, Israel. "Their swords are weapons of violence.
>
> O my soul, come not into their secret council, unto their assembly let not my honor be united [for I knew nothing of their plot], because in their anger they slew men ... and in their self-will they disabled oxen."

Genesis 49:5–6 (AMP)

Israel linked the fate of Simeon and Levi when prophesying. His word choice is noteworthy. He spoke of "the secret of their council" (their united strength). When jointly united, the influence of these two brothers has incredible potential and dynamic ability. They are "equally headstrong," warned Israel. "Let me not enter their secret (i.e., *cowd*; *close deliberation*; by implication, *intimacy* or *consultation*).[3] "The knowledge of the secrets of the kingdom of God has been given to you," Jesus told His followers (Luke 8:10, NIV).

He said to them, "To you it has been given to [come progressively to] know (to recognize and understand more strongly and clearly) the mysteries and secrets of the kingdom of God, but for others they are in parables, so that, [though] looking, they may not see; and hearing, they may not comprehend."

Luke 8:10 (AMP)

Many are ever seeing by never perceiving and ever hearing but never understanding. But Jesus did not leave it there; He also spoke of the influence of the heart (our inner man). Our hearts are often calloused (hardened) so that we cannot rightly appropriate what is heard or seen. "Otherwise," He declared, "we would rightly see with our eyes and hear with our ears, and understand with our hearts (the dynamic of Levi within the creative scheme of God).

Reuben's "excellence" (his creative potential within the Lord's orchestrated plan of healing) has fallen from grace into disregard. Likewise, the combined influence of Simeon and Levi has become scattered within the community of man (Jacob), and their joint influence has been dispersed in Israel (the spiritual family of God). But this no longer needs to be so, because Jesus has come and reversed this curse. "Blessed are your eyes because they see," said Christ, "and your ears because they hear" (Matthew 13:16, NIV). Jesus came to set the captive free, proclaiming: "I tell you the truth, many prophets and righteous men longed to see what you see but did not see it, and to hear what you hear but did not hear it" (v. 17, NIV). Praise God, because Christ has restored unto you and me the legacy of Reuben and the joint influence of Simeon and Levi. This is the prerogative and the agency of His Holy Spirit.

God has sent His Son to purchase (to ransom, to redeem, to atone for) our freedom; that we might be adopted and have sonship conferred upon us. Now, because we are recognized as God's children (heirs of Abraham, Isaac and Jacob), the Lord has sent His Holy Spirit into our hearts. Therefore, we are no longer slaves (bond servants) but sons, and if sons, we are also heirs by the aid of God through Christ. Now that we are acquainted with and understand and know the true God, or rather, are understood and known by God, we are no longer restrained by the weak and beggarly and worthless, elementary things that have previously enslaved us (Galatians 4:4–9). Like Elisha, who dealt a lethal blow to the "bad" waters at Jericho's fountainhead (2 Kings 2:21–22), the Messiah has applied heaven's salt to the source of our life's flow by way of His divine conception—Israel. Thus says the Lord: "I ... have healed these waters; there shall not be any more death, miscarriage or barrenness [and bereavement] because of it" (2 Kings 2:21, AMP). Furthermore, the bitter waters that once spewed forth from Jericho (that which is symbolic of mankind's rebellion and sin) remain healed to this day. Its barrenness that robbed us and our children of health and caused misery (miscarriage) is cured (i.e., repaired, made whole). Praise God! When in partnership with the gospel of God's good news, we can be confident of this. "He who began a good work in us will carry it on to completion (*epiteleo*, *Strong's* NT:2005). "I am convinced and sure of this very thing," Paul wrote to the Philippians (Philippians 1:6b, AMP), "that He Who began a good work in you will continue ... developing [that good work] and perfecting and bringing it to full completion in you." The Greek *epi-* of *epiteleo* is a primary preposition meaning *superimposition* (of time, place, order, etc.). Through its use, we know that God's work in us who believe is fully complete—its full expression is realized.

Israel's prophecies regarding Reuben, Simeon, and Levi (Genesis 49) are important because they still affect us today. Reuben's preeminence (his influence) is still "turbulent" (unfocused) for many people and is the fountainhead of much chaos. Simeon and Levi (the oracles of hearing with understanding and affiliation, respectively) have awesome power when in concert but, when misapplied, garner a terrible outcome. We are self-will and in our stubbornness and folly hamstring the ox (our plowing-engine). Thus, said Israel, "Let not my soul (i.e., *nephesh*) enter their council. Let not my honor be united to their assembly ... they hamstrung an ox" (Genesis 49:6, NKJV). Israel's remarks concerning his *nephesh* (soul) testify of inner resolve what we are to ourselves.

> The real difficulty of the term [*nephesh*] is seen in the inability of almost all English translations to find a consistent equivalent or even a small group of high-frequency equivalents for the term. The KJV alone uses over 28 different English terms for this one Hebrew word. The problem with the English term "soul" is that no actual equivalent of the term or the idea behind it is represented in the Hebrew language. The Hebrew system of thought does not include the combination or opposition of the terms "body" and "soul," which are really Greek and Latin in origin. The Hebrew contrasts two other concepts which are not found in the Greek and Latin tradition: "the inner self" and "the outer appearance" or, as viewed in a different context, "what one is to oneself" as opposed to "what one appears to be to one's observers." The inner person is *nepesh*, while the outer person, or reputation, is *shem*, most commonly translated as *name*.[4]

From Israel's remarks, it is understood that the combined influence of hearing with understanding (Simeon) and heart affection (Levi) is profoundly important and strongly influences one's inner person, what we are to ourselves. *Nelson's Illustrated Bible Dictionary* says the word *soul* often refers to the inner life of man, "the seat of his emotions, and the center of human personality."[5] The first use of the Hebrew word *nepish* in the Old Testament expresses this meaning: "The Lord God formed the man from the dust of the ground and breathed into his nostrils the breath of life, and the man became a living being [*nepish*]" (Genesis 2:7, NIV). This is what makes us distinct from all other animals.

The united principles of hearing with understanding (Simeon) and heart-felt connection with it (Levi) bequeaths the soul. "Simeon and Levi are brothers," [declared their spiritual-head]. "Let not my soul enter their council; Let not my honor be united to their assembly" (Genesis 49:5–6, NKJV). In the context of Israel's prophetic utterance, consciousness (i.e., the Reubenic and Simeonic principles of kingdom power) are engaged and energized through the agency of human will (i.e., the Levitic principle of connectedness). Their synergistic exuberance, in and through the human soul (*nephesh*), is formidable.

"O my soul," declared Israel, "come not thou into their secret; unto their assembly, mine honor, be not thou united" (Genesis 49:6a, KJV). Israel's reference is important because "our soul is our honour; by its powers and faculties we are distinguished from, and dignified above, the beasts that perish."[6] By his declaration, Israel does not profess his abhorrence of such practices in general but his own innocence in the matter of the Shechemites.

The combined strengths of Simeon and Levi, when acting in concert, go well beyond their individual capacities and capabilities. For this reason, we must never forsake our special revelation of God and its unique knowhow. Bring it to fruition through the agency of wholehearted affiliation and agreement (the Levitic principle). Make it personal, as did Simeon and Levi when avenging their sister, Dinah. Fully engage that which is rightly seen and heard. As Deepak Chopra explains:

> Consider the way three people might observe the same sunset. The first person is obsessing over a business deal and doesn't even see the sunset, even though his eyes are registering the photons that fall on [his] retinas. The second person thinks, "Nice sunset. We haven't had one in a while." The third person is an artist who immediately begins a sketch of the scene. The differences among the three are that the first person sent nothing out and received nothing back; the second allowed his awareness to receive the sunset but had no awareness to give back to it—his response was rote; the third person was the only one to complete the circle: He took in the sunset and turned it into a creative response that sent his awareness back out into the world with something to give.[7]

Deepak Chopra concludes: "If you want to fully experience life, you must close the circle."[8]

I cannot say enough about Israel's prophetic declaration concerning the united front and fate of Simeon and Levi. Israel is their Pied Piper of destiny. Thus, he declared, "I divide them in Jacob [man's fleshly countenance], and I scatter them in Israel [mankind's spiritual disposition]" (Genesis 49:7b, YLT). Jacob's people were whole and unbroken until the time of Israel's prophecy. They were a family of men; twelve strong brothers united in common cause and effect. But their posterity became divided and scattered as declared by heaven; that is, until God's Christ came to reside with us. Through Jesus we are restored to wholeness; the heritage of the united brothers (Israel's sons) is ours once again!

"Blessed are your eyes because they see, and your ears because they hear," the Lord declared (Matthew 13:16, NIV). Jesus Christ has come to put us back together again like Humpty Dumpty. Therefore, hear what says the Lord and come into absolute, whole-hearted affiliation with it. You will be surprised at the result; how God will work in and through you. His twelve foundational principles of supernatural increase will energize your soul. The one whose soil is good and hears the Word of God with understanding; "He produces a crop, yielding a hundred, sixty or thirty times what was sown" (Matthew 13:23b, NIV). Blessed be Shiloh (which means the Peacemaker), the Lord Jesus Christ, Who has come to restore peace (i.e., *shalom*; soundness, health, prosperity, and wellbeing in general) to the community of God (Israel)! "The scepter shall not depart from Judah, nor a lawgiver from between his feet, until Shiloh come; and unto him shall the gathering of the people be," prophesied Israel (Genesis 49:10, KJV).

Chapter Five Evaluation

1. The "excellence" of true and right sight is dramatically presented in this chapter. Read Numbers 13 and notice the spies' response after reconnoitering God's Promised Land (v(v). 31–33). "We saw [*ra'ah*] ... and *we are in our own eyes* as grasshoppers; *and so we were* in their eyes" (v. 33, YLT, emphasis mine). Their *seeing* determined their destiny. In Jesus' words, they were "ever hearing but never understanding" and they were "ever seeing but never perceiving" (Matthew 13:14, NIV). Their hearts had become calloused (i.e. dull or unresponsive) and consequently they were unwilling to "turn" (v. 15, NIV). As a result, the entire community of people lifted up their voices and wept aloud (Numbers 14:1). This eventually led to whining and complaining (v. 2) and some spoke of turning back to Egypt (v. 3). Others even considered the prospect of stoning their leadership (v. 10). "How long will these people treat Me with contempt? How long will they refuse to believe in Me, in spite of all the miraculous signs I have performed among them?" said the Lord (v. 11). And it all began wayward glance. They looked and saw, but did so errantly. Be careful how you begin your creative miracle. *Seeing* through God's eyes is the beginning of miracles. How do you *see*? Are you constantly looking back?

2. We've embarked on a journey of discovery to learn the secrets of the kingdom of heaven (Matthew 13:11). You may recall the marching orders given by Moses to the twelve spies. Read Numbers 13:18–20. Before the spies went into Canaan's land, Moses' instructions were to "*see* what the land is like" (Numbers 13:18a, NIV, emphasis mine). We first come into our Godly heritage by seeing. The verb used here basically connotes seeing with one's eyes, but can also be used in the sense becoming consciously aware of, or perceiving. There were a number of things Moses wanted them to observe. They were to see what the land was like, but also see the strength of the people who lived there, the nature of

the land (whether good or bad), and the kind of towns there (whether unwalled or fortified). Moses also admonished the spies to do their best to bring back some of the land's fruit. My purpose in writing this book is to help you procure the land's ripe fruit. So far, we've only scratch the surface of God's producing principles "the exceeding greatness of His power to usward who believe, according to the working of His mighty power?" (Ephesians 1:19, KJV). Read the full story of the spies in Numbers 13. In your opinion, why is the specific time of their exploration identified as forty days? What does the number forty imply? Explore the use of *forty* in the Scriptures and then extend these truths to your own discovery of truth. What is implied?

3. The majority of the spies said the land they explored devours its inhabitants (Numbers 13:32). "We seemed like grasshoppers in our own eyes, and we looked the same to them," they declared (v. 33, NIV). In light of what we've discovered about the seeing principle within the Lord's creative scheme (i.e. the Reubenic Principle), notice the role their eyes play in the procurement of God's fullness. Conversely, two of the spies who also went into the land and saw the same things said, "We should go up and take possession of the land, for we can certainly do it" (v. 30, NIV). These men modeled what Jesus encouraged in Matthew 13:16–17. The Lord's "muchness" is ours in Christ Jesus, but we must take possession of it by coming into absolute, wholehearted agreement with the Lord's intention. This is where the Levitic and Judaic Principles come into play.

4. Finally, reread the story of Benjamin's birth in Genesis 35:16–20. This was Israel's last-born son and, consequently, he represents the final of God's twelve truths concerning His muchness. What are the implications of this son's name change and how do they apply to you?

CHAPTER SIX

The Secret Things of the Lord

> The secret things belong to the Lord our God, but those things which are revealed belong to us and to our children forever.
>
> Deuteronomy 29:29a (NKJV)

> He [Jesus] said to them, "Therefore every teacher and interpreter of the Sacred Writings who has been instructed about and trained for the kingdom of heaven and has become a disciple is like a householder who brings forth out of his storehouse treasure that is new and [treasure that is] old [the fresh as well as the familiar]."
>
> Matthew 13:52 (AMP)

Jacob lived large in keeping with the Lord's "muchness." With divinely apportioned greatness, Israel ruled as God.[1] He was a prince with power who prevailed with God and men (Genesis 32:28).

One day, Jacob called for his sons and said: "Gather around so I can tell you what will happen to you in days to come. Assemble and listen, sons of Jacob; listen to your father Israel" (Genesis 49:1–2, NIV). It was *Jacob* who called to his sons together as a community, but it was *Israel* who prophesied over them.

Matthew Henry comments: "It was of use to them to attend him in his last moments, that they might learn of him how to die."[2] Oh that we would all learn from God how to die!

> …What he said to each he said in the hearing of all the rest; for we may profit by the reproofs, counsels, and comforts, that are principally intended for others. His calling upon them once and again to gather together intimated both a precept to them to unite in love, (to keep together, not to mingle with the Egyptians, not to forsake the assembling of themselves together,) and a prediction that they should not be separated from each other, as Abraham's sons and Isaac's were, but should be incorporated, and all make one people.[3]

Reuben's fate was first foretold because he was Jacob's firstborn son. But having defiled his father's couch, the bed of procreation, Reuben brought great reproach upon himself and on his family. Thereby, he forfeited the prerogatives of his birthright and was stripped by Israel of his rightful place among his brethren.

Matthew Henry notes:

> No judge, prophet, nor prince, is found of that tribe, nor any person of renown except Dathan and Abiram, who were noted for their impious rebellion against Moses. That tribe, as not aiming to excel, meanly chose a settlement on the other side Jordan. Reuben himself seems to have lost all that influence upon his brethren to which his birthright entitled him; for when he spoke unto them they would not hear, ch. 42:22. Those that have not understanding and spirit to support the honours and privileges of their birth will soon lose them, and retain only the name of them. The character fastened upon Reuben, for which he is laid under this mark of infamy, is that he was unsta-

ble as water. (1.) His virtue was unstable; he had not the government of himself and his own appetites: sometimes he would be very regular and orderly, but at other times he deviated into the wildest courses. Note, Instability is the ruin of men's excellency. Men do not thrive because they do not fix. (2.) His honour consequently was unstable; it departed from him, vanished into smoke, and became as water spilt upon the ground.[4]

Then, as Jacob looked upon the community of men who stood around his deathbed, his eyes became fixed on Simeon and Levi, for they were the sons next in age to Reuben. These united brothers had treacherously and barbarously destroyed the Shechemites, and Israel held this against them. In self-will, they were governed by passion rather than prudence, and Israel cursed their lust. "Shameful dispersions are the just punishment of sinful unions and confederacies," remarks Matthew Henry.[5]

It's important to note that Israel, when prophesying the fate of his sons, didn't curse the persons of Simeon and Levi; that is, who and what they signified within God's holy family. "I will scatter them in *Jacob*, and disperse them in *Israel*" the aged saint prophesied (Genesis 49:7, NIV). Once again, the demarcation between *Jacob* and *Israel* is distinct. "I will divide them in Jacob and scatter them in Israel," he prophesied (Genesis 49:7, AMP).

Now it was Judah's turn to hear his fate; that which would befall mankind through him. As Jacob turned his full attention to his fourth-born son, visions of future happenings were opened, and Israel beheld a growing and enduring tribe of men. "Judah," declared Israel, "you are he whom your brothers shall praise; Your hand shall be on the neck of your enemies; Your father's children shall bow down before you" (v. 8, NKJV).

"God was praised for him (Genesis 29:35), praised by him, and praised because of Him," says Henry.[6]

> As the oracle of praise, Judah's brethren would praise God because of him. Those that are to God for a praise shall be the praise of their brethren...The prerogatives of the

birthright which Reuben had forfeited, the excellency of dignity and power, were thus conferred upon Judah.[7]

In Israel's vision, Judah was compared, not to a rampant, raging lion that was the terror of the forest, but to a lion that was strong and courageous. As such, he was immensely qualified to command and for conquest when in battle. He is formidable as a lion's whelp and would win great victories. In keeping with Judah's heritage, God's people wage war, not for the sake of war, but for the sake of peace. We are a couchant lion that enjoys the satisfaction of God's power and success, but without creating exasperation and vexation to others. "This," says Henry, "is to be truly great."[8]

The root of Judah's name stresses the activity of praise (vigorous confession, acclamation, and recognition of God). "Now will I praise [*yadah*] the Lord!" declared his mother when she finally recognized her own part in the divine plan of her salvation (Genesis 29:35, AMP). *Yadah*'s root (*yad*) means *to use* (i.e., *hold out*) *the hand; physically to throw* (a stone, an arrow) *at or away; especially to revere or worship* (with extended hands).[9] Additionally, *yad* refers to an open hand as opposed to a clenched fist. *The McClintock and Strong Encyclopedia* notes that praise is "an acknowledgement made of the excellency or perfection of any person or action. 'The desire of praise,' says an elegant writer, 'is generally connected with all the finer sensibilities of human nature. It affords a ground on which exhortation, counsel, and reproof can work a proper effect.'"[10] Praise should always improve, never corrupt, and must always elevate and never debase.

The *International Standard Bible Encyclopedia* notes that *praise* of God is a prominent theme throughout the Scripture. It is "the appropriate response of God's creatures to His majesty and His saving deeds."[11] This same encyclopedia also notes that true praise of God, as distinguished from false praise, is first of all an inward emotion of joy. "The mouth expresses the praise of the heart (cf. Psalm 51:15 [MT 17]; 71:8) by telling about the great things that God has done…"[12]

When Israel was prophesying the fate of his son from his deathbed, he declared that Judah's hand would be on the neck of his enemies. Notice his emphasis on action as well as his reference to Judah's hand. "Like a lion he crouches and lies down, like a lioness—who dares to rouse him?" (Genesis 49:9b, NIV). Certainly, Judah made mistakes, even as you and I have made mistakes. But as Israel's son of praise, he always sought to make things right with his father and his family. For example, he offered himself as surety for Benjamin and pleaded on his behalf before the Egyptians). That's the wonder of praise. We must always confess our sins, praise the Lord for what He's done, thank Him for His manifold gifts, and then go forth with an open hand. We must always speak of God's inspired gifts and revelations, sing of them, dance before Him, and lift up holy hands because of them. Praise is the exercise of God's abundance toward you!

At first, the language of Israel's prophecy is somewhat enigmatic. He declared, "The scepter will not depart from Judah, nor the ruler's staff from between his feet" (Genesis 49:10a, NIV). Then he added, "He will tether his donkey to a vine, his colt to the choicest branch; he will wash his garments in wine, his robes in the blood of grapes. His eyes will be darker than wine, his teeth whiter than milk" (v(v). 11–12, NIV). Why would anyone bind his donkey to a choice vine and, thereby, ruin its fruit? Why would someone wash his garments in wine? No one in Old Testament times would tether his donkey to a choice vine. Nor would anyone waste his precious wine by washing clothes in it. "This is the language of hyperbole," says Warren Wiersbe. "It describes a land so wealthy and a people so prosperous that they can do these outrageous things and not have to worry about the consequences. During the Kingdom Age, when the Messiah reigns, people will enjoy health and beauty (v. 12), because the devastating enemies of human life will have been removed.[13]

All this is the consequence of true and right praise. Judah ushers in the treasures of God. Hence, when Jacob and the family of Israel moved to Egypt, it was Judah whom Jacob sent ahead to make all things ready (Genesis 46:28). Also, after the death of Joshua, the question was raised up as to who would be the first to go up and fight for Israel against the Canaanites. The Lord answered, "Judah is to go; I have given the land into their hands" (Judges 1:2, NIV). Notice again the reference to the hands of Judah. I do not believe this is by accident. Judah was to live up to his name; praise is to raise one's hands unto the Lord in the performance of His holy will concerning you.

Judah is the fourth of the Lord's producing principles. When rightly joined with his brethren (the oracles of seeing, hearing, and heart affiliation), things are accomplished. Until the coming of *Shiloh* (the Peaceful One of God) his influence (the power of true and right confession, acclamation, and appropriate response) overshadowed the sway of his elder brothers (Reuben, Simeon, and Levi). He is described as a Star coming forth from *Jacob*, a Scepter (i.e., a tribe) rising from *Israel* (don't miss the interplay between the two natures of man—Jacob and Israel). *Shiloh* will rise to rule over the nations, and the Gentile's will hope in Him (Romans 15:12). Then will come all joy and peace so that we might overflow (i.e., be caused to super-abound, increase or excel) with confidence by the power of the Holy Spirit (v. 13).

Chapter Six Evaluation

1. Reuben was Jacob's firstborn son and, as such, is representative of his father's might, the beginning of Jacob's strength. But because he tried to usurp his father's authority, Reuben's excellency (i.e., his dignity and power) were forfeited. Consequently, his offspring failed to excel and shamefully chose to settle on the eastern side of the Jordan. Read this story in Numbers 32. On the other side of the Jordan was God's good and spacious Promised Land. However, Reuben said to Moses, "If we have found favor in your eyes, let this land be given to your servants as our possession." Reuben settled short of God's fullness. "Do not make us cross the Jordan," they declared (Numbers 32:5, NIV). From Moses' response, we see his displeasure; first, because it seems the Reubenites were trying to avoid the battles necessary to procure God's best (the land that flows with milk and honey), and second, their lack of persistence was a discouragement for the others (v(v). 6–7). "This is what your fathers did when I sent them from Kadesh Barnea to look over the land," said Moses. "After they went up to the Valley of Eshcol and viewed the land, they discouraged the Israelites from entering the land the Lord had given them" (32:8–9, NIV). I wonder how many of us are on the Jordan's wrong side by choice. Have you stopped short for one reason or another? Understand that this may be the result of unfocused vision and clouded eyes. But, thank God, Jesus Christ has come to restore sight to the blind. Therefore, pray that God will once again open your eyes to see with holy vision that which He's called you to do. The beginning of strength is in your restored sight.

2. Moses didn't pull any punches when dealing with Reuben's weak-heartedness. "And here you are, a brood of sinners, standing in the place of your fathers and making the Lord even more angry with Israel," he spat. "If you turn away from following Him, He will again leave all this people in

the desert, and you will be the cause of their destruction" (Numbers 32:14–15, NIV). In your own experience, does this same sin plague the Church today? Does your society flounder for lack of resolve to do what is right? Give examples if within a small study group.

3. We observed in Genesis 49 that the tribe of Judah was prophesied to become very formidable, not only through great victories, but also peaceably and quietly through true and right praise. The heritage of Judah is not to make war for the sake of war, but for the sake of peace. Always remember this when passionately following your own inspired dreams. Never forget that Judah is compared, not to a raging lion that is always tearing and pouncing, but to a couchant lion that enjoys the satisfaction of his power and success. He is not seen as creating vexation to others. Here is a great lesson we should all learn as we move into our rightful place with God. Do not use your power and divinely enabled influence to lord over other people. Instead, love them and help establish a peaceful existence. Sadly, this lesson has been lost amongst many of God's people, both today and in the past. Do you agree?

4. Perhaps one of the more enigmatic points of Israel's prophecies concerns the "scepter" that will not depart from Judah (Genesis 49:10a). According to Adam Clarke on this verse, the Jews have quibbled over the word *shebet* (Strong's OT:7626) which is translated "scepter." Some say the word does not signify a staff or rod as many suppose, but, as in a very ancient manuscript of the Pentateuch, the word *shebet* signifies a tribe. In essence, what Israel was prophesying was that Judah would continue as a distinct tribe until the coming of the Messiah. "After his coming," comments Clarke, "it [the tribe of Judah] was confounded with the others so that all distinction has been ever since lost."[14] This is also my understanding and is in complete accord with Christ's sayings in Matthew 13:11–17. By his own experience, Israel knew

that the combined strengths of his firstborn sons (Reuben, Simeon, and Levi), if not rightly channeled through praise (the lifting up of our hands unto the Lord), could be easily corrupted and turned to evil. This is seen in Reuben's power grab, as well as in the cold, calculating fury of Simeon and Levi that turned to cruelty. Without *Shiloh's* accompanying peace and rest (i.e., *Shiloh*—God's Peacemaker), the Lord's supernatural potency of compounded increase and strength is ripe for abuse. If not rightly channeled through praise, it can literally drive men crazy. Have you ever experienced this, especially within the operation of churches you've attended?

CHAPTER SEVEN

Commitment Determines Destiny!

> The Lord said to Moses, "Send some men to explore the land of Canaan, which I am giving to the Israelites. From each ancestral tribe send one of its leaders."
>
> Numbers 13:1–2 (NIV)

Poised at the entrance of Canaan's good and spacious land were throngs of God's people. Previously, the Lord had declared the Promised Land's excellence. It was a good and spacious land that flowed with milk and honey (Exodus 3:8). He guided Israel to it (Exodus 32:34; 33:2, 14) and kept them along the way (Exodus 23:20). Now their assignment was to explore the land.

"From each ancestral tribe send one of its leaders," declared the Lord. "See what the land is like" (Numbers 13:2, 18, NIV). What is the nature of the land into which we are called? Is it a good land or bad? What are the habitations therein and are the land's occupants strongly entrenched? Is its soil fertile? Are there trees? God enjoins each of us to check out (i.e., reconnoiter, evaluate) our heritage.

Additionally, we must also undertake to procure a testimony; some of the land's fruit as a witness (Numbers 13:18–20).

Every tribe was to be equally represented in the reconnaissance of the Lord's promised blessings. None were, nor should any in the future, be excluded. Every one of God's people has a responsibility and a share. "Be of good courage," declares the Lord (Numbers 13:20b, NKJV).

Forty days later (the time of testing) the spies returned with an amazing testimony. God's bounty was so great that a branch with one cluster of grapes was brought back. It was so large, full, and ripe that the cluster of grapes required two of them to carry it. They also brought with them pomegranates and figs. But they also brought one more thing; they brought back word of terrible giants, fortified cities, and a strong people. "We saw the descendants of Anak there. The Amalekites dwell in the land of the South; the Hittites, the Jebusites, and the Amorites dwell in the mountains; and the Canaanites dwell by the sea and along the banks of the Jordan," they said (Numbers 13:28b-29, NKJV).

Israel baulked at this. They hesitated!

"Go up and possess it and do not fear or be discouraged," said God previously. But the people became fearfully agitated. I suppose they thought they could just walk in and God would hand it to them on a silver platter. But this is not God's way. He leads us to the threshold of gracious provision but it is our prerogative to partake thereof. He will never force His goodness upon us! As it is said, "You can lead a horse to water but you can't make him drink." Each of us has a responsibility.

With the bad news, the mood within the camp turned bleak and dismal. The spies' evil report spread like contagion throughout the camp because there is always a ready group of followers eager to hear and believe the worst. Hence, the children of Israel became apprehensive and rebelled against the command of the Lord. They whined, "The land is a land that devours its inhabitants, its men being of great stature. We are like grasshoppers in our own sight!" (Numbers 13:32–33, NIV). This, then, became a self-fulfilling prophesy. We must never call ourselves anything less than does God!

If you follow the progression of events, you will also discover rudiments of your own demise. First, the spies surveyed the land set before them by God. "See what it is like," said the Lord (Numbers 13:18a). Then, after reconnoitering (seeking and searching), the spies had a choice. Would they align themselves with God's spoken word, or would they baulk in fear? Sadly, their confession turned bitter and they wailed. "We were *in our own sight* as grasshoppers, and so we were *in their sight*," said the majority of spies (Numbers 13:33b, AMP). Their seeing was the beginning of their undoing—it was clouded and tainted. Seeing (*ra'ah* in the Hebrew) is always the initiate of either blessing or cursing.

Then they gave the children of Israel a bad report. "The land through which we have gone as spies is a land that devours its inhabitants, and all the people whom we *saw* (*ra'ah*) in it are men of great stature. There we *saw* [*ra'ah*] the giants [the descendants of Anak who were giants]; and we were like grasshoppers in our own sight, and so we were in their sight" (Numbers 13:32–33, NKJV, emphasis mine).

They looked and looked again, and their eyes (*'ayin*) became a fountainhead of affliction. Twice used, *'ayin* not only depicts the anatomical eye but also is used to express weakness or hurt.[1] Thus, the children of Israel spoke of turning back and returning to the previous bondage.

> That night all the people of the community raised their voices and wept aloud. All of Israel grumbled against Moses and Aaron, and the whole assembly said to them, "If only we had died in Egypt! Or in this desert! Why is the Lord bringing us to this land only to let us fall by the sword? Our wives and children will be taken as plunder. Wouldn't it be better for us to go back to Egypt?" And they said to each other, "We should choose a leader and go back to Egypt."
>
> Numbers 14:1–4 (NIV)

What are the lessons of this story? Why is it included in God's narrative of Israel? First and foremost, it concerns the release of the Lord's multitudinous blessings. It is necessary that we liberate our increase. This begins with seeing. That which is divinely apportioned is within our grasp, but it must be seen and understood in keeping with God's holy word. Then we must claim it, actively gathering it to ourselves. And, as always, there are giants standing in the way. In our present age and in the context of our lives today, these giants may represent mounting debts, seemingly impossible circumstances, and roadblocks such as aberrant notions and religious traditions of men. They may also include family conflicts, afflictions and disabilities. Whatever they are, our mountains of adversities are not above the Lord; His name stands high above them all. As a result, begin by faithfully placing one foot in front of the other. With assured steps you must begin your assent. Forsake that which lies behind and move with confidence toward a brighter tomorrow; realizing that, in all these things, we are more than conquerors through Him Who loves us. We must be convinced that neither death nor life, neither angels nor demons, neither the present nor the future, nor any powers, neither height nor depth, nor anything else in all creation, are able to separate us from the love of God that is in Christ Jesus our Lord (Romans 8:38–39).

Dead men's bones litter the landscape that leads to and from God's precious land of increase and promise because few there are who truly avail themselves of God's holy blessings. Jesus likened it to a gate. He declared, "For wide is the gate and broad is the road that leads to destruction, and many enter through it. But small is the gate and narrow the road that leads to life, and only a few find it" (Matthew 7:13–14, NIV).

I believe it is for this reason that Jacob beheld angels ascending *and* descending upon his stairway that rested on the earth with its top reaching to heaven (Genesis 28:12). To me this means that it was a two-way avenue. Those ascending angels bear our grief and sorrows unto the Lord; while those that descend carry His Good New of comfort and peace.

Another lesson from Numbers 13 and 14 concerns the witness of the few who chose to side with God. Joshua and Caleb, two from among the crowd of spies, didn't agree with the majority opinion. They didn't deny the presence of the Canaanite men who were of great stature. Neither did they refute the courage of the Canaanites. They had also seen that the people of the land were strong and lived in fortified cities. These were all undeniable truths. But, contrary to the majority opinion of the committee, Joshua and Caleb didn't side against God. In Jesus words, they were of a different mindset than the naysayers who, in Christ's words, were like whitewashed tombs; beautiful outwardly but full of dead men's bones on the inside (Matthew 23:27). The committee of ten negatively-minded spies was a group of people who individually could do nothing and collectively decided nothing could be done."[2] They lacked faith and were discouraged at the prospect of entering the land. Sadly, their discouragement quickly spread throughout the camp like a contagion. Doubt turned to unbelief, and unbelief became rebellion against the will of God.

> "Sin," [say those with a bad report], "cannot be destroyed in this life—it will always dwell in you—the Anakim cannot be conquered—we are but as grasshoppers against the Anakim," etc., etc. Here and there, a Joshua and a Caleb, trusting alone in the power of God, armed with faith in the infinite efficacy of that blood which cleanses from all unrighteousness, boldly stand forth and say: "Their defense is departed from them, and the Lord is with us, let us go up at once and possess the land, for we are well able to overcome." We can do all things through Christ strengthening us: he will purify us unto himself, and give us that rest from sin here which his death has procured and his word has promised.[3]

The corruption of unbelief quickly spread throughout the camp and the people raised their voices toward heaven in causeless discontent (Numbers 14:2). Like foolish children, they imagined monsters lurking behind every door and under every bed. They were ever hearing but never understanding; ever seeing but never perceiving. Their hearts became calloused and, without eyes to see and ears to hear, they turned against God. Hence, they gave credit to, and aligned themselves with, the evil report.

The world's mourners are numerous and their sorrows work death among us. Hence, the people began to grumble and spoke of returning to Egypt. Those of slave mentality were the most vocal among them. "Would that we had died in Egypt! Or that we had died in this wilderness! Why does the Lord bring us to this land to fall by the sword? Our wives and little ones will be a prey. Is it not better for us to return to Egypt?" (Numbers 14:2b-3, AMP). Boo-hoo! Sob!

"Here is a most wicked, blasphemous reflection upon God himself, as if he had brought them hither on purpose that they might fall by the sword, and that their wives and children, those poor innocents, should be a prey," says Matthew Henry.[4]

The report of Joshua and Caleb is one we should all hear and remember. They declared, "The land we passed through and explored is exceedingly good" (Numbers 14:7, NIV). It'ss a truth worth repeating because its our heritage in God. Our destiny is not just good; it is *exceedingly* (i.e., superlative) good! Praise the Lord!

Then the two witnesses added, "If the Lord is pleased with us, He [God] will lead us into that land, a land flowing with milk and honey, and will give it to us, only do not rebel against the Lord. And do not be afraid of the people of the land, because we will swallow them up. Their protection is gone, but the Lord is with us. Do not be afraid of them" (v(v). 8–9, NIV). I love how the Amplified Bible frames verse nine. "Only do not rebel against the Lord, neither fear the people of the land, for they are bread for us. Their defense and the shadow [of protection] is removed from over them, but the Lord is with us. Fear them not" (AMP).

Notice that Joshua and Caleb appealed to the people's sense of awareness, their special knowingness of God. They spoke in terms people understood. These were the same people who saw Egypt's defenses removed. They had also experienced the shadow of the Lord's protection (His pillar of cloud by day and His pillar of fire by night), as well as His signs and wonders. They knew all about such things but quickly forgot them when facing giants. "The land through which we have gone as spies is a land that devours its inhabitants," they declared.

Sadly, multitudes of people live like grasshoppers in a land sprouting with blessing. Instead of being uplifted, they are devoured. They are defenseless rather than defended. "Do not rebel against the Lord," [argues Joshua], "neither fear the people of the land, for they are bread for us" (Numbers 14:9a, AMP).

But the people wouldn't listen and from the Lord's response we see how serious the matter had become. They had spurned that which they knew (their divine awareness) and, as a result, the glory of the Lord appeared at the Tent of Meeting. The appearance was not just to Moses and Aaron, but to all the Israelites. "How long will these people treat me with contempt?" said the Lord to Moses. "How long will they refuse to believe in me, in spite of all the miraculous signs I have performed among them? I will strike them down with a plague and destroy them, but I will make you into a nation greater and stronger than they" (Numbers 14:10–12, NIV).

This story bears witness to the importance of heart-affection (The Levitic Principle of connectedness and affiliation). The Lord has set before us a future of life and prosperity, or a destiny of death and destruction (Deuteronomy 30:1). The choice is ours and is a matter of the heart.

> I call heaven and earth as witnesses today against you, that I have set before you life and death, blessing and cursing; therefore choose life, that both you and your descendants may live; that you may love the Lord your God, that you may obey His voice, and that you may cling to Him, for He is your life and the length of your days; and that you may dwell in the land which the Lord swore to your fathers, to Abraham, Isaac, and Jacob, to give them.
>
> Deuteronomy 30:19–20 (NKJV)

God calls each of us to faithfulness. Our comprehending minds, affections, and wills must be actively employed in the Lord's business. He also divinely empowers us to *live* in His full vitality. But the tone of God's message is clear—we must wholeheartedly come into affection and affirmation with that which we know. If our hearts turn away, we shall surely perish and our days in the land shall not be prolonged. This was the fate of the disbelieving generation of Israel who sided with the ten spies. God calls heaven and earth (the spiritual and the natural) as His witnesses.

It was a new generation of Israel that finally stood poised upon the threshold of God's Promised Land. Unlike their predecessors who had rebelled against the Lord, this generation of people had heard the declarations of God and were ready and eager to cross the Jordan to engage the enemy. They were ready to step into their God-given heritage. Their heart-attitude was different from that of their fathers. They trusted God!

In a previous chapter I alluded to the story of Peter's confession of Christ. "Who do people say the Son of man is?" Jesus asked His disciples (Matthew 16:13, NIV). Some say John the Baptist; others say Elijah; and still others say Jeremiah or one of the prophets," they replied. It seems the disciples were unwilling to fully commit themselves, perhaps because their minds and hearts were not yet made up. Hence, Jesus pressed the issue. He demanded an answer because we must always be firmly committed if we are to advance. Jesus demanded an honest answer. "But what about *you*? Who do *you* say I am?" (v. 15, NIV, emphasis mine). While the other disciples stumbled over their answer, Simon Peter blurted out his honest reply. "You are the Christ, the Son of the Living God," he exclaimed.

By his admission, Simon Peter declared his intuitive vision of the Lord Jesus Christ. By intimation, he'd also made up his mind to unreservedly live in the light of that revelation. Heaven and earth were his witnesses and, hence, the epithet *Simon Peter* is used by the Gospel writer to emphasize Simon's human temperament and Peter's spiritual ("rock-like") nature. Simon Peter was the Lord's inspired man. Hence, he declared his wholehearted agreement and affiliation to his Lord and Savior.

When determining the man's affections, Jesus had two questions for the man. First, He pointedly asked, "But what about *you*?" (Matthew 16:15a, NIV, emphasis mine). Then Jesus said, "Who do *you* say I am?" (Matthew 16:15, NIV, emphasis mine). Two very poignant questions framed by God that demand our honest reply. The first question demands to know our affections. This is the third of God's Producing Principles, the Levitic Principle). The second question ("Who do *you* say I am?") implies requisite action. Was Simon Peter prepared to step-up to the plate and follow the Lord, no matter what? This is the fourth of God's divine principles in His holy scheme of healing and deliverance, the Judaic Principle of praise (the opening of one's hand unto God).

Luke concludes this incident with one additional comment:

> Then He [Jesus] said to them all, "If anyone desires to come after Me, let him deny himself, and take up his cross daily, and follow Me. For whoever desires to save his life will lose it, but whoever loses his life for My sake will save it. For what profit is it to a man if he gains the whole world, and is himself destroyed or lost?"
>
> Luke 9:23–26 (NKJV)

Not one of them was excluded from Christ's emphatic decree—"He said to them all." In other words, we each must decide for ourselves. "But what about you?" He asks. "Who do you say I am?"

The choice is ours to make! "Commitment determines the destiny ahead in this world for each one of us."⁵

Our decision of wholehearted commitment is fundamental to the Lord's declaration of divine prosperity (His "muchness"). It is the heritage of all God's people who obey Him and turn their hearts toward Him. Even as the Lord made the patriarchs (Abraham, Isaac, and Jacob) prosper with "muchness" (His plentitude in every work), so too will He do so for you and me. We shall excel in His increase.

> And the Lord thy God will bring thee into the land which thy fathers possessed, and thou shalt possess it; *and he will do thee good* [*yatab*: causatively to make well, literally sound or figuratively successful], and multiply thee above thy fathers... [He] will make thee *plenteous* [*yather*] in every work of thine hand, in the fruit of thy body, and in the fruit of thy cattle, and in the fruit of thy land, for good.
>
> Deuteronomy 30:5, 9 (KJV)

As Moses expounded these virtues, he probably paused as he considered the alternatives—the Lord's next thought. Our natural inclination is to quickly excuse ourselves for living "small" (that is, existing beneath God's divinely apportioned capacity and capability of plenteous increase). But God's command is to reach for it.

> He will bring you to the land that belonged to your fathers, and you will take possession of it. He will make you more prosperous and numerous than your fathers. The Lord your God will circumcise your hearts and the hearts of your descendants, so that you may love him with all your heart and with all your soul, and live. The Lord your God will put all these curses on your enemies who hate and persecute you. You will again obey the Lord and follow all his commands I am giving you today. Then the Lord your God will make you most prosperous in all the work of your hands and in the fruit of your womb, the young of your livestock and the crops of your land. The Lord will again delight in you and make you prosperous, just as he delighted in your fathers, if you obey the Lord your God and keep his commands and decrees that are written in this Book of the Law and turn to the Lord your God with all your heart and with all your soul.
>
> Now what I am commanding you today is not too difficult for you or beyond your reach. It is not up in heaven, so that you have to ask, "Who will ascend into heaven to get it and proclaim it to us so we may obey it?" Nor is it beyond the sea, so that you have to ask, "Who will cross the sea to get it and proclaim it to us so we may obey it?" No, the word is very near you; it is in your mouth and in your heart so you may obey it.
>
> See, I set before you today life and prosperity, death and destruction. For I command you today to love the Lord your God, to walk in his ways, and to keep his commands, decrees and laws; then you will live and increase, and the

Lord your God will bless you in the land you are entering to possess.

> Deuteronomy 30:5–16 (NIV), emphasis mine.

The wonderful thing about the Lord's promise is that it is not too difficult, incomprehensible, or ethereal (beyond reach). His promises are here with us and for us…"very nigh unto thee… that thou mayest do [*'asah*] it" (v. 14, KJV). Among other things, the verb *'asah* implies a moral obligation. "The numerous texts in which this concept occurs attest to the importance of an ethical response to God which goes beyond mere mental abstraction…"[5] The Lord will make us abundantly prosperous in every work if we obey His voice, keep His commandments and His statutes, and turn to Him will our whole mind and heart and with all our being (v. 10).

Chapter Seven Evaluation

1. This chapter underscores the importance of appropriate response to the Lord's benevolence. The story of the twelve spies in the thirteenth chapter of Numbers shows the consequence of inappropriate response. Read Deuteronomy 30:16–20. Verse 16 contains the Lord's blessing if we obey Him, love Him, and then walk in His ways to keep His commandments. Notice again the elements of the Lord's orchestrated plan of well-being. To properly obey we must first see and hear the word of God (the Reubenic and Simeonic Principles, respectively). Then we must love the Lord as our God (the Levitic Principle of connectedness). Finally, we must keep His commandments and His statutes and His ordinances. This is the last principle shown to Leah, the wife of Jacob, through the birth of her fourth son, Judah. In this way, God promises us life and multiplication, and blessedness in the land which we shall possess. What does verse 17 say about the mind and the heart? Additionally, what is the consequence if you or I will not hear and are enticed away to worship other gods?

2. Think about the Lord's emphatic proclamation in Deuteronomy 30:19. Why does the Lord say, "I call heaven and earth *to witness* [*'uwd*] this day ... "? (v. 19, AMP, emphasis added). By calling heaven and earth as witnesses, is God suggesting that the principles outlined herein are repeatable, both in the natural and in the spiritual? *'Uwd* means to duplicate or repeat, and, by implication, to "testify (as by reiteration); intensively, to encompass, restore (as a sort of reduplication)."[6] That which God has declared has universal applications and is to be universally applied.

3. You may be thinking this is too good to be true. Is it really this easy? Are God's orchestrated plans for our lives within easy reach? Once again, read Deuteronomy 30:11–14.

4. Numbers 13:28–29 gives a detailed report of the names of the peoples who occupied Canaan's land. The descendants of Anak were there, but we forget about the others: the Amalekites in the South of the land, the Hittites, the Jebusites, and the Amorites occupied the mountains, and the Canaanites dwelled by the sea and along the banks of the Jordan. Why are the enemies of God and their territories so definitively identified? Perhaps you baulk (begin well but stop) because you feel your particular enemy is too big or ferocious. Even in this God leaves little room for excuses. All the formidable tribes of Canaan are mentioned.

5. What must we do if we are given to griping and complaining? The people heard the discouraging report and forgot everything they learned along the way. They listened to the ten spies who spoke negatively instead to the two who encouraged the people, saying, "Let us go up at once and take possession, for we are well able to overcome it" (Numbers 13:30, NKJV). In a previous incident not too dissimilar, what did God say to the people. When given to gripe, I am forever reminded to "stand still." Read Exodus 14:13; Numbers 9:8; 2 Chronicles 20:17; and Job 37:14. What are the Lord's instructions in confusing times when we are unsure which way to turn or when we are given to fear?

6. Perhaps one of the greatest lesson from the incident recorded in Numbers 13 and 14 concerns our confession. The ten faithless spies said, "We are not able to go up against the people, for they are stronger than we" (Numbers 13:31, NIV). Guard your confession! It was all about perceived "strength." How strong are you in the Lord? Are you able to stand against a determined consortium of enemies who occupy all the strategic places of your promised blessing? Guard your confession of strength!

7. Read Joshua and Caleb's response in Numbers 14:6–9. How does their witness apply to you? What does verse 7 say regarding the land to which we are called? Furthermore,

take to heart the words of verses 8 and 9. Read them aloud and claim them as your own.

8. Read Deuteronomy 28:1 and 28:58. Notice that "commitment" is a daily choice. If in a group setting, have each member write down a brief definition of *commitment*. Share these and then discuss the basic nature of *commitment* as it applies to the group.

9. The generation of people to whom Moses spoke lived a noncommittal life and consequently fell under a curse. *The Teacher's Commentary* on Deuteronomy 27–34 says, "The invitation to commitment is an open one! It is never too late for the believer to return to God. The door remains open to the people of God. All the Lord asks is that we respond to Him.... If you will not hear, then destiny becomes history."[7]

CHAPTER EIGHT

The Wind Ran Out of Breath

Ears that hear and eyes that see—the Lord has made them both.

Proverbs 20:12 (NIV)

"Go and tell this people," [said the Lord], 'Hear and hear continually, but understand not; and see and see continually, but do not apprehend with your mind. Make the heart of this people fat; and make their ears heavy and shut their eyes, lest they see with their eyes and hear with their ears and understand with their hearts and turn again and be healed.'"

Isaiah 6:9–10 (AMP)

Unto you it is given to know the mystery of the kingdom of God: but unto them that are without, all these things are done in parables: That seeing they may see, and not perceive; and hearing they may hear, and not understand...

Mark 4:11–12a (KJV)

> All these things Jesus spoke to the multitude in parables; and without a parable He did not speak to them, that it might be fulfilled which was spoken by the prophet, saying: "I will open My mouth in parables; I will utter things kept secret from the foundation of the world."
>
> Matthew 13:34–35 (NKJV)

Multitudes of people had gathered to hear the prophet articulate the ways and means of God's kingdom. But Jesus didn't speak to them in lofty, theological terms. Instead, He painted simple pictures from everyday life. His parables (similitudes or plain comparisons borrowed from daily living) captured the people's imaginations and aroused their interest. They are a mirror in which we see ourselves and a window through which we see God.

Sadly, much of what Jesus said was lost upon the multitudes who heard Him. Christ's words fell on deaf ears, and His parables were only darkened lanterns. "Listen," Jesus repeatedly cautioned (Matthew 13:18; 21:33; Mark 4:3; 7:14; and Luke 9:44; 18:6, NIV). "Consider carefully how you listen," He said (Luke 8:18, NIV). It's important how we respond to the truth, because this will determine what further truths God will teach us.

"Listen!" Jesus said to capture the people's attention (Mark 4:3a, NIV). Then Christ unfolded one of His most profound and well-known parables—The Parable of the Sower. Jesus spoke of seeds that were sown, some that fell by the wayside, others on stony ground, and some among thorns. Only a handful of seeds fell on good ground. The unfolding story of each seed was then told. Those that fell by the wayside were quickly devoured by the birds of the air. Those that fell on stony ground found no depth of soil. They sprang up but quickly withered in the hot sun for lack of root. The fate of those seeds that fell among the thorns was not much better. They grew up but were choked out before they could measurably increase.

But it wasn't the dead and dying seeds that were the Lord's focus. His emphasis was on the fate of the few fortunate seeds that were sown in good soil. They didn't wither or die. Neither were they choked out by ruinous weeds. Instead, these few seeds produced a tremendous increase; some thirty, sixty, and others one-hundred fold. In Christ's story, one plus one didn't simply add up to produce two. The compounded increase of God grows by magnitudes of ten and hundreds.

"He who has ears to hear, let him hear," Jesus declared (Mark 4:9, NIV). We must always be careful to gather to Him and rightly hear Him speak. This is the second law of God's kingdom increase—the Simeonic principle that was revealed to Leah (Genesis 29:33). Jesus placed a great deal of importance on the hearing of God's Word. "In one form or another," notes Warren Wiersbe, "the word *hear* is used thirteen times in Mark 4:1–34. Obviously, our Lord was speaking, not just about physical hearing, but about hearing with spiritual discernment. To 'hear' the Word of God means to understand it and obey it (see James 1:22–25)."[1]

The disciples stirred uneasily as they listened because, despite the Lord's warning about hearing with an understanding heart, they didn't fully comprehend. Their hearing was dull and confused. Had sin blinded them to the truth? Had its turbulence stirred up an undercurrent of misunderstanding? They lacked the Lord's prosperity as promised through Moses.

> Then the Lord your God will make you most prosperous in all the work of your hands and in the fruit of your womb, the young of your livestock and the crops of your land. The Lord will again delight in you and make you prosperous, just as he delighted in your fathers, if you obey the Lord your God and keep his commands and decrees that are written in this Book of the Law and turn to the Lord your God with all your heart and with all your soul.
>
> Deuteronomy 30:9–10 (NIV)

"Why does He speak in parables?" they privately grumbled amongst themselves. But Christ's intention was for them and us to think on His revelations, imagine them for ourselves, and perceive their implication. They must be personally employed to be of use. As noted by *The Bible Exposition Commentary* on Mark 3:13–19,

"A parable is a story or figure placed alongside a teaching to help us understand its meaning. It is much more than 'an earthly story with a heavenly meaning,' and it certainly is not an 'illustration,' such as a preacher would use in a sermon. A true parable gets the listener deeply involved and compels that listener to make a personal decision about God's truth and his or her life."[2]

Later, when He was alone, Jesus' disciples privately gathered to Him and asked for an explanation.

"To you it has been given to know the mystery of the kingdom of God; but to those who are outside [the unknowing crowd], all things come in parables [similes, riddles]," Jesus patiently explained (v. 11, NKJV).

Quoting a well-known passage from Isaiah, Jesus said: "Seeing they may see and not perceive, and hearing they may hear and not understand; Lest they should turn, And their sins be forgiven them" (Mark 4:12, NKJV). The sad truth is that many *see* (i.e., *blepo*) but but few *perceive* (*eido*); many hear but not with understanding. *Blepo* denotes simple voluntary observation[3] while *eido* means to *consider, know*, or *have knowledge*.[4] The people's casual attitude toward heaven's mysteries kept them from true awareness. "Seeing they see but do not perceive," said Jesus, "and hearing they hear but do not understand."

Then Jesus said something quite remarkable. Often missed, the passage challenges our own lack of understanding. "Do you not understand this parable?" He asked. "How then will you understand *all* the parables?" By implication, it is our prerogative to hear all (i.e., *ginosko*[5]) of Christ's sayings. Nothing is to be kept secret! *Ginosko* is a prolonged form of a primary verb which means *to know absolutely*. *The Exegetical Dictionary* remarks that *ginosko* references notice or observation of hidden intent (Mark 12:12 par. Matthew 21:45/Luke 20:19; Matthew 22:18; John 16:19; cf. also Mark 15:10).[6] We are meant to be "in the know," because the gospel advances according to our awareness. According to Christ, there is nothing hidden that should forever remain a mystery. "Is a lamp brought to be put under a basket or under a bed?" [Jesus asked so as to make His point]. "Is it not to be set on a lampstand? For there is nothing hidden which will not be revealed, nor has anything been kept secret but that it should come to light" (Mark 4:21–23, NKJV).

"Therefore," Jesus concluded, "consider carefully what you hear (v. 24a). The Amplified Version says, "Be careful what you are hearing." Then said Jesus, "The measure [of thought and study] you give [to the truth you hear] will be the measure [of virtue and knowledge] that come back to you—and more [besides] will be given to you who hear" (v. 24, AMP).

This brief passage gives all the essential ingredients of kingdom increase and productivity (i.e., seeing, hearing, valuing, and doing). It is a swelling chorus that makes good music—God's holy symphony of doing. It begins like a mustard seed, small but with huge potential to grow into a great tree that gives shelter to all who abide in its shadow (Mark 30:31–32). "[Things are hidden temporarily only as a means to revelation]," said Jesus. "For there is nothing hidden except to be revealed, nor is anything [temporarily] kept secret except in order that it may be made known" (Mark 4:22, AMP). The Lord's emphasis falls on the contrast between small beginning and the enormous profits in the end. Jesus's challenge is to "consider carefully what you hear." If it were not possible, He would not have said so. Thus, Jesus challenged, "With the measure you use, it will be measured to you—and even more. Whoever has will be given more; whoever does not have, even what he has will be taken from him" (Mark 4:24–25, NIV).

Our lesson is clear—do not despise small beginnings with God, especially your unique recognition and understanding (*ginosko*) from God's own hand. Your flash of inspiration has tremendous potential (ability and competency) over all the power (strength, violence) of the enemy (Luke 10:19). Therefore, allow your devout revelation to grow and flower into perfection. Test it and prove it to be of God (1 Samuel 3:7–9).

Jesus privately shared these wondrous things of God with all those who were closest to Him. Mark's gospel tells us that He explained everything *fully* (Mark 4:34, AMP). As Christians and fellow heirs with Christ Jesus, you and I also have this special privilege through the Holy Spirit to rightly hear the revelations of God. The Holy Spirit is God's Spirit of truth Who guides us into all truth. "He will speak only what He hears, and He will tell you what is yet to come," said Jesus. "He will bring glory to Me by taking from what is Mine and making it known to you. All that belongs to the Father is Mine. That's why I said the Spirit will take from what is Mine and make it known to you" (John 16:13b-15, NIV).

Following Christ's remarkable revelation of kingdom increase and productivity, He and His disciples got into a boat to cross to the other side (Mark 4:35). Little did the disciples know it was a practical test to see how much they had learned. It is never enough to merely hear God's truths; they must also be repeated—put into practice.

As the men began to cross to the other side of Galilee's Sea, the gentle breeze freshened, became blustery, and then turned into a furious gale of hurricane force wind that churned the quiet sea into frothy mass of giant waves. The disciples frantically bailed and struggled against the rising water at their feet.

Were these men out of God's perfect will? Absolutely not, for it was Jesus Himself Who had said, "Let us cross over to the other side" (Mark 4:35, NKJV). Wittingly or unwittingly, in one way or another, we are all in the process of crossing over from one reality to another. It's on "the other side" that new dimensions of truth, as well as a new destiny, await. But between here and there is a storm that assails us. It tests our resolve, tugs at our heart's fabric, and examines our faith. We've heard Christ's commandments, now will we rely on His holy enabling? God would not put us into a boat only to sink it! Nothing can hinder the working out of our plans when God is with us. Jesus promises a guaranteed safe arrival if only we will trust Him!

Jesus earlier spoke of eyes that see with perception and ears that hear with understanding. He also spoke of turning unto our salvation. Is this our part in the Lord's plan of salvation? Jesus must have sensed the disciples' confusion and consequently asked, "Why are you so fearful? How is it that you have no faith?" (v. 40, NKJV). I particularly like the Amplified Bible's version. He said to them, "Why are you so timid and fearful? How is it that you have no faith (no firmly relying trust)?" It's all about our firmly relying trust.

"Master, don't you care that we are perishing?" the disciples cried out fearfully. Of course He cared. It was for this reason He delayed. There was divine intention in the storm. Despite their rowing and much cursing, they couldn't prevail against the mighty tempest. The gale-force winds were of supernatural design and meant to test their burgeoning faith—their revelation of divine truth. They needed to learn the importance of a trust that is solid and steadfast.

The Lord rose. "Hush now!" He commanded. "Be still (muzzled)!" (Mark 4:39, AMP).

Immediately, the wind ceased; sinking to rest as if exhausted by its beating. The result was a great calm, a perfect peacefulness.

From Christ's demeanor when in the midst of the storm, the text suggests that the disciples already possessed the wherewithal to effectively confront the wind and waves. It was not in their strength or cunning, because this was tried and failed. All that was necessary for overcoming the mighty tempest was a firmly relying trust in God. The disciples had already seen and heard wondrous truths (the secrets of the kingdom of God). Now it was up to them to rely upon it and effectively turn.

Chapter Eight Evaluation

1. It's said that when you were born, you were crying and everyone around you was smiling. Live your life in such a way that, at the end, you're the one who's smiling, and everyone around you is crying. Two very engaging questions are addressed in this chapter. The first was posed by the disciples who were beset by a ferocious windstorm. Waves beat against their small boat, they bailed, and, all the while, Jesus was in the stern asleep on a pillow. They finally awoke Him and said, "Teacher, do You not care that we are perishing?" (Mark 4:38, NKJV). What is it that now buffets you? What tempest has suddenly risen and, even now, threatens to overturn your life? Take some time to think about your answer. Write it down. If within a group setting, and if your personal storm is not too personal, honestly share your fears, your emotions, etc. You'll feel better for it! Above all, remember that Jesus is in your boat. He knows your grievances and sees your needs. In fact, He's been there, done that! He's accompanied men who desperately struggled against contrary winds.

2. Now it's time to come clean. Does it seem that sometimes the Lord is coolly detached and oblivious to your troubles? Is He seemingly asleep on a pillow in the stern of your skiff? Judging from His reaction when awakened, what does this story in Mark 4 reveal about the Lord? Was Jesus really insensible to the storm?

3. Now consider the second question posed in this story. It was asked by a demoniac who resided on "the other side." Chasing after the storm as it does, it is very relevant to our own spiritual condition. Read Mark 5:1–20. The man who was demon possessed asked Jesus, "What have I to do with You?" (v. 7a, NKJV). For that matter, what have you to do with Christ? Remember the context wherein it was composed? In

light of God's revealed truths (the secrets of the kingdom of God), what do you have to do with Christ?

4. The fourth and fifth chapters of Mark's Gospel contain all the essential ingredients of Kingdom increase and productivity (i.e., seeing, hearing, valuing, and turning). It is a swelling chorus that makes great music! It is the Lord's holy symphony of doing that begins like a mustard seed in smallness but grows to become hugely profitable and beneficial. "He who has ears to hear, let him be hearing [and let him consider, and comprehend]," said Jesus (Mark 4:9, AMP). From Christ's Parable of the Sower we learn that there are four kinds of hearts that hear and respond to God's unveiled truths. First, there is the hardened (calloused) heart (Mark 4:4, 15) that resists God's Word and brings it to no effect (i.e. the birds come and snatch it away). There are also those who are shallow of heart (v(v). 5–6, 16–17). This sort of person is like the thin, rocky soil typically found in Palestine. Without sufficient depth of soil, his or her spiritual roots are shallow and cannot sufficiently resist the pressures of draught or the scorching heat of the sun. Are you of this sort? Are God's wondrous truths joyfully heard and accepted but you've found that the price is too high to necessarily make them Your own? Has your exuberance waned because of persecution or difficulty? Warren Wiersbe warns that it is easy for the fallen human nature to counterfeit "religious feelings" and thereby give a professing Christian feelings of false confidence.[7] The third type of heart is one that is crowded with spiritual weeds that are not plucked-up. Consequently, this type of hearer readily receives God's word but doesn't truly repent. Consequently, the cares of this world (i.e. the desire for riches, lusts for things, etc.) leave little room for the good seed to grow and mature. Finally, there is the fruitful heart (Mark 4:8, 20). It is wondrously changed as evidenced by spiritual fruit. Our challenge is to examine our own heart and life in light of these four types of heart. God's seed has been cast forth and has fallen to you and me. But what have

you done with it? What precious nuggets of divine truths have you heard from God's Own lips? What have you done with them and do they produce fruit?

5. What was Jesus's command to the man who was miraculously set free from his various demons? Read Mark 5:18–20. What was required of him? For that matter, what is now required of you and me? How does the story in Mark 5 apply to you and your testimony?

6. Once you've discerned the Lord's will as it concerns you, it is your responsibility is to live it and share it. The testimony of him who is divinely enabled is guaranteed to produce wonder and amazement. Read Mark 4:24–25. What is Christ's promise?

7. The challenge of this chapter is to not despise or disregard God's small beginnings (His precious nuggets of divine truth uniquely shared with you). Allow His holy inspirations, visions, and special anointings to grow and fully mature. "Consider Abraham!" says the apostle Paul. "He believed God, and it was credited to him as righteousness" (Galatians 3:6, NIV). Did he know all things about God or was Abraham's overall knowledge of God limited? This is evidenced by the name(s) he gave to God which suggest that his divine revelations were very specific and to the point. Also consider the man's age. He was ninety-nine years old and still called Abram. As such, he was an imperfect man to whom God said, "Walk before me and be blameless. I will confirm My covenant between Me and you and will greatly increase you (Genesis 17:1–2, NIV). But it was only after Abram had fallen facedown in complete surrender to the Lord that He was empowered unto divine fruitfulness. Abram became the God-empowered man named Abraham who possessed a full realization of the multiplying God. His blessing was exceeding increase (i.e. the Lord's *over and above* "muchness"). Now it's up to you! Recall your special knowingness and rediscover it know-how. In confirmation, read

the account of Genesis 20:1–7. It is very important for you to realize that in your moment of divine revelation of God (your eureka-moment), you also became God's custodian or steward. As such, you are blessed with requisite capacity and capability. Consider this: What good are newly opened eyes if there is no requisite power to live the dream? Consider Abraham! (Galatians 3:6). He was a man not unlike you or me. In a flash of inspiration, he saw God (the Lord Who Provides, the Seeing God), and was thereby empowered to likewise "see" and "see to it." He was the Lord's prophet of increase. As such, he could counteract decrees and curses of decrease (Genesis 20:7).

8. Take a moment and consider your present trials and temptations. Perhaps you may want to write them down. Coming on the heels of Christ's kingdom parables revealed in Mark 4, the demoniac's question is purposely placed to make you and me evaluate our own particular position with God. Christ is asking, "Do you bring a lamp (the light of God's revealed truth) to put it under a bowl or a bed, or do you put it on a stand to light the whole house (Mark 4:21)?

CHAPTER NINE

Divine Conceptions: God's Conclusion

> And she conceived again and bore a son, and said, "Now I will praise the Lord." Therefore she called his name Judah. Then she stopped bearing.
>
> Genesis 29:35 (NKJV)

We've come a long way on our progressive journey of spiritual discovery. Our study is aptly concluded by five vital words strategically placed at the close of Leah's narrative. Her story of miraculous deliverance from self-loathing and mediocrity ends with the emphatic proclamation, "then she stopped having children" (Genesis 29:35b; NIV).

Having experienced the Lord's generative power of divine conception, Leah brought forth life-changing principles of supernatural strength and vitality. Through her firstborn sons (Reuben, Simeon, Levi, and Judah), she learned the ways and means of God keys to kingdom increase that loose and bind (Matthew 16:19; 18:18). "See," declares the Lord, "I set before you today life and prosperity, death and destruction. For I command you today to love the Lord your God, to walk in His ways, and to keep His commands, decrees and laws; then you will live and increase, and the Lord your God will bless you in the land you are entering to possess" (Deuteronomy 30:15–16, NIV).

Heaven's harmony, when rightly sung, rejuvenated Leah's dull and dreary existence. In contrast, she was given completeness, soundness, and God's *shalom*—well-being of the whole person (Mark 5:34).[1] After much trouble and grief, God's "muchness" was finally hers to enjoy. Thus, her last statement through her son, Judah, was: "This time I will praise [literally, hold out the hand]" (Genesis 29:35, NIV). Judah epitomized Leah's final realization. Then, for a time, she ceased bearing children because God had finished His work in her. The divine symphony of doing (*'asah*) in and through her was accomplished because she'd finally opened her hand to the Lord. Now, all things were possible for her.

This was later confirmed by Jesus. A certain man in the crowd had brought his demon-possessed son to His disciples to drive it out. Jesus said to them, "O unbelieving generation, how long shall I stay with you?" (Mark 9:19a, NIV). I prefer the Amplified Version that says He answered them, "O unbelieving generation [without any faith]! How long shall I [have to do] with you?"

The boy's distraught father begged Jesus to do something. "If you can do anything," he pleaded, "take pity on us and help us."

Jesus reply forms the highpoint of this discussion. Don't miss it because it is the heritage of all believers who rightly apply God's divine principles of blessing and increase.

"If you can?" said Jesus. "Everything is possible for him who believes" (v. 23, NIV).

At once the boy's father gave a tearful plea, "Lord, I believe! [Constantly] help my weakness of faith!" (v. 24, AMP).

In many respects we are akin to that distraught father who was at his wit's end. Likewise we are like Leah who is introduced in the Bible as greatly disadvantaged. The Scriptures say she had eyes that were weak *and* dull looking while her younger sister, Rachel, was beautiful and attractive (Genesis 29:16–17). The word "dull" as used in the Bible is translated elsewhere as tedious or uninteresting. This comparative statement embodied her dreary existence. And to top it all off, she was also unloved. Is it any surprise that Rachel, Leah's younger sister, was also her father's darling—his pride and joy? And, if this wasn't bad enough, Jacob loved Rachel (v. 18a). Poor Leah!

Much is implied in the relatively short narrative of Leah's life. Her plight depicts the lives of countless multitudes of people who are less gifted, disadvantaged, undesirable, and miserable. For one reason or another, they lack the love and attention so longingly desired. Like Leah, they are always second best—a miserable afterthought. Her lovelier sister was much preferred. Rachel was everyone's favorite. And then there was Leah.

Within every family, and in most situations, there is a "Rachel" and there is a "Leah." There is one who is seemingly advantaged and another who is somehow less advantaged. Perhaps you can identify with Leah's sad hopelessness. Like Leah, you live in the long-reaching shadow of another. Consequently, it seems you are always behind the proverbial eight ball; you want a descent shot at life but there is always the eight ball between you and it. In this, you are not alone. Praise God because He's provided a way of escape His Divine Conception!

The Lord sees your plight. Hence, the Scriptures tell us that that "when the Lord *saw* [*ra'ah*] that Leah was not loved, He opened her womb" (Genesis 29:31a, NIV, emphasis added). This passage firmly rests on the Lord's precept of seeing with discernment, enjoyment, and experience. According to Warren Wiersbe, "the name sounds like 'he [God] has seen my affliction.'"[2] Reuben, and all he represents, is the Lord's foremost conception within Israel. "See!" declared Leah when he was born.

"The conceptions of which the OT speaks concern children who were to play an important part in redemptive history," says *The Theological Wordbook*.[3] Conceptions are markers of munificence (largesse). They represent "the selective, monergistic power of God."[4]

But despite the fact that God *saw* Leah, Jacob's affections remained unchanged. More was required. Hence, Leah's schooling continued and she *conceived* again (v. 33). God had *heard* her plea and a second son was born into the family of God. "Because the Lord *heard* that I am not loved, He gave me this one too," Leah proclaimed

(Genesis 29:33, NIV, emphasis mine). The name Simeon means *one who hears* and implicates *hearing* (i.e., attentive understanding) in God's orchestrated plan of "loosing"—His scheme of procreation that brings forth blessing with increase.

When Reuben was conceived and born into the community of God, Israel, I believe Leah was given a special prowess or ability to see and "see it through." But what good is seeing if we see unclearly (without right reckoning or understanding). Hence, God's second principle, the ability to *rightly hear*, lends comprehension to things seen. Indeed, what good is seeing without the interpretive ability to understand and apply with know-how? What good are precognitive dreams without an awakening? Hence, when Jesus healed a blind man's eyes, He asked, "Do you see anything?" (Mark 8:23, NIV).

But the man did not see with focused intent and saw only blurred images. Jesus therefore again placed His hands on the man's eyes. This time, they were fully opened and the man saw with perception. The Scriptures say his sight was restored, and "he saw everything clearly" (Mark 8:25b, NIV). Much is implied within this short text. The Amplified Bible says, "He put His hands on his eyes again; and the man looked intently [that is, fixed his eyes on definite objects], and he was restored and *saw everything distinctly* [even what was at a distance]" (emphasis mine). It is always God's intent that His people see everything distinctly, even what is at a distance.

Having conceived within her womb Israel's first two sons, you would think that Leah's salvation was assured. But even though she was seen by God and could likewise see with opened eyes, and in spite of the fact that she had understanding with know-how, Jacob's love was still as far from her as night is from day. Leah remained unloved, reviled, and unfulfilled within the family of God, Israel. What more was necessary to free her from the repressive bonds? Lead needed more!

Hope blossomed afresh when Leah conceived again, her third time. The Lord's children were coming forth, one after another in a prescribed fashion, as markers of His largesse. In the process, Leah was growing; edified and enabled with know-how.

This time, when Leah conceived, she was convinced that her destiny was about to take a turn for the better. She believed that her issues were finally resolved, once and for all. Repeatedly, the word *hara* (translated *concieved*) is used of her deliverance. She conceived (Genesis 29:33a, NIV), once more she conceived (v. 34a, NIV), and she conceived again (v. 35a, NIV).

"Now *this time* will my husband be a companion to me, for I have borne him three sons," Leah declared (v. 34a, AMP, emphasis mine). She named her third son *Levi* (companion), the root of his name meaning *to twine*, and by implication, *to unite*.[5] Leah's third conception within Israel unveils the wonder of affiliation and intimate connection. Within God's scheme of deliverance, we must each come into absolute, wholehearted agreement with things divinely seen and heard.

But Leah reckoned too heavily on husband's response and afterward was disappointed when Jacob's affections remained unchanged. We each love what we love, and our affections are only altered as we each see fit. Hence, it was not until the advent of her fourth son, the Lord's last holy conception in this merciful dispensation, that Leah was finally vindicated. "She conceived again, and when she gave birth to a son she said, 'This time I will praise the Lord.' So she named him Judah" (Genesis 29:35a, NIV). We know this is His last movement in Leah's song of deliverance because of the final five words that conclude this chapter. The narrative says, "Then she stopped having children" (v. 35b, NIV). It was as if God put an exclamation mark at the end of His hallowed work. Judah's conception was God's last testimonial of truth in His orchestrated plan of salvation. The Amplified Bible says, "Then [for a time] she ceased bearing." Thus ends the chapter in this narration.

Leah had finally come to realize that her insightful revelations of truth held no sway over her husband. His resolve and will were his own because he was a free moral agent who must assemble or dissemble for himself. On the other hand, her *knowingness* was sufficient for *her* need; to see her through and to give her all she needed for freedom and to live unbounded.

The Lord's revelations in and through Leah's conceptions were all she needed to fully activate her God-given blessing. She became one (i.e., whole-heartedly connected) to her special knowingness and she opened her hand unto it. These are the third and fourth conceptions of God within Israel, respectively. We must actively and affectionately become our vision's companion!

With Judah's conception and birth, Leah finally came to realize her own part within the Lord's holy scheme of deliverance. *She*, not Jacob, had to turn in the direction of her revealed knowledge. It is never enough to merely see and hear (Matthew 11:15; 13:9, 15–16). We must also vigorously agree and associate with our special knowingness and know-how. Then we must also rightly appropriate it and turn accordingly. This is the inner meaning of "praise"—the opening of one's hand unto that which God has specifically revealed.

In 1979, Dr. Paul Yonggi Cho, pastor of the world's largest church, published a book titled *The Fourth Dimension*. Therein, Pastor Cho quotes Ironside's commentary on the two distinct types of God's Word as it appears in the New Testament. *Logos*, according to Ironside, is "the said Word of God," and *rhema* is "the saying Word of God."[6] Cho believes it was the *Logos of God*, "the said Word of God," that created the world. *Logos* is the general Word that stretches from Genesis to Revelation.[7] *Rhema*, on the other hand, is the "quickened" word of God. "*Rhema* is a specific word to a specific person in a special situation."[8]

"The spoken word has powerful creativity," notes Pastor Cho, "and its proper usage is vital to a victorious Christian life. This spoken word, however, must have a correct basis to be truly effective."[9] He therefore espouses something he refers to as "the law of incubation" that activates faith. It consists of several key elements. "First," he writes, "to use your faith, you must be able to envision a clear-cut objective...You must *see* your objective so vividly and graphically that you can feel it in your emotions."[10] "Secondly," he writes, "if you have a vivid picture, you should have a burning desire for those objectives...You should have a burning desire for a goal, and you must keep on seeing that goal accomplished."[11] Dr. Cho's second key is what I've called God's Levitic principle; the conception that links the first essential elements of divine blessing (right seeing and right hearing) to His last, the Judaic principle of active participation. We must have a burning desire for things seen and heard and then rightly "turn" (Matthew 13:15; Mark 4:12). Two scriptures are quoted by Cho to make his second point: "The desire of the righteous is given" (Proverbs 10:24b, YLT), and "Delight thyself on Jehovah, And He giveth to thee the petitions of thy heart" (Psalm 37:4, YLT). "When you have a clear goal, and have this desire burning in your heart to a boiling point," writes Dr. Cho, "then you should kneel down and pray until you receive the substance, the assurance."[12]

Pastor Cho's "envisioning" espouses the divine principles of seeing and hearing—the conceptions of Reuben and Simeon within God's kingdom. We must understand and contextualize our inspired thoughts (God's *rhema*) in light of His creation (i.e., His *Logos*). Consciously apply (give substance to) that which is divinely inspired (conceived).

You may recall an earlier reference I made to the life and ministry of the prophet Ezekiel. Ezekiel opens his book with the statement: "In the thirtieth year, in the fourth month, on the fifth day, while I was among the exiles by the Kebar River, the heavens were opened, and I *saw* (i.e., *ra'ah*) visions of God" (Ezekiel 1:1, NIV, emphasis added). The Hebrew *ra'ah* is used over thirty times by the prophet Ezekiel to describe his heavenly experiences. Furthermore, the concept of "right hearing" (i.e., *shama'*) is also prevalent in Ezekiel's writings. For example, it is recorded seven times that Ezekiel also *heard* (i.e., *shama'*) the word of the Lord (Ezekiel 1:24, 28; 2:2; 3:12; 9:1; 10:13, and 43:6). But it was not through his divinely appointed visions and hearing that the prophet affected the destiny of those people around him. God's command was that the prophet also partake of his divine revelation to make it his own. "Son of man," [said the Lord,] "*hear* that which I am speaking unto thee...open thy mouth and eat that which I am giving unto thee" (Ezekiel 2:8, YLT). The prophet had to literally incorporate the word of God into his being so that it became a living part of him (Ezekiel 3:1). "All My words that I speak unto thee," said God, "receive with thy heart" (Ezekiel 3:10). Thus, Ezekiel partook of his revelation by coming into a vital connectedness (i.e., association) with it. In these passages, we see affect of Israel's three eldest sons. Furthermore, the divine conceptions are made complete via Israel's fourth son, Judah. "Son of man," [commanded the Lord], "eat what you find; eat this scroll, and go, *speak* to the house of Israel." (Ezekiel 3:1, NKJV, emphasis mine). Ezekiel's calling required that he *actively participate* with the revealed word (open his hand unto it). As Pastor Cho said, "*Claim and speak* the word of assurance, for your word actually goes out and creates. God spoke and the whole world came into being. Your word is the material which the Holy Spirit uses to create."[13]

We must show evidence of our faith to make it work. To change our reality, we must actively participate with things envisioned, precognitive dreams, special visions, etc. Dr. Cho equates the giving of commands as one such path. "The church today has lost the art of giving commands," he observes. "On the bank of the Red Sea Moses begged, 'Oh God, help us! The Egyptians are coming.' God rebuked him, saying, 'Moses, why are you crying to me? Give the command and the Red Sea shall be divided.'"[14]

Miracles don't come by blindly stumbling about. The divine conceptions of God revealed through Leah's sorrow and subsequent deliverance show you and me that there are laws within the spiritual realm that must be satisfied. They form the foundation of Israel; the first of four of which are embodied in the persons of his first four sons. The Lord will not do anything apart from you and me. He co-operates with us through the agency of His Holy Spirit to accomplish great and wonderful things. But the challenge is to energize your revelation by taking that which is specially known (i.e., things seen in the spirit realm and then conceptualized and understood), capture it within your heart and mind to make it your own, and then actively open your hand unto it. Thus, Ezekiel had to *eat* of his revelation. "Do not rebel like that rebellious house," said the Lord. "Open your mouth and eat what I give you" (Ezekiel 2:8b, NIV). Speak it, confess it, and live it! Jeremiah said: "Thy words have been found, and I eat them, and Thy word is to me for a joy, and for the rejoicing of my heart, for Thy name is called on me, O Jehovah, God of Hosts. I have not sat in an assembly of deriders, nor do I exult, because of thy hand—Alone I have sat, for [with] indignation Thou hast filled me" (Jeremiah 15:16–17, YLT, emphasis mine). In the language of the text, Jeremiah "found" the divine revelation, implying he didn't passively receive but interactively saw and heard it.

The root of Judah's name (*yadah*) means *literally, to use* (i.e., hold out) *the hand*; *physically, to throw* (a stone, an arrow) *at or away;*

especially to revere or worship (with extended hands); *intensively.*"[15] Thus, Leah's response following the conception and birth of her fourth son didn't reference either the Lord or her husband. "This time," she declared, "*I* will praise the Lord!" Her last affirmation mentions only her own part in the divine scheme of change and refreshment. Thereby, she was signaling her intention to *actively participate* with God in His "loosing" process. Vigorous connectedness, the Levitic and Judaic principles, is the final key that unlocks the door of divine procreation. Lively entanglement is the affirmation of truth that sets us free. Thus, Leah announced her intention to extend her hands toward the Lord without reservation. "This time *I* will praise the Lord," she avowed, holding back nothing (Genesis 29:35, NIV, emphasis mine). Unreservedly, Leah was determined to align herself with things seen and heard (i.e., her special knowingness).

I'll conclude with three words of caution. First, understand that years of reproach, struggle, and misfortune often exact a heavy toll upon the human psyche. Without doubt, it is often difficult to see yourself as does God, as anything more than a cast off or an ugly inconvenience. Early in Leah's marriage, her desire was to be loved and accepted (Genesis 29:32, 33 and 34). She wished for a place of honor and respect within her home, the household of Israel. But how is this possible for one who is naturally disadvantaged? It was only by the time of her final conception (Judah) that she finally realized her own part in God's orchestrated plan of salvation and deliverance. Against all odds and every opposition, she opened her hands to God in praise! Without reservation she declared, "This time *I* will praise the Lord!" (Genesis 29:35, NIV, emphasis mine). Without a doubt, it was very difficult for Leah to see herself as did God. But with knowingness also comes know-how. Trust the Lord!

Praise is evidenced by uplifted or extended hands to God. It is the reach of faith! *Yadah*, the root of Judah's name, means *to use or hold out the hand* (i.e., to revere or worship with extended hands). Said God, "I desire and delight in *dutiful, steadfast love and goodness,* not sacrifice, and the knowledge of and acquaintance with God more than burnt offerings" (Hosea 6:6, AMP, emphasis mine). Praise, then, is the dutiful, steadfast affirmation of one's knowledge and acquaintance with the Lord, despite all odds. *Unger's Bible Dictionary* says *praise* is *an approval or admiration ... for blessings received.*[16]

After the Israelites had been freed from their Egyptian bondage, they were relentlessly pursued by Egypt's mighty army. Freedom is not easily achieved and the Egyptian taskmasters were loath to let them go. With the Egyptian army in hot pursuit, Israel baulked. "Was it because there were no graves in Egypt that you brought us to the desert to die?" they complained to Moses. "What have you done to us by bringing us out of Egypt? Didn't we say to you in Egypt, 'Leave us alone; let us serve the Egyptians'?" (Exodus 14:11–12a, NIV).

When relentlessly pursued, we often become weak kneed and whiny. If you are given to such complaints and despondency, if you are talking of turning back, God declares, "Do not be afraid. Stand firm [i.e., *yatsab*], and you will see the deliverance the Lord will bring you today. The Egyptians you see today you will never see again. The Lord will fight for you; you need only to be still" (v(v). 13–14, NIV). To *stand firm* means *to present oneself in readiness for service* (see Zechariah 6:5). This same verb testifies of holding your ground when challenged (2 Chronicles 11:13). This is what it means to praise God. No matter what, and despite all challenges to the contrary, hold fast to that which God has specially bestowed.

My second word of caution in such matters concerns your understanding regarding God and who you are in Christ. Never call yourself anything less than does the Lord! When your back is to the wall, and against all odds, stand firm. Consider Abraham (Galatians 3:6a, NIV). Everyone undoubtedly thought him strange, perhaps a fool. He called himself *Abraham* (father of a multitude) when he was old and had no heir. Yet he resolutely clung to his special appellation. He "believed in *and* adhered to *and* trusted in *and* relied on God, and it was reckoned *and* placed to his account *and* credited as righteousness (as conformity to the divine will in purpose, thought, and action)" (Galatians 3:6, AMP).

My third word of caution concerns your heart's confession. Know who and what you are but also make sure your special cognition (i.e. vision, dream, awakening, etc.) wholly lines-up with God's revealed Word. Does that which moves you contradict the Bible? When Jesus was accused of driving out demons by the power of Beelzebub, the prince of demons, He said, "Every kingdom divided against itself will be ruined, and every city or household divided against itself will not stand. If Satan drives out Satan, he is divided against himself. How then can his kingdom stand?" (Matthew 12:25–27, NIV). God's kingdom stands because He is not divided against Himself. Is your special insight (i.e., your unique knowingness which set's your soul afire) God-breathed? If so, it will never align itself against what the Bible says. Measure what you know by the end result. Does it engender a gentler love and compassion? Beware your own volition and willful carnality that often will lead you astray. I find myself drawn to Chuck Swindoll in this regard. He admonishes us to carefully test what we may think to be a prompting from the Lord.

> He doesn't speak to us audibly as He did in those days, and what may feel like a compelling unction from the Holy Spirit may just as well be your own hidden desire. It is true that you have living within you the Holy Spirit of almighty God, and He always gives good guidance. But you also carry with you many pounds of carnal flesh that makes wrong seem right. A transformed mind will tell the difference, but that doesn't take place overnight. Maturity comes with time and experience; it's a product of a growing intimacy with the Almighty.[17]

Swindoll's advice is sound. We must always put our inclinations to the test. "The Lord will honor His truth by confirming it for you. What has it taught you?"[18]

All things are finally tied together in and through Leah's final conception within Israel—our *active participation* (the oracle of Judah). When coupled with his siblings (the divine conceptions of the Lord through Reuben, Simeon, and Levi) miraculous changes are wrought. By *willful affiliation* and *vigorous participation*, we energize God's holy intentions. This is the Lord's parenthetical statement, His holy declaration, in and through Leah. Nothing more remained to be done, His work was finished! Hence, the twenty-ninth chapter of Genesis concludes with the summative statement, "Then she stopped having children."

> She [Leah] conceived again, and when she gave birth to a son, she said, "This time I will praise the Lord." So she named him Judah. *Then she stopped having children.*
>
> Genesis 29:35 (NIV), emphasis mine.

"Consider carefully what you hear," declares the Lord. "With the measure you use, it will be measured to you—and even more. Whoever has will be given more; whoever does not have, even what he has will be taken from him" (Mark 4:24–25, NIV).

Now the challenge is yours and mine! Knowing the innermost workings of God's kingdom and His increase, will you extend your hands toward the Lord in praise? How will your story end? Your parenthetical statement and mine are yet to be fully written.

Chapter Nine Evaluation

1. It is time that we all begin to properly *praise* the Lord with open hands. What has God done in you? Have you properly received it and *turned*? Do you live up to it? I urge you to grab hold of that which God has done for you!

2. Do you lack? If so, what would you do if you knew you could not fail? Would you live differently if you knew, beyond all shadow of doubt, that God is on your side? Join forces with God and receive Jesus Christ as your Savior and Lord. "To as many as did receive *and* welcome Him, He gave the authority (power, privilege, right) to become the children of God, that is, to those who believe in (adhere to, trust in, and rely on) His name—Who owe their birth neither to bloods nor to the will of the flesh [that of physical impulse] nor to the will of man [that of a natural father], but to God. [They are born of God!]" (John 1:12–13, AMP).

Appendix: The Science of "Seeing"

Genesis by Observership

John Archibald Wheeler was an eminent American theoretical physicist and colleague of Albert Einstein and Niels Bohr. He was a professor of physics at Princeton University between 1938 and 1976 and the director of the Center for Theoretical Physics at the University of Texas at Austin from 1976 to 1986.[1] During the Second World War, Dr. Wheeler participated in the development of the atomic bomb under the Manhattan Project and later worked on the development of the hydrogen bomb with Project Matterhorn. While at Princeton, Wheeler coined the word *wormhole* to describe hypothetical tunnels in space-time. Later, in 1967 during a talk at NASA's Goddard Institute of Space Studies, Wheeler also first used the term *black hole*.

Wheeler had a colorful way with words. For example, his doctrine of "It from Bit" suggests that the origin of all things physical is information-theoretic. Otherwise put, "every *it*—every particle, every field of force, even the space-time continuum itself—derives its function, its meaning, its very existence entirely... from the apparatus-elicited answer to yes-or-no questions, binary choices, bits."[2] Wheeler's "It from Bit" doctrine theorizes that every item of the physical world has at its base an immaterial source and explanation.

> That which we call reality arises in the last analysis from posing of yes-no questions and the registering of equipment-evoked responses; in short, that all things physical are information-theoretic in origin *and that this is a participatory universe.*[3]

Wheeler's "Participatory Anthropic Principle" formulates that conscious observers are the creators of reality. Minds make the universe manifest—it is a work in progress. Does the universe really exist if we are not looking?

John Wheeler was also known for his phrase "genesis by observership." He speculated that our observations contribute to the creation of physical reality, that reality exists not because of its physical components, but, rather, because of the act of observing the universe. "Information may not be just what we *learn* about the world," he wrote, "it may be what *makes* the world."[4]

When I first heard Wheeler's provocative ideas, especially his notion of *genesis by observership*, I was struck with their relevance to the creative processes clearly outlined in the Bible. At the time, I was embroiled in a seminary course on the book of Genesis. In particular, I was pondering the relevance of God's *seeing* in the initial creative scheme (Genesis 1). The scriptures repeatedly note, seven times in all, that God "saw" (Genesis 1:4, 10, 12, 18, 21, 25, and 31). I remember wondering why the recurring statements of God's "observership" were emphasized. How did His *seeing* (*ra'ah* in the original language of the Bible) and His affirmations (declarations of "goodness") advance reality? Seeing with comprehension and implied affiliation were essential elements of the overall creative scheme. Being mentioned seven times for emphasis, it's as if God is thumping us on the head, saying, "Wake up to My creative processes!" I remember asking my students, for I was teaching at the time, if the recurring statements of God's "observership" somehow set the stage for that which would follow—the producing principles revealed to Abraham, Isaac, and Israel. I also challenged my student's with Christ's provocative statements from His Parable of the Sower. From the very beginning, God's Word confirms what Wheeler later came to refer to as *genesis by observership*. Additionally, I remember wondering how the repeated statements of *goodness* (Genesis 1:4, 10, 12, 18, 21, 25, and 31) add to creation's story. The assertions of God's approval seemingly undergird His creative process as a necessary ingredient. It wasn't enough that God simply said, "Let there be light," and there was light. Somehow, His beholding of creation's *goodness* added a degree of relevance and durability to it. Furthermore, the repeated statements imply His requisite affiliation and connectedness with all things seen.

"To Wheeler," said Tim Folger in *Discover Magazine*, "we are not simply bystanders on a cosmic stage; we are shapers and creators living in a participatory universe."[5]

> According to the rules of quantum mechanics, our observations influence the universe at its most fundamental levels. The boundary between an objective "world out there" and our own subjective consciousness that seemed so clearly defined in physics before the eerie discoveries of the 20th century blurs in quantum mechanics. When physicists look at the basic constituents of reality—atoms and their innards, or the particles of light called photons—what they see depends on how they have set up their experiment. A physicist's observations determine whether an atom, say, behaves like a fluid wave or a hard particle, or which path it follows in traveling from one point to another. From the quantum perspective, the universe is an extremely interactive place.[6]

A classic demonstration of how observation influences reality is the two-slit experiment. Light is known to have a dual nature, behaving like tiny, compact particles (photons) and sometimes like waves spread out in space. In the two-slit experiment, a stream of photons (minuscule packets of light) is focused on two parallel slits. When photon detectors are set up beside each slit, allowing the observation of the photons as they pass, the photons act like particles, passing through one slit or the other to expose a strip of photographic film behind. But something bizarre happens when the photon detectors are removed. Instead of the two distinct clusters of dots on the photographic film (characteristic of particulate energy), a pattern of alternating light and dark stripes appears. The clusters corresponding to where individual photos hit after randomly passing through one slit or the other disappear, and the photons begin to behave like waves. Each individual photon seems to spread out and surge against both slits at once. Incredibly, the outcome of the experiment depends on the observer—what he is trying to assess. If he sets up photon detectors next to the slits, the photons behave as ordinary particles that traverse along one route or the other, but never both at the same time. If the observer removes the photon detectors, the photons seem to travel both routes simultaneously, as would be expected of waves. The alternating bright streaks in the pattern of alternating light and dark stripes correspond to where waves overlap; the dark strips on the film indicate that alternate waves have cancelled each other out. The outcome of the classic two-slit experiment depends on the observer—what he is trying to measure.

It's tempting to dismiss the above findings as mere oddities except when considering the role of observership in shaping reality. But other experiments have shown the same results. For example, in a 1984 experiment at the University of Maryland, physicists set up a light source and an ingenious arrangement of mirrors to provide a number of possible photon routes. They were able to show that a photon's path was not fixed until a measurement was made. Even more baffling is that such measurements were made *after* the photons had left the light source and were already on their way through the circuit of mirrors. By the time the physicists decided which measurement to make, the photon had already found that path! If they chose to locate the photon on one particular pathway, it was already traveling along that route! If they chose a different pathway, it was there! The physicist's measurements made in the present somehow determined the photon's past. By their measurements, the observers could retroactively force the photons along one particular pathway or another, even though the photons had already begun their circuitous flight through the course of mirrors and before the detectors were positioned. It is a mind-boggling idea—"a tenuous lead, a clue that the mystery of creation may lie not in the distant past but in the living present."[7]

Take a moment to consider the implications of the above statement—that creation does not necessarily lay buried within the distant past but within *our living present*. The universe, our lives, etc. are a work in progress. As conscious observers, we partake in the creation of a participatory universe. As Stanford University physicist Andrei Linde put it:

> "The universe and the observer exist as a pair...We are together, the universe and us. The moment you say that the universe exists without any observers, I cannot make any sense out of that. I cannot imagine a consistent theory of everything that ignores consciousness. A recording device cannot play the role of an observer, because who will read what is written on this recording device? In order for us to see that something happens, and say to one another that something happens, you need to have a universe, you need to have a recording device, and you need to have us. It's not enough for the information to be stored somewhere, completely inaccessible to anybody. It's necessary for somebody to look at it. You need an observer who looks at the universe. In the absence of observers, our universe is dead."[8]

If you find the above information confounding, join the crowd. But don't let it put you off, because quantum discoveries substantiate what the Bible has said all along. God has created a garden of life founded on principles of *seeing* and *hearing*. We shape and reshape reality based on our focused intentions and conscientious awareness. We are created in the image and likeness (i.e., similitude, after the same manner) of God (Genesis 1:26–27). Within each of us lies the same untapped reserves of potential. But we must grow in coherence with the word of God. "According to your faith will it be done to you," said Jesus (Matthew 9:29, NIV). Nothing is too difficult for God's people. With faith as small as a mustard seed, we can say to any mountain, "Move from here to there and it will move. Nothing is impossible for us (Matthew 17:20). Conversely, we inhibit many miracles because of our lack of faith (Matthew 13:58; 14:31).

Andrei Linde tells a very interesting story in this regard:

> I come from Russia, where there is a fairy tale about two frogs in a can of sour cream. The frogs were drowning in the cream. There was nothing solid there; they could not jump from the can. One of the frogs understood there was no hope, and he stopped beating the sour cream with his legs. He just died. He drowned in sour cream. The other one did not want to give up. There was absolutely no way it could change anything, but it just kept kicking and kicking and kicking. And then all of a sudden, the sour cream was churned into butter. Then the frog stood on the butter and jumped out of the can. So you look at the sour cream and you think, 'There is no way I can do anything with that.' But sometimes, unexpected things happen."[9]

The Reubenic Principle of Seeing

> The limit to our ability to observe the universe determines the boundaries of reality. Physical reality and observability are tied together. If you and I cannot observe it, it does not exist... or is it perhaps, if it exists, it is because you and I observe it?
>
> Evan H. Walker[1]

I began this appendix by quoting the eminent American theoretical physicist John Wheeler. Wheeler had a colorful way with words, popularizing the expression *black hole* to depict gravitational collapse.

He also coined the word *wormhole* to describe hypothetical tunnels in space-time. In particular, it was his provocative idea, something he called *genesis by observership*, which captured my attention. Wheeler believed that our observations contribute to the creation of physical reality. "To Wheeler we are not simply bystanders on a cosmic stage; we are shapers and creators living in a participatory universe."[2]

In a 1983 interview and later quoted by Dennis Overbye in the *New York Times* (April 14, 2008), Wheeler said: "If there's one thing in physics I feel more responsible for than any other, it's the perception of how everything fits together."[3]

God's *seeing*, as depicted in the Creation text (Genesis 1:4, 10, 12, 18, 21, 25, and 31), denotes much more than a mere glance. His *seeing* (*ra'ah* in the original language) signifies observation with discernment; it is an expression of perception. According to the Keil and Delitzsch Commentary:

> God's seeing is not a mere expression of the delight of the eye or of pleasure in His work, but is of the deepest significance to every created thing, being the seal of the perfection which God has impressed upon it, and by which its continuance before God and through God is determined.[4]

It is this *fitting together of things* that is the subject of *The Divine Conception*. How do things properly fit together? If we can only discover this, we can then begin to reshuffle the deck of cards dealt us and revitalize our destinies.

The mechanics of *The Divine Conception* are delineated throughout the entirety of scripture. Christ alluded to them when speaking of humankind's suffering. "Though seeing, they do not see," He preached. "Though hearing, they do not hear or understand" (Matthew 13:13a, NIV). He then identified our problem as a matter of the heart (the seat of our mental and physical powers and capacities). "For this people's heart has become calloused [become insensitive or dull]," He declared (v. 15a, NIV). It is because we hardly hear with our ears and have closed their eyes that we don't understand and remain unhealed (are less than whole).

You may recall that Abraham first met "the Seeing God," *Jehovah-jireh*, upon the lofty heights of Moriah (Genesis 22:14). He called that place The Lord Will Provide (literally, see to it). "And to this day it is said, 'On the mountain of the Lord it will be provided.'" (v. 14b, NIV).

What Abraham didn't understand, however, was that such awakenings are also accompanied with ability to see them through. Thus, he too could "see to it" as did the Lord. He was God's emissary of fruitfulness with ability to counteract curses of decrease and infertility. "He is a prophet, and he will pray for you and you will live," [declared the Lord]. "But if you do not return her [Sarai], you may be sure that you and all yours will die" (Genesis 20:7, NIV). This is the epitome of Christ's wholeness as explained in Matthew 13:15.

We've studied at length Hagar's visitations whereby aspects of the Lord's divinity were revealed to her. She called Him *El-Roi*, The God Who Sees Me (Genesis 16:13a), declaring, "I have now *seen* the One who *sees* me" (v. 13b, NIV, emphasis mine). Henceforth, I believe that she, like Abraham, was granted ability. God increased her with a multitude of descendants (Genesis 16:10). He gave her capacity and capability in keeping with His visions.

Subsequently, the scriptures also reveal that Isaac shared in his father's most holy anointing of increase (Genesis 26). He could reap where others could not (v(v). 12–15). "We saw clearly that the Lord was with you," said Abimelech to him (v. 28, NIV).

Likewise, Isaac's son took up that same mantle of anointing. As *Israel*, Jacob prevailed with God and with men (Genesis 32:28). Appropriately, his firstborn son was named *Reuben*. The root of Reuben's name, *ra'ah*, signifies true and right sight. Reuben was the beginning of his father's strength (Genesis 49:3a). As declared by Israel, he was "excelling in honor, excelling in power" (Genesis 49:3b, NIV). "Redeem all your firstborn sons," declares the Lord. "No one is to appear [*ra'ah*] before Me empty handed [ineffectually]" (Exodus 34:20, NIV).

Sadly, Reuben abused his power and sinned against his father's bed of procreation (i.e., proliferation). Hence, his father declared his fate among men. "Turbulent as the waters, you will no longer excel," Israel prophesied (Genesis 49:4a, NIV). The Amplified Bible renders this same passage, "unstable *and* boiling over like water, you shall not excel *and* have the preeminence [of the firstborn]..."

Reuben's special strength and ability within the family of men has since become ineffectual (i.e., flawed, imperfect). He lost his privileged place of strength's beginning within Israel (1 Chronicles 5:1–2). "As Jacob's firstborn son, Reuben should have been a strong man with dignity, who brought honor to his father and family, but he was a weak man who disgraced his family by defiling his father's bed."[5]

Israel's prophetic words regarding Reuben's heritage is fascinating. "Turbulent as the waters," he declared (Genesis 49:4a, NIV). He would no longer "excel" in honor and power (Genesis 49:4a, NIV) so that Reuben's influence within the community of man would become chaotic and muddled. Israel's word choice, "turbulent as the waters," is remarkable in that quantum mechanics (the science of matter and energy at its most finite limits) has shown that light (that which impacts our eyes so that we see) and water have much in common in their wave properties. When focused, waves amplify their energies, and vision is clear and sharp. The focused energy of the laser is only one example. In like manner, harmonious waves of water join together to form huge, rogue waves with tremendous potential. We are all familiar with the destructive force of tsunamis.

Despite the fact that Reuben lost his privilege as strength's beginning within Israel, *seeing* is still God's foundational principle at the heart of the universe. It is a complicated web of relationships in which the observer is an integral part.

> A careful analysis of the process of observation in atomic physics has shown that the subatomic particles have no meaning as isolated entities, but can only be understood as interconnections between the preparation of an experiment and the subsequent measurement. Quantum theory thus reveals a basic oneness of the universe. It shows that we cannot decompose the world into independently existing smallest units. As we penetrate into matter, nature does not show us any isolated "basic building blocks," but rather appears as a complicated web of relations between

the various parts of the whole. These relations always include the observer in an essential way. The human observer constitutes the final link in the chain of observational processes, and the properties of any atomic object can only be understood in terms of the object's interaction with the observer. This means that the classical ideal of an objective description of nature is no longer valid.[6]

Paul Davies, author of *God & The New Physics*, states:

When Newton invented his laws of mechanics, people took this to be the death of the freewill concept. According to Newton's theory, the universe is like a giant clockwork, unwinding along a rigid, pre-determined pathway towards an unalterable final state.... Then along came the new physics with its relativity of time and space and its quantum uncertainty. The whole issue of freedom of choice and determinism went back into the melting pot.[7]

Because of inherent "turbulence" prophesied by Israel, Reuben's legacy of perception faded into ignominy. Very few descendants of Reuben are distinguished as leaders in the Holy Scriptures. Furthermore, the tribe declined in numbers between the Exodus and the entrance into the Promised Land (Numbers 1:20–21; 2:11; 26:7). Additionally, Dathan and Abiram, Reubenites by birth, joined with Korah in rebellion against God's appointed leadership. The scriptures say they "became insolent and rose up against Moses" (Numbers 16:1–2, NIV). Thousands died as a consequence.

But Reuben's rejection and subsequent loss of strength and influence was not without reprieve. When questioned as to His ministry, Jesus said His mission was to proclaim freedom for the prisoners and *recovery of sight* for the blind. "The Spirit of the Lord is on Me," He proclaimed, "because He has anointed Me to preach good news to the poor. He has sent Me to proclaim freedom for the prisoners and *recovery of sight* for the blind, to release the oppressed, to proclaim the year of the Lord's favor" (Luke 4:18–19, NIV, emphasis mine). It is obvious from this passage that Jesus wasn't speaking of people who were physically sightless. His reference was to spiritual sightedness at the higher levels of perception. Consequently, our prerogative as fellow heirs with Christ is to see God, behold His handiwork, and have ability to "see to it." "The eye is the lamp of the body," said Jesus. "If your eyes are good, your whole body will be full of light. But if your eyes are bad, your whole body will be full of darkness. If then the light within you is darkness, how great is that darkness!" (Matthew 6:22–23, NIV).

With the advent of quantum physics, science has now born out the importance of the human observer and his "observership" in the creative process (i.e., the bed of procreation). Quantum theory has demolished the conventional concepts of solid objects and of nature's stringent deterministic laws. Capra emphatically states:

> At the subatomic level, the solid-material objects of classical physics dissolve into wave-like patterns of probabilities, and these patterns, ultimately, do not represent probabilities of things, but rather probabilities of interconnections. A careful analysis of the process of observation in atomic physics has shown that the subatomic particles have no meaning as isolated entities, but can only be understood as interconnections between the preparation of an experiment and the subsequent measurement.[8]

Quantum theory has given the observer with a vital role in the nature of physical reality. No longer is there a strict separation between determinism and free will as once believed. "There is concrete experimental evidence against the notion of 'objective reality,'" states Paul Davies. "This appears to offer human beings a unique ability to influence the structure of the physical universe in a way that was undreamt of in Newton's day."[9]

Reuben's diminished capacity and ability need no longer restrain you or me. With the advent of Christ, our sight is recovered!

In conclusion, the importance of the observer and observership in the creative process (i.e., the bed of procreation) is now proven by the new physics. But the process of seeing with a measured eye is only the beginning of strength. It is the first part of God's holy equation and must be accompanying by understanding (hearing) for clarity and applicability. This is the legacy of Simeon, Israel's second son, and will be discussed in the next section. The Simeonic principle, when linked with the third and fourth dynamics of God's creative protocol—the Levitic and Judaic Principles—divinely equips us for liberty in Christ. After Jesus proclaimed freedom for the prisoners, recovery of sight for the blind, and release of the oppressed (i.e., the year of the Lord's favor), He declared, "Today this scripture is fulfilled in your hearing" (Luke 4:21, NIV).

The Simeonic and Levitic Principles

Seeing is the preeminent principle of God's kingdom. As Israel's firstborn son, Reuben became the first sign of his father's strength. Consequently, he is worthy of a double portion of all his father's blessing (Deuteronomy 21:17). But, as previously noted, without proper understanding and wisdom as to relevance and applicability, his sightedness was of little value. Hence, God's Reubenic principle faded into ignominy. From this we learn the value of coupling our gifted sightedness with the Simeonic and Levitic principles of hearing with requisite affiliation and agreement (companionship), respectively. These are the Lord's second and third doctrines within His creative scheme of deliverance. When brought to fruition by requisite action (the Judaic Principle) we are supplied to abundance. We sow our seed on good soil, hearing and accepting the word so as to produce a crop that is thirty, sixty and one-hundred times what is sown (Mark 4:20).

These principles are dramatically shown in Matthew's tale of Jesus' miraculous feeding of the multitude. Evening was quickly approaching and the huge, swelling crowd of people that followed Jesus was hungry. "This is a remote place, and it's already getting late," observed the disciples. "Send the crowds away, so they can go to the villages and buy themselves some food." (Matthew 14:15, NIV).

But Jesus seized on the moment to teach His disciples a valuable lesson regarding kingdom increase. "They do not need to go away," He said. "*You* give them something to eat."

The disciples were bewildered. Where would *they* find the resources to feed the multitude? It would take at least eight months wages to pay the check.

Their eyes were on the problem, not the solution. Thus, Jesus began by redirecting their eyes. Taking what they had from their hands, five loaves of bread and two fish, Jesus looked up to heaven (v. 19). I am confident the disciples' eyes also turned upward as Jesus turned their gaze heavenward. Then Jesus blessed (*eulogeo* in the original text) the food in their hearing. "He gave thanks and broke the loaves" (Matthew 14:19a, NIV). In other words, He praised God with open hands. After giving thanks, Jesus broke the bread and fish into twelve small portions and distributed the pieces to His disciples. Although it is unstated, I am confident they each looked at their paltry portion and thought, "What am I to do with so small an amount?" His disciples' intent (their reasoning and mental faculties) was tested. God's blessings went from His hands to their hands; and from their hands to those of the needy.

With a shrug of their shoulders and perhaps an anxious sideways glance at their fellows, they set out on their assigned tasks. They each took their seemingly insignificant portion to their group and began to distributed. Thereby, they companioned the Lord's cause which is the ideal of Levitic connectedness. They gave out of their supposed need to discover, in the end, that they had more than enough to feed the starving multitude. But they had to be rightly joined with Christ to do so.

Matthew tells us "they [the hungry masses] all ate and were satisfied" (Matthew 14:20a, NIV). Another version says everyone was "filled" (NKJV). The Bible in Basic English adds that the multitude "all took of the food and had enough" (BBE). This is the essence of contentedness. The entire world hungers for that which is the prerogative of God's people. With gifted hands we mete out satisfaction and happiness (that which fulfills). All this begins by first looking toward heaven (God), refocusing our eyes, understanding what is possible when we believe, and then becoming companions with God in His work.

Afterward, the disciples picked up twelve basketfuls of broken pieces that were left over. They were a token of God's unity and completeness. Only then, after the people had been fed and fully satisfied, did Jesus dismiss the crowd. No one in the Christ's camp went away hungry. He would not suffer them to faint from exhaustion or collapse along the way as they returned home at day's end (Matthew 15:32).

As the twilight of evening began to fall, Jesus commissioned His disciples to go on ahead of Him. Without reservation, the merry band got into a boat and began their journey to the other side of Galilee's sea. But as they went, and when they were a considerable distance from land, a fierce storm broke forth upon them. Jesus went out to meet them, walking on the water, but the disciples saw Him and were terrified. "It is a ghost!" they screamed with fright (Matthew 14:26, AMP).

"Take courage! It is I," said Jesus. "Don't be afraid." Then He later challenged Peter, and all who were with him: "You of little faith, why did you doubt?" (v. 31, NIV)

After feeding the multitude of people with only five loaves of bread and two small fishes, and after taking part in the miracle themselves, the disciples should have learned valuable lessons regarding God's kingdom increase. But from their reaction to Jesus when they saw Him walking on the water, and from Peter's subsequent show of unbelief, the disciples still had much to learn. Christ's rebuke suggests that they had ability to overcome the storm but didn't benefit by it. They had all they needed to defeat their fears and doubts, and also sufficient strength to succeed in the face of adversity, but failed to appropriate it.

Jesus got into a boat to cross to the other side. Life is forever a series of such crossings from one truth or reality to another. Jesus, being aware of his disciples' consternation (for they had insufficient provision for the journey), said to them, "Why do you reason because you have no bread? Do you not yet perceive or understand (i.e., *suniemi* in the Greek)? Is your heart still hardened? Having eyes, do you not see? And having ears, do you not hear? And do you not remember? When I broke the five loaves for the five thousand, how many baskets full of fragments did you take up?" (Mark 8:17–19, NKJV). Expressed is our ubiquitous concern and Jesus's response. The weight of insufficient provision is eased by right discernment, understanding, and an established heart (Isaiah 6:9,10; Jeremiah 5:21).

The root of understanding (*suniemi* in the language of the Bible) is *hiemi*, which means *to put together*, i.e., (mentally) *to comprehend; by implication, to act piously*.[1] It is a moral reflection so as to put together the individual pieces, the union of facts, or the amalgamation of features to form a whole. We must collect together the individual pieces and then rightly assemble them as we do a puzzle. Only then can we adequately address our lack and insufficiency. "Therefore do not be foolish, but understand (*suniemi*) what the Lord's will is," writes Paul (Ephesians 5:17, NIV).

The Biology of Belief is a groundbreaking treatise on biology's new frontier, one that has the potential to radically change our understanding of life. The author, Bruce H. Lipton, PhD, is a former medial school professor and research scientist.

> My new understanding of the nature of life not only corroborated my stem cell research but also, I realized, contradicted another *belief* or mainstream science that I had been propounding to my students—the *belief* that allopathic medicine is the only kind of medicine that merits consideration in medical school. By finally giving the energy-based environment its due, it provided for a grand convergence uniting the science and practice of allopathic medicine, complementary medicine, and the spiritual wisdom of ancient and modern faiths.[2]

On a personal level, Dr. Lipton knew at the moment of insight that he'd gotten himself stuck simply by *believing* that he was fated to have a spectacularly unsuccessful personal life. "I thought I was one of those people victimized by a missing or mutant happiness gene," he writes.[3]

> "There is no doubt that human beings have a great capacity for sticking to false *beliefs* with great passion and tenacity, and hyper-rational scientists are not immune. Our well-developed nervous system, headed by our big

brain, is testament that our awareness is far more complicated than that of a single cell. When our uniquely human minds get involved, we can choose to perceive the environment in different ways, unlike a single cell whose awareness is more reflexive.

> "I was exhilarated by the new realization that I could change the character of my life by changing my *beliefs*. I was instantly energized because I realized that there was a science-based path that would take me from my job as a perennial 'victim' to my new position as 'co-creator' of my destiny."[4]

Through his studies of cell communities (which he describes in Chapter One of his book, *Lessons from the Petri Dish*), Bruce Lipton came to realize that we are not "victims of our genes, but master of our fates, able to create lives overflowing with peace, happiness, and love."[5] He describes his *eureka moment* in terms he best understands—the dynamics of super-saturated solutions in chemistry:

> These solutions, which look like plain water, are fully saturated with a dissolved substance. They are so saturated that just one more drop of the solute causes a dramatic reaction in which all the dissolved materials instantly coalesce into a giant crystal.... I experienced a moment of insight that transformed me, not into a crystal, but into a membrane-centered biologist who no longer had any excuses for messing up his life.[6]

Have you ever had such a moment, a *eureka moment*, when realization suddenly flooded into your soul? At such times, the pieces of life's puzzle abruptly fall into place, and, out of the blue, you see how they fit together. Such *go-ahead* moments are part and parcel with God's Simeonic principle—His hearing dynamic in the creative scheme of events.

After eating the forbidden fruit, the eyes of Adam and Eve were abruptly opened, and they became conscious of their nakedness

(Genesis 3:7). Then, when they heard the sound of the Lord walking in the garden, they were filled with fear. They'd heard His footsteps in the past, but never like that. There was something in them that caused dread and panic. Hence, in the downward spiral of events that followed, Adam and Eve hid among the trees, shunning the Lord's presence.

Matthew Henry comments on the steps of their transgression. "They were not steps upward," he remarks, "but downward towards the pit—steps that take hold on hell."[7] Of note is that their steps are the same as those that also take hold of heaven. "First, she [Eve] saw," Henry observes.

> She should have turned away her eyes from beholding vanity; but she enters into temptation, by looking with pleasure on the forbidden fruit. Observe, a great deal of sin [and blessing, whichever the case may be] comes in at the eyes. At these windows, Satan throws in those fiery darts, which pierce and poison the heart. The eye affects the heart with guilt as well as grief. Let us therefore ... make a covenant with our eyes, not to look on that which we are in danger of lusting after (Proverbs 23:31; Matthew 5:28). Let the fear of God be always to us for a covering of the eyes (ch. 20:16).[8]

First, Eve saw. Then the passage adds that she saw that the fruit of the tree was *good*; that is, pleasing to the eye and desirable for gaining wisdom (Genesis 3:6a). Here, in a nutshell, are the first two principles of the Lord's creative scheme—the dynamics of Reuben and Simeon.

But it is never enough to merely look and comprehend with understanding. Eve also had to divorce herself from her affections and affiliation with God. Thus, by partaking of the fruit and eating thereof, she joined with the devil in her disobedience and, because sin loves company, she shared it with Adam. The cycle was complete. Eve gave some of the ill-gotten fruit to her husband who was with her, and they both ate (v. 6b). This was the consummation of the deadly deed—the combined operations of Levi and Judah were coupled with those of Reuben and Simeon.

Suddenly, their eyes were jointly opened and knowingness flooded into their souls. They knew good *and* evil (Genesis 3:5). God warns us to be careful because His creative principles have the potential for both good and evil, blessings and curses. Thereafter, He called heaven and earth as His witnesses. He declared, "I have set before you life and death, blessings and curses. Now choose life, so that you and your children may live and that you may love the Lord your God, listen to his voice, and hold fast to him. For the Lord is your life, and he will give you many years in the land he swore to give to your fathers, Abraham, Isaac and Jacob" (Deuteronomy 30:19–20, NIV).

The story of Adam and Eve concludes with the summative statement, "Then the eyes of both of them were opened, *and they realized*" (Genesis 3:7, NIV, emphasis mine). "The devil did not take it, and put it into her (Eve's) mouth," comments Matthew Henry, "whether she would or no; but she herself took it. Satan may tempt, but he cannot force; may persuade us to cast ourselves down, but he cannot cast us down (Matthew 4:6)."[9] Eve reached out and took the fruit and consumed it and gave of it to her husband. The Judaic principle of active participation was the final act of her doing (in this case, for evil).

> She gave it to him, persuading him with the same arguments that the serpent had used with her, adding this to all the rest, that she herself had eaten of it, and found it so far from being deadly that it was extremely pleasant and grateful. Stolen waters are sweet.... Those that have themselves done ill are commonly willing to draw in others to do the same. As was the devil, so was Eve, no sooner a sinner than a tempter.[10]

"Where are you?" said God when He came looking for the couple. But Adam and Eve had hidden themselves because they heard Him in the garden and *realized* (*yada'*; to ascertain by seeing, recognize) the shame of their nakedness before Him.

"I heard (*shama'*; the root of Simeon's name which means to hear intelligently) You in the garden, and I was afraid because I was naked; so I hid" said Adam ashamedly (v. 10, NIV).

"Who told you that you were naked?" demanded the Lord, knowing that they had sin. God didn't ask because He needed information. Being God, He is all knowing. Rather, He asked for Adam and Eve's sake, to give them the opportunity to understand their deception and confess their sin. His question is also rightly asked so that you and I might grasp the steps of our own demise. We begin with disobedience and then progress down the avenue of doubt to disaffection. Finally, we put feet to our sins and consummate our creation (in this case, that which brings havoc and disarray).

God could have justly destroyed Adam and Eve. When asked pointblank if he'd eaten of the tree, Adam did not readily admit his sin. Instead, he blamed both God and his wife! When God questioned Eve, she put the blame on serpent. She didn't say, "The serpent that *You* created, but perhaps thought it. "There were excuses but no confessions."[11] Joined hand in hand, Adam and Eve were willing partners, having actively participated together. God's desire, in His benevolent questioning of the couple, was to help them. But they would not avail themselves of His aid.

Mark's gospel records the story of a certain blind man from Bethsaida. The man's neighbors, the townspeople of Bethsaida, begged Jesus to *touch* him (Mark 8:22, NIV, AMP, NKJV). But Jesus didn't immediately heal the man. Instead, He first took the blind man by the hand and led him outside the village. Why did Jesus do this? How did His "taking the man's hand" affirm the restorative process? I believe it is the same process at work within the fall of Adam and Eve. We lightly skip over this seemingly innocuous passage without realizing its relevance in the solution of our own various ills.

By taking the man's hand, Jesus demonstrated the essential element of affiliation. By this simple act, God joined with the man and his predicament. Christ would not flippantly work His miracle without the necessary bond of fellowship. Hence, the two of them joined hands, one with the other. This is the avenue of whole-hearted attachment in the operation of God's deliverance—the essential

Levitic connection. It is a necessary ingredient of our healing and its continuance. "Blessed are the pure in heart," said Jesus, "for they shall see God" (Matthew 5:8).

Why did Christ lead the man outside his hometown of Bethsaida? I think the townspeople's unbelief and skepticism had a chilling effect upon God's restorative processes. This is perhaps why Jesus later forbade the man to return to his native Bethsaida. The atmosphere of that place was deleterious to the miracle and its continuance. Somehow, our faith and belief or contrary doubts and disbelief affect the atmosphere of God's revival and its persistence. It was for this reason that Jesus didn't do any miracles in His own hometown (Mark 6:5). Matthew remarks, "He did not do many miracles there because of their lack of faith" (13:58, NIV). Moreover, Jesus denounced several other cities because His miracles brought no repentance (Matthew 11:20). True repentance means we must rethink our ways and feel compunction. The *Theological Dictionary of the New Testament* notes that the Greek verb translated as *repent* means *to change one's mind, adopt another view,* or *change one's feelings*.[12] Only by turning and joining with God can we avail ourselves of His great strength and power.

Quantum theory and atomic physics have revealed there is an essential interconnectedness within the universe. All things are joined together, as if hand in hand. We cannot decompose the world into independently existing parts. There is "a universal interwovenness that always includes the human observer and his or her consciousness."[13]

> At the atomic level, "objects" can only be understood in terms of the interaction between the processes of preparation and measurement. The end of this chain of processes lies always in the consciousness of the human observer.[14]

A fundamental feature of the atomic reality is the universal interconnectedness of things and events. As Niels Bohr put it, "Isolated material particles are abstractions, their properties being definable and observable only through their interaction with other systems."[15] Quantum theory has forced us to see the universe as a complicated web of relations between the various parts of a unified whole. Says the noted physicist Werner Heisenberg, "The world thus appears as a complicated tissue of events, in which connections of different kinds alternate or overlap or combine and thereby determine the texture of the whole."[16] Capra refers to this as the "web philosophy" in modern physics, which describes the world as "a perfect network of mutual relations where all things and events interact with each other in an infinitely complicated way."[17]

After taking the man's hand to lead him to a place less congested and less distracting, Jesus laid His hands upon the man's eyes. He touched him (Mark 8:22).

"Do you see anything?" asked Jesus (Mark 8:23, NIV). Miraculously, the man's sight was restored but was distorted and impaired. This is the "turbulence" prophesied by Israel when declaring the fate of Reuben in the affairs of humankind.

The scripture says the man "looked up" and said, "I see people; they look like trees walking around" (v. 24, NIV). The phrase, "looked up" summarizes the beginning of all miracles. Be free of that which hinders you by "looking up," according to the dictate of God. The verb used here also means *to look through, penetrate by vision*, or *to look fixedly*.[18] How much of life do we miss because our glance is cursory and lacks understanding or perception? Mankind's *seeing* has its type in God's seeing, so my challenge and yours is to always begin by *looking up* so as to rightly see with penetrating vision.

To rightly see is divin, and as the passage in Mark 8:24 reveals, God's intention is that His people see with clarity. Consequently, Jesus once again applied His hands to the man's unfocused eyes, and this time, the man looked intently. His sight was fully restored, and he saw everything distinctly, "even what was at a distance" (Mark 8:25b, AMP). The Creator's intention is not clouded, obstructed vision, but focused discernment.

> God's seeing is not a mere expression of the delight of the eye or of pleasure in His work, but is of the deepest significance to every created thing, being the seal of the perfection which God has impressed upon it, and by

which its continuance before God and through God is determined.[19]

Jesus came to bestow unimpaired capacity and capability. With seeing ability, His people begin the participatory process as fellow initiators with God (Genesis 1:26–27; 20:7; Matthew 7:7–8) so as to rightly assemble life's pieces into a meaningful whole (Matthew 13:13–23). "Hearken unto me every one of you, and understand," declared the Lord (Mark 7:14, KJV). Later, Jesus questioned His followers, saying, "Do you have eyes but fail to see, and ears but fail to hear?...Do you still not understand?" (Mark 8:18–21, NIV). "Turbulent as the waters, you will no longer excel," declared the Lord to His seeing son (Reuben) who'd abused his power (Genesis 49:4a, NIV). But, praise God, no longer is instability and its subsequent lack our heritage. "The eye is the lamp of the body," declares the Lord. "If your eyes are good, your whole body will be full of light" (Matthew 6:22, NIV).

It is no accident that the biblical narrative of the blind man's restoration falls on the heels of Christ's most pressing question, "Do you still not understand?" (Mark 8:21, NIV). The Amplified Bible says, "And He kept repeating, 'Do you not yet understand?'" (v. 21, AMP) Clarity of understanding is central to our liberty and salvation in Christ. Why else do we have this story?

Follow the Lord's lead. Take His hand and be led outside your village of doubt. Leave behind that which restrains you (i.e., distractions, confusion, doubts, and whatever else that hinders you). Then allow Jesus to caress your eyes. "Look up, and lift up your heads; for your redemption draweth nigh" (Luke 21:28, KJV).

"Look carefully then how you walk!" admonishes the Apostle Paul. "Live purposefully and worthily and accurately," he writes in his letter to the Ephesians, "not as the unwise and witless, but as wise (sensible, intelligent people), making the very most of the time [buying up each opportunity], because the days are evil. Therefore do not be vague and thoughtless and foolish, but understanding [*suniemi*] and firmly grasping what the will of the Lord is." (Ephesians 5:15–17, AMP).

> Hear [*shama,'* hear intelligently with implication of attention and obedience], O Israel. The Lord our God, the Lord is one. Love the Lord your God with all your heart and with all your soul and with all your strength [the Levitic Principle]. These commandments that I give you today are to be upon your hearts. Impress them on your children. Talk about them when you sit at home and when you walk along the road, when you lie down and when you get up. Tie them as symbols on your hands and bind them on your foreheads. Write them on the doorframes of your houses and on your gates.
>
> Deuteronomy 6:4–9 (NIV)

Thus, the man's sight was fully restored, and he saw everything clearly (*telaugos; in a far-shining manner*).[20] The prefix of *telaugos, tele*, refers to the uttermost limit, and *auge* is a reference to *radiance*.[21] *Thayer's Greek Lexicon* says this word implies "full of light"[22] and *Strong's Concordance* says *auge* refers to a ray of light.[23]

I believe it is no small coincidence that the blind man was living in Bethsaida's vicinity. Furthermore, it was also important to the man's continued healing vitality that he not return again to that den of unbelief. Hence, Jesus sent him home, saying, "Don't go into the village" (Mark 8:26, NIV). "Woe to you, Bethsaida!" said Christ. "For if the miracles that were performed in you had been performed in Tyre and Sidon, they would have repented long ago, sitting in sackcloth and ashes" (Luke 10:13, NIV). Bethsaida epitomizes all that is wrong with society when the united strengths of Simeon and Levi are dispersed (diluted). The brother's swords are weapons of violence (Genesis 49:5). Their "council" and "assembly" has awesome potential within God's kingdom, but cursed is their anger and wrath, for it is fierce and cruel. "I will divide them in Jacob and scatter them in Israel" declared the Lord (Genesis 49:6–7, NKJV). These two brothers, when acting in concert as self-willed siblings, have the potential of anarchy, violence, and injustice. "Into their secret, come not, O my soul!" declared Israel. "Unto their assembly be not united, O mine honor. For in their anger they slew a man, and in their self-will eradicated a prince" (Genesis 49:6, YLT). Their anger and fury parallels "as they pleased," which is suggestive of unbridled self-indulgence ("just for sport," NLT). Just imagine the different outcome if, instead of unbridled anger and pleasure, the united strength of Simeon and Levi were turned to good. When acting in concert in your life and mine, unimaginable peace and wellbeing would result.

So it was that Jesus sent the man with radiant eyes home. His testimony had tremendous potential to greatly impact those whom he knew. He was God's empowered emissary of diving sight. Even as Eve shared her fruit with her husband (in that case to his detriment), the sighted man's duty was to share his special fruit for the betterment of all who knew him. To paraphrase Bruce Lipton, he was taken from his job as a perennial "victim" to a new position as "co-creator" of his destiny.[24]

The King James translation renders Genesis 49:6 as "O my soul, come not thou into their *secret*," suggestive of "intimacy" or "intimate consultation."[25] *The Theological Wordbook of the Old Testament* says, "The word stresses that intelligent [well-informed] counsel can be a key to good success (Proverbs 15:22)."[26] Israel's disassociation with his two sons, Simeon and Levi, demonstrates their joint sway within the affairs of men. They are powerful spiritual allies!

For all these reasons, I strongly urge you to test and approve what is the will of God (His good, pleasing, and perfect will) concerning you (Romans 12:2). Test your special knowingness and knowhow by the standard of God's Word as it is revealed in the Bible. From the lessons of Simeon and Levi, ask yourself if your path leads to justice and wellbeing—God's *shalom* (i.e., His completeness, wholeness, welfare, and health)—or death and wanton disregard of life. When rightly applied, the joint council of Simeon and Levi has tremendous potential for good and ease or distress and evil. Understand that ill intent can quickly escalate toward evil and destruction. "Take heed to yourselves, lest you forget," warned Moses (Deuteronomy 4:23a, AMP).

> The relationship is one of harmony and wholeness, which is the opposite of the state of strife and war: "I am for peace: but when I speak, they are for war" (Psalm

120:7). *Shalom* as a harmonious state of the soul and mind encourages the development of the faculties and powers. The state of being at ease is experienced both externally and internally. In Hebrew it finds expression in the phrase *beshalom* (*in peace*): "I will both lay me down in peace [*beshalom*], and sleep: for thou, Lord, only makest me dwell in safety" (Psalm 4:8).[27]

Whole-hearted agreement encompasses the whole being. It is our affiliation and commitment (the Levitic principle) that energizes our testimony. The combined influence of Simeon and Levi is irresistible (Genesis 49:5).

It has long been recognized that two types of understanding or modes of consciousness exist. The "rational" is derived from everyday experiences and belongs to the realm of the intellect (i.e., differentiated, divided, and determinate thoughts). "Intuitive knowledge," on the other hand, is discernment that transcends intellectual thinking and sensory perception; it is a direct insight that lies outside the realm of the intellect and is often obtained by watching rather than thinking. Fritjof Capra observes that these sudden realizations usually occur when the thinking-mind is quieted. "When the rational mind is silenced, the intuitive mode produces an extraordinary awareness; the environment is experienced in a direct way without the filter of conceptual thinking."[28] This is a non-sensory apprehension of reality. Perhaps it is for this reason for God's dual proclamation regarding Jacob *and* Israel: "I will scatter them [Simeon and Levi] in *Jacob* [possibly suggestive of the rational mind] and disperse them in *Israel* [the intuitive (spiritual) nature]" (Genesis 49:9b, NIV).

Importantly, other religions beside Judaism also recognize one or more of the producing principles revealed in the Holy Scriptures. For example, the notion of observation is embodied in the name for Taoist temples, *kuan*, which originally meant *to look*.[29] Taoists regard their temples as places of observation. Seeing is regarded as the basis of knowing in Buddhist schools; the first item of the Eightfold Path which is the Buddhist's prescription for self-realization. Knowing without seeing is impossible and is the beginning of strength (Genesis

49:3). But knowing with contextual understanding and inherent applicability must also be accompanied by vigorous affiliation and affection. This is the repeated affirmation of Genesis, which establishes God's seeing with agreement (Genesis 1:4, 10, 12, 18, 21, 25, and 31). The Lord observed with sentience and then invested Himself into His creation (i.e., its light, waters, land, the animals, humankind, etc.). The result was fruitfulness, productiveness, and fertility. It was good!

The principles in God's dynamic scheme of increase (right seeing and hearing, affiliation, and vigorous participation) are woven into the fabric of all creation. For example, we see them in operation in Babel's tower (Genesis 11). Verses 5–9 record the Lord's conversation regarding man's inherent capacity and capability. The story begins with the Lord's "seeing." He came down to see (*ra'ah*) the city and the tower that the men were building. Then said the Lord, "If as one people speaking the same language [hearing with implied agreement and affiliation—the joint principles of Simeon and Levi] they have begun to do this, then nothing they plan to do [the fourth principle of active participation—Judah] will be impossible for them. Come, let us go down and confuse [i.e., confound, mix up, cause them to ineffectually hear] their language so they will not understand [i.e., *shama'*] each other" (Genesis 11:6–7, NIV). So the Lord scattered (*puwts* in the original language) them from there over all the earth, and they (i.e., dashed apart into pieces) the people's communal understanding; confounding them. As long as they were one people with one language, they were an unstoppable force capable of almost anything. "They are one people and they have all one language," [observed the Lord,] "and this is only the beginning of what they will do, and now nothing they have imagined they can *do* [*'asah*: accomplish, advance] will be impossible for them" (Genesis 11:6, AMP, emphasis mine). Interestingly, the word translated *scatter* is the same word used in Genesis 49:7, where God said He would "scatter" the joint influence of Simeon and Levi throughout Jacob (i.e., the community of man).

God's Fourth Principle of Deliverance

The act of putting into practice (i.e., *'asah*; accomplishing or advancing) one's unique awareness is God's fourth concept within Israel—Judah. No deliverance is complete without it (Mark 4:12). It is God's final declaration through Leah. She named her fourth son Judah, declaring, "This time I will praise the Lord" (Genesis 29:35b, NIV). Only then was she able to escape her awful fate. Leah turned to do that which was previously revealed through Judah's siblings—Reuben, Simeon, and Levi. With that, the Word of God emphatically states she stopped having children (v. 35c). The Lord's work in and through Leah was finished, at least for a time.

We live in a universe designed by God that is participatory by nature. As noted by Capra, "In atomic physics, then, the scientist cannot play the role of a detached objective observer, but becomes involved in the world he observes to the extent that he influences the properties of the observed objects."[1] This involvement of the observer is perhaps the most important feature of quantum theory and, as John Wheeler suggested, we should consider replacing the word "observer" with "participator." Quoting John Wheeler, Capra writes:

> Nothing is more important about the quantum principle than this, that it destroys the concept of the world as "sitting out there," with the observer safely separated from it by a 20-centimeter slab of plate glass. Even to observe so miniscule an object as an electron, he must shatter the glass. He must reach in. He must install his chosen measuring equipment. It is up to him to decide whether he shall measure position or momentum. To install the equipment to measure the one prevents and excludes his installing the equipment to measure the other. Moreover, the measurement changes the state of the electron. The universe will never afterwards be the same. To describe what has happened, one has to cross out the old word "observer" and put in its place the new word "participator." In some strange sense the universe is a participatory universe.[2]

God's fourth conception within Israel, His Judaic principle of requisite action, is never more dramatically portrayed than in the narrative of Abraham's meeting with God on Moriah's mountaintop (Genesis 22). He'd previously "looked up" and saw the place in the distance (v. 4), suggesting he knew beyond all shadow of doubt what must be done. "God Himself will provide (literally, *see*; *ra'ah*)," he told his son (v. 8).

"Abraham! Abraham!" called God to him from heaven (v. 11).

"Here I am," the man replied with intent. By now he was no stranger to God. He knew the deity of God.

"Do not lay a hand on the boy," [said the Lord]. "Do not do anything to him. Now I *know* that you fear God, because you have not withheld from me your son, your only son" (v. 12, NIV, emphasis mine). "Knowingness" (*yada'*) anchors this passage. It underscores the importance of awareness and discernment in the divine scheme of blessing.

Then Abraham "looked up" (NIV), lifting his eyes (NKJV) to *see* (i.e., *ra'ah*) the ram caught by its horns (v. 13a). We must each look up from our various diversions and preoccupations to behold the Lord's provision.

But one more thing still remained for Abraham to do. He'd lifted his eyes to see, but, of necessity, he also had to catch hold (i.e., *'achaz* in the original text) of God's intended sacrifice. *'Achaz* means *to seize* (often with the accessory idea of holding in possession).[3] *The Theological Wordbook of the Old Testament* notes that the verb's sixty-eight occurrences in Scripture are "rather evenly divided between the literal and metaphorical, both positive and negative. The basic idea of the root is 'to take hold of.'"[4] Thus, Abraham went over and took the ram and sacrificed it.

> Then Abraham looked up and glanced around, and behold, behind him was a ram caught in a thicket by his horns. And Abraham went and took the ram and offered it up for a burnt offering and an ascending sacrifice instead of his son!
>
> Genesis 22:13 (AMP)

What would have been the outcome if Abraham had not rightly answered the Lord's call, if he failed to look up so as to see, or if he failed to "turn" (Mark 4:12) toward the Lord? With eyes fully opened, he'd heard the Lord's voice, he came into agreement with the divine purpose, and then he actively participated with God to bring it to fruition. Thus, God said, "Now I know!" (Genesis 22:12).

God's people are destroyed for lack of knowledge (i.e., Godly skill and cunning) (Hosea 4:6). Bezaleel, one of the inspired builders of God's Holy Tabernacle, was said to be filled "with the spirit of God, in wisdom, and in understanding, and in knowledge, and in all manner of workmanship" (Exodus 31:3, KJV). Regarding his divine enablement, Warren Wiersbe writes: "The Holy Spirit gave Bezaleel and Aholiab the wisdom to know what to do and the ability to do it. In like manner, God has given gifts to His people today so that the church might be built up (1 Cor 12–14; Eph 4:1–17; Rom 12:1). Bezaleel and Aholiab did not do all the work themselves but taught others who assisted them."[5]

"The Lord will provide," Abraham had previously said to his son (Genesis 22:8). Indeed, He did. God literally *saw* to it!

The Lord's response to Abraham's unswerving dedication shows the importance of God's fourth conception within Israel, our participatory obedience, which is the Judaic principle of divine increase.

> "Now I know that you honor and obey God," [said the Lord]..."I make a vow *by My Own name*—the Lord is speaking—that I will richly bless you. Because you did this and did not keep back your only son from me, I promise that I will give you as many descendants as there are stars in the sky or grains of sand along the seashore. Your descendants will conquer their enemies. All the nations will ask me to bless them as I have blessed your descendants—*all because you obeyed* [i.e., *shama'*] My command."
>
> Genesis 22:12a, 15–19 (TEV), emphasis mine.

An aspect of the Lord's divine nature was revealed to Abraham on that fateful day. It had something to do with His revealed name—*Jehovah-jireh*, The Lord Will Provide. "By my Own name I will bless you," declared God. At a loss for words, Abraham called the name of the place *Jehovah-jireh*.

> Abraham looked up and there in a thicket he saw a ram caught by its horns. He went over and took the ram and sacrificed it as a burnt offering instead of his son. So Abraham called that place *The Lord Will Provide. And to this day it is said*, "On the mountain of the Lord it will be provided (*Jehovah-jireh*)."
>
> Genesis 22:13–14 (NIV), emphasis mine.

The *place* was named according to the Lord's manifestation. I believe this suggests that a lingering essence of God's revealed nature remained in that locale—the immediate vicinity of His manifestation. It seems the locale was somehow invested (charged) with the dignity of God's holy presence. The space being altered, it became sacred to the ancients. Lest you think I've lost my mind in this regard, the same is said of the place where Moses met the Lord (Exodus 3). In that instance, God said to him, "Do not draw near this place. Take your sandals off your feet, *for the place where you stand is holy ground*" (v. 5, NKJV, emphasis added). Moreover, when God's cloud rested upon the Tent of Meeting, the tabernacle was somehow charged with God's majesty (His glory) so that no one, not even Moses, could enter.

> Then the cloud covered the Tent of Meeting, and the glory of the Lord filled the tabernacle. Moses could not enter the Tent of Meeting because the cloud had settled upon it, and the glory of the Lord filled the tabernacle.
>
> Exodus 40:34–35 (NIV)

Warren Wiersbe comments that "no matter how expensive the tabernacle was, without the presence of God it was just another tent."⁶ The Lord's *shekinah* glory resided in the tabernacle and it guided the Israelites on their pilgrim journey.

I firmly believe that Abraham did not call upon the name of God *in general* whenever he worshipped on his altar located on Moriah's height. Although unstated, I think Abraham worshipped with dignity in keeping with his specific revelation of God; the divine nature inhabiting the place. I believe he worshipped *Jehovah-jireh*, The Lord Will Provide. Furthermore, the writer of 2 Chronicles applies the name of Moriah to the mount on which Solomon's Temple was built, possibly associating it with the sacrifice of Isaac (2 Chronicles 3:1). Genesis 22:14 also suggests a similar association with this mountain.

Altars were routinely built to honor the specific nature of the revealed Lord. Often, it is said that the saints called on *the name of the Lord* (Genesis 28:18–22; 33:20; 35:7; Exodus 17:15), suggesting their worship was very specific and to the point. For example, when Gideon was gripped by fear and trepidation because of his many enemies, the Lord appeared to him and declared, "Peace! Do not be afraid" (Judges 6:23a). At that moment, I believe Gideon was instantaneously infused with God's *shalom* (i.e., the Lord's welfare and overwhelming peace). Thereafter, Gideon built an altar to the Lord at that site and called it *The Lord Is Peace—Jehovah-shalom* (v. 24a). The Lord's *shalom* (that specific aspect of God's revealed character) somehow inhabited that place and still remains today (v. 24b). Because God's *shalom* is still in residence to this day, I believe that if I were to find it and worship accordingly, I too would experience something of God's *peace* (the resident influence) as revealed to Gideon. "To this day it still stands," declares the Word of God (v. 24b, AMP). Upon that altar, I would not praise God *in general*. Neither would I praise *Jehovah-jireh* at Gideon's altar. I would praise the Lord very specifically, according to the nature and character of God that was purposely revealed there—*Jehovah-shalom*.

Consciousness somehow shapes or alters physical reality, the place where it exists. For this reason, Moriah's mountaintop was sacred and became the center of Jewish culture (2 Chronicles 3:1). On that same site, David was told to go up and build an altar to the Lord. At that time, it was a threshing floor that belonged to

Araunah, the Jebusite (2 Samuel 24:18). When Araunah asked why the king was there, David said, "To buy your threshing floor so I can build an altar to the Lord, that the plague on the people may be stopped" (v. 21, NIV). "I will give all this to the king," said Araunah. "May the Lord your God accept you." But the king replied, "No, I insist on paying you for it. I will not sacrifice to the Lord my God burnt offerings that cost me nothing." So David bought the threshing floor and the oxen and paid fifty shekels of silver for them [which is the price of redemption]. He built an altar to the Lord there and sacrificed burnt offerings and fellowship offerings, and the Lord answered him in behalf of the land, and the plague that was on Israel was stopped (v. 25).

Solomon later built the temple of the Lord in Jerusalem on that same site, which was on Mount Moriah, where God had appeared to his father, David (2 Chronicles 3:1).

Space can literally become charged with an aspect of God's persona, His divine essence, wherever He is in residence. There are numerous examples of this found throughout Scripture. For example, the Lord appeared to Moses in the flames of a burning bush in the desert near Mount Sinai. "Take off your sandals, for the place where you are standing is holy ground," declared God (Exodus 3:5, Acts 7:33, NIV). It was in that same vicinity that God later met Moses and told him to put limits for the people around the mountain. "Tell them," declared the Lord, "'Be careful that you do not go up the mountain or touch the foot of it. Whoever touches the mountain shall surely be put to death'" (Exodus 19:12, NIV). Thereafter, there was "a regular burnt offering instituted at Mount Sinai" as a pleasing aroma, an offering made to the Lord by fire (Numbers 28:6, NIV). The King James Version of the Bible says it was "a continual burnt offering, which was ordained in Mount Sinai for a sweet savor, a sacrifice made by fire unto the Lord." Additionally, the immediate area surrounding the Tent of Meeting was invested with the divine presence of God. It was like a cloud, and Moses could not enter the Tent of Meeting, because God's glory settled upon the area to fill the tabernacle (Exodus 40:35).

In 2001, William Tiller, Walter Dibble, and Michael Kohane published their groundbreaking work on the role of human consciousness in a variety of specific target experiments. They were able to prove that our view of the world we live in strongly shapes the way we think about "space" and its interaction ("conditioning") to influence matter and events within its vicinity. Their research concentrated on four target experiments: (1) Water target experiments to increase the pH of water in equilibrium with air; (2) Water target experiments to decrease the pH of the same type of water in equilibrium with air; (3) *In vitro* thermodynamic activity of the liver enzyme, alkaline phosphatase (ALP); and (4) the ATP/ADP ratio of the energy story molecule, adenosine triphosphate [ATP], to its chemical precursor, ADP, in fruit fly larvae to make them more physically fit. In each of the four target experiments, Tiller et al. applied only human consciousness in the form of specific human intentions. For example, they made no direct chemical additions to the water to change its pH, etc. Their experimental procedure was novel; they used surrogate hosts, simple electronic circuits, to supply the conscious intent that was applied directly to each target experiment. This was because the average human consciousness tends to fluctuate greatly so that a specific consciousness state cannot be highly reproducible from experiment to experiment. Consequently, they captured a specific human intention in a suitable host (a "black box," so to speak) so that the variability of the intention's strength over time, or from experiment to experiment, would be small and manageable. The host device they selected was an electronic circuit of the pre-integrated circuit vintage that was housed in a plastic black box. They called these simple electrical devices IIEDs (Intention Imprinted Electrical Devices). Four well-qualified meditators, each with several decades of regular meditative practice, sat around these devices and proceeded to mentally connect coherently with them so as to "imprint" specific intentions. Thus, their specific "intentions" could be maintained by these simple electrical devices in an uninterrupted flow that was free of outside distractions. Using these simple electronic IIEDs, Tiller et al. thereby maintained focused intentions, previously erratic and feeble, so that they were "more consistent, more direct, and more ordered."[7] The researchers would then place the activated IIEDs (intention imprinted electrical devices) in the proximity of their target experiment—for example, a vessel of water that was being monitored for pH level. In this way, they were able to demonstrate that the water pH could be moved upwards or downwards (depending on the specific intention imprinted into the device). Additionally, their specific *in vitro* enzyme target experiments showed that specific activated IIEDs were able to significantly increase the thermodynamic activity of the enzyme in complete accord with the imprinted intention. *In vivo* studies with fruit flies showed that specific intention increased the ATP/ADP ratio in developing fruit fly larvae, making them more fit by reducing larval development time. Tiller *et al* were able to produce data showing "that the local symmetry, and thus the local physics, changed in very significant ways as a result of continued IIED use in that locale. This is thought to occur," they concluded, "via changes in the degree of order present in the physical vacuum."[8]

Why do we often fail to fully appropriate the adequacy of God? Is it because we are too easily distracted by outside influences and mundane pursuits? Jesus warned of such things in His parable of the Sower (Mark 4:13–20). Conversely, Abraham gave God his undivided affection and was subsequently blessed (Genesis 22:12–18). "Because you have done this," declared the Lord, "I will surely bless you" (v(v). 16–17a, NIV).

In their book, Tiller et al. explain their "conditions for repeatability." They state:

> It is well known that most individual humans have intentions that swing widely over time so that the time-averaged effect over weeks to months is usually of small magnitude. Individual humans having long practice with one of the available inner-self-management techniques [e.g., meditation, healing prayers, concentrated prayer sessions, etc.] ... do much better ... [9]

The sway of focused group intention, meditation, and prayer is well documented throughout the Bible. In one notable example, a scripture says that numerous saints had gathered to wait upon the Lord. "They all joined together constantly in prayer," records Luke, the author of Acts (Acts 1:14a, NIV). Another translation says, "All of these with their minds in full agreement devoted themselves steadfastly to prayer, [waiting together] (AMP). They were one in spirit and purpose to know and do the will of God:

> They persevered in the work to which they had given themselves. They had strong faith in Him whose words had brought and now kept them together. When that faith was tried by delay it bore the test. Continuance in prayer would increase the sense of power at the throne of grace; and this would intensify the longing for the promised blessing. This confident expectation ought to appear in all Christian assemblies, for there are Divine promises yet to be fulfilled.[10]

On the day when the Church first began, peace and unity prevailed. "The day of murmuring had not yet come (Acts 6:1)," comments T.S. Dickson. "Union is strength. A divided Church cannot long remain a praying Church. God answers prayer when it is offered by few or many 'with one accord.' The promise is addressed to those who are 'agreed.'"[11]

Tiller et al. writes: "One may presume that most of these outwardly-directed fluctuations of intention from a large number of uncorrelated individuals tend to cancel each other out because their amplitudes lie in the linear regime."[12] For this reason, Tiller et al. used IIEDs that were "imprinted" to produce their intended result. A select group of four meditators were used who, during a 1–2-hour focused meditation session, imprinted the devices. Using this technique, Tiller and his colleagues were able to eliminate much of the swing or fluctuation of outwardly directed intention of individuals by themselves. From their perspective, the experimental results were influenced by: "The imprinter's training, degree of inner self-management, internal coherence, group cooperative coherence, heart focus, and intentions," as well as other factors, such as "the degree of inner-management and internal coherence of the actual experimenters," "the held attitudes of heart and mind of the experimenters during the course of the experiments," and "the number of times the experiment is repeated in the particular locale."[13]

Using the above techniques, Tiller et al. demonstrated that continued use of an activated IIED at a particular locale eventually led to the "conditioning" of that space. Desired oscillations in air temperature, pH, etc. often continued long after the IIED originally causing the conditioning was removed. The implications of this for religion are enormous because Tiller's findings confirm the affect of spiritual influences on space. Altars, for example, are sacred places invested with our directed intentions (coherent prayers, supplications, and holy meditations). They become charged with God's abiding presence so that the locality is curiously altered. Bethel, for example, was where Abram called on the name of the Lord (Genesis 13:3–4). Later, Jacob discovered the same place and called it "awesome" (awe-inspiring) and "the gate of heaven" (Genesis 28:17, NIV). "This is none other than the house of God," he declared because of the Lord's enduring presence residing there. (v. 17b, NIV). Additionally, the Lord identified Himself with the place calling Himself "the God of Bethel" (31:13, NIV). Jacob's responsibility was to settle there and build an altar because Bethel was his sacred place of communion (Genesis 35:1). Hence, from that time forward, the Israelites went to Bethel to inquire of the Lord (Judges 20:18, 26; 21:2). King Jeroboam, recognizing the spatial integrity of Bethel, also established an altar there that was contradictory to the Lord's spirit that inhabited the place (1 Kings 12:28–30). Consequently, the Lord sent a prophet to cry out against its corrupting influence. "O altar, altar!" said the man concerning this altar. "This is what the Lord says: 'A son named Josiah will be born to the house of David. On you he will sacrifice the priests of the high places who now make offerings here, and human bones will be burned on you.'" (1 Kings 13:1–2, NIV). In anger, King Jeroboam stretched out his hand *from the altar* and said, "Seize him!" As testimony of God's abiding presence at Bethel, the king's outstretched hand immediately shriveled up so that he couldn't pull it back.

Bethel proves that God's spirit can literally inhabit a particular locality. The Holy Scriptures are replete with such examples: Abraham's altar on Mount Moriah (Genesis 22:13–14), the sacred ground where Moses' met with God (Exodus 2:5; 19:11–13), the area around the Tent of Meeting (Exodus 29:42–43, Exodus 40:33–34), and Gideon's altar that still stands today (Judges 6:24).

From this short treatise on altars and the affect of attitudes and directed intentions on their vicinity, and in the light of recent revelations in the field of quantum mechanics, there is little doubt that all creation is indeed invested with the Lord's divine awareness. As His children, and as the spiritual heirs with Abraham, we are co-creators with God. The statement, "and God saw that it was good" is the beginning of our strength. Repeated seven times in the opening chapter of the Bible for emphasis, this testimonial lends credence to what John Wheeler, the eminent American theoretical physicist, called "genesis by observership." As conscious observers, we partake in the creation of a participatory universe. The Lord's seeing with understanding, as well as His unqualified participation in His created work (i.e. personified by His walking in the garden—Genesis 3:8) form the underlying principles upon which all creation and creativity is founded. Israel (the man who prevailed with God as His prince with power), is founded upon precepts espoused in his firstborn sons. Reuben is Israel's son of seeing. Simeon espouses the dignity of hearing with understanding. Levi establishes commonality as a bond. Finally, Judah personifies our active involvement in the creative process. Thus, we see and hear; becoming aware. Then, as we come into active accord as a companion, we turn unto a new reality (Mark 4:12). To "turn" means to let go from oneself (from one's power or possession).

You too can tap into this creative reserve of strength and vitality. As Jesus said, "The secret of the kingdom of God has been given to you. But to those on the outside everything is said in parables so that, 'they may be ever seeing but never perceiving, and ever hearing but never understanding; otherwise they might turn and be forgiven!'" (Mark 4:11–12, NIV). If you don't understand this, how will you understand anything? When a lamp is brought to light your path, you do not bury it or darken it. It is meant to be put upon a stand so that its illumination can be enjoyed. "For whatever is hidden is meant to be disclosed," said Jesus, "and whatever is concealed is meant to be brought out into the open. With the measure [we] use, it will be measured to [us]-and even more. Whoever has will be given more; whoever does not have, even what he has will be taken from him" (Mark 4:22, 24–25, NIV).

Endnotes

Introduction

1 KJV references the King James Version of the Holy Scriptures. Capitalization of certain pronouns referring to the Father, the Son, and the Holy Spirit is, in most cases, the author's own.

2 Theological Wordbook of the Old Testament on *ša'ar* (Strong's OT:7778). Copyright © 1980 by The Moody Bible Institute of Chicago. All rights reserved.

3 NKJV references the New King James Version of the Bible. Capitalization of certain pronouns referring to the Father, the Son, and the Holy Spirit is, in most cases, the author's own.

4 AMP references the Amplified Bible.

5 Keil and Dlitzsch Commentary on the Old Testament (Genesis 16:13–14): New Updated Edition, Electronic Database. Copyright © 1996 by Hendrickson Publishers, Inc. All rights reserved. Emphasis mine.

PART ONE: BEGINNINGS

Chapter One: In the Beginning, God Saw...

1. OT:7200 is *Strong's* Reference Number. "OT" is an Old Testament reference while "NT" refers to the New Testament.

2. Vine's Expository Dictionary of Biblical Words on SEE, *ra'ah* (OT:7200). Copyright © 1985. Thomas Nelson Publishers.

3. Theological Wordbook of the Old Testament on *wisdom* (Strong's OT:2450). Copyright © 1980 by The Moody Bible Institute of Chicago. All rights reserved. Used by permission.

4. J. Bolton in *The Biblical Illustrator* on Genesis 1:31. Copyright © 2002, 2003, 2006 Ages Software, Inc. and Biblesoft, Inc.

5. *Ibid.*

6. *Ibid.*

Chapter Two: The Eye of the Beholder

1. Biblesoft's New Exhaustive Strong's Numbers and Concordance with Expanded Greek-Hebrew Dictionary on *'abad*, OT:5647.

2. Biblesoft's New Exhaustive Strong's Numbers and Concordance with Expanded Greek-Hebrew Dictionary on *shamar* (OT:8104).

3. *Ibid.*

4. Keil & Delitzsch Commentary on the Old Testament (Genesis 1:24–31), emphasis added.

5. *Ibid.*

6 The Wycliffe Bible Commentary on Gen. 1:26–30, Electronic Database. Copyright (c) 1962 by Moody Press.

7 Biblesoft's New Exhaustive Strong's Numbers and Concordance with Expanded Greek-Hebrew Dictionary on 'asah (OT:6213). Copyright © 1994, 2003, 2006 Biblesoft, Inc. and International Bible Translators, Inc.

8 Homilist in *The Biblical Illustrator* on Genesis 2:5. Copyright © 2002, 2003, 2006 Ages Software, Inc. and Biblesoft, Inc.

9 J. Parker in *The Biblical Illustrator* on Genesis 2:5.

10 *Ibid.*

Chapter Three: Creativity and the Dynamic Process

1 Theological Wordbook of the Old Testament on 'asah (*Strong's* OT:6213).

2 Vine's Expository Dictionary of Biblical Words on bara' (*Strong's* OT:1254).

3 John E. Hartley, New International Biblical Commentary, Hendrickson, Peabody, Mass (2000), p. 53–54.

4 Lexical Aid to the Old Testatment, *Hebrew Greek Key Sudy Bible* on bara' (OT 1254), AMG Pub. (1990).

5 Lexical Aid to the Old Testatment, *Hebrew Greek Key Sudy Bible* on 'asah (OT: 6213), emphasis added.

6 Biblesoft's New Exhaustive Strong's Numbers and Concordance on 'asah (OT:6213).

7 Fri Capra, *The Tao of Physics*, Shambhala, Boston, MA, (2000), p. 27.

8 Capra, p. 28.

9 Capra, p. 31.

Chapter Four: When the Patriarchs Met God

1. NASU references the New American Standard-Updated Version of the Holy Scriptures.

2. Matthew Henry's Commentary on the Whole Bible (Genesis 12:4–5), PC Study Bible Formatted Electronic Database Copyright © 2006 by Biblesoft, Inc. All Rights reserved.

3. Biblesoft's New Exhaustive Strong's Numbers and Concordance on *shem*, OT:8034, emphasis mine.

4. International Standard Bible Encyclopaedia on *Names of God*, Electronic Database Copyright (c)1996 by Biblesoft, emphasis added.

5. The New Unger's Bible Dictionary on GOD. Originally published by Moody Press of Chicago, Illinois. Copyright (c) 1988.

Chapter Five: What's In a Name?

1. Jamieson, Fausset, and Brown Commentary on Genesis 17:5, Electronic Database. Copyright © 1997, 2003, 2005, 2006 by Biblesoft, Inc. All rights reserved.

2. Nelson's Illustrated Bible Dictionary on NAME, Copyright (c)1986, Thomas Nelson Publishers, emphasis mine.

3. *Ibid.*

4. John E. Hartley, New International Biblical Commentary, Hendrickson, Peabody, Mass (2000), p. 171.

5. Adam Clarke's Commentary, Electronic Database. Copyright (c) 1996 by Biblesoft.

6 Biblesoft's New Exhaustive Strong's Numbers and Concordance with Expanded Greek-Hebrew Dictionary on *katartizo* (NT:2675).

7 William Hendriksen, New Testament Commentary, Exposition of Paul's Epistle to the Baker Book House, Grand Rapids, Mich. (1989), pp. 407–408, emphasis added.

8 *Ibid.* p. 409.

Chapter Six: Prophet of Exceeding Increase

1 Paul Yonggi Cho, The Fourth Dimension, Logos International, Plainfield, New Jersey (1979), p. 30.

2 Biblesoft's New Exhaustive Strong's Numbers and Concordance with Expanded Greek-Hebrew Dictionary on *nabat* (OT:5027).

3 Vine's Expository Dictionary of Biblical Words on "Look" (*nabat, Strong's* OT:5027).

4 Keil and Delitzsch Commentary on the Old Testament (Genesis 15:1–6).

5 The Bible Exposition Commentary on the Old Testament (Genesis 15:7–21): © 2001–2004 by Warren W. Wiersbe. All rights reserved.

6 McClintock and Strong Encyclopedia on Bless, Electronic Database. Copyright © 2000, 2003, 2005, 2006 by Biblesoft, Inc.

7 The New American Commentary, Matthew 4:1–2.

8 Nelson's Illustrated Bible Dictionary on KNOWLEDGE.

9 International Standard Bible Encyclopaedia on KNOWLEDGE.

Chapter Seven: "On the Mountain of the Lord It Will be Provided"

1. Easton's Bible Dictionary on PROPHET, PC Study Bible formatted electronic database Copyright © 2003, 2006 Biblesoft, Inc. All rights reserved.

2. The Hebrew-Greek Key Study Bible, Lexical Aids to the New Testament on FAITH (NT:4102), AMG, Chattanooga, TN (1990).

3. Biblesoft's New Exhaustive Strong's Numbers and Concordance on *yada'* (OT:3045).

4. *Ibid.*

5. J.R. Lucas, 'Minds, Machines and Gobel,' *Minds and Machines* (ed. A.R. Anderson; Prentice-Hall, 1964), p. 57.

Chapter Eight: "I Have Met El Roi"

1. Matthew Henry's Commentary on the Whole Bible (Genesis 16:7–9), PC Study Bible Formatted Electronic Database. Copyright © 2006 by Biblesoft, Inc. All Rights reserved.

2. Bible Knowledge Commentary/Old Testament (Genesis 16:7–16), Copyright © 1983, 2000 Cook Communications Ministries; Bible Knowledge Commentary/New Testament Copyright © 1983, 2000 Cook Communications Ministries. All rights reserved.

3. The Bible Knowledge Commentary/ Old Testament (Genesis 16:7–16).

4. *Ibid.*

5. International Standard Bible Encyclopaedia on KNOWLEDGE, Electronic Database Copyright © 1996, 2003, 2006 by Biblesoft, Inc.

6. Biblesoft's New Exhaustive Strong's Numbers and Concordance with Expanded Greek-Hebrew Dictionary on *epiginosko* (NT:1921).

7. Exegetical Dictionary of the New Testament on Strong's 1921 © 1990 by William B. Eerdmans Publishing Company. All rights reserved.

8. *Ibid.*

9. Introduction to Biblical Hebrew, Scribner's Sons, 1971, p. 168. From Theological Wordbook of the Old Testament on *hinneh* (Strong's 2009). Copyright © 1980 by The Moody Bible Institute of Chicago. All rights reserved.

Chapter Nine: Room Enough

1. Biblesoft's New Exhaustive Strong's Numbers and Concordance with Expanded Greek-Hebrew Dictionary on *'atsam* (OT:6105).

2. International Standard Bible Encyclopaedia on NUMBER, Electronic Database Copyright © 1996, 2003, 2006 by Biblesoft, Inc. All rights reserved.

3. Smith's Bible Dictionary on JESUS, PC Study Bible formatted electronic database Copyright © 2003, 2006 by Biblesoft, Inc.

4. Biblesoft's New Exhaustive Strong's Numbers and Concordance with Expanded Greek-Hebrew Dictionary on *yasha'* (OT:3467).

5. Easton's Bible Dictionary on *Jesus*, PC Study Bible formatted electronic database Copyright © 2003, 2006 Biblesoft, Inc. All rights reserved.

6 Biblesoft's New Exhaustive Strong's Numbers and Concordance with Expanded Greek-Hebrew Dictionary on *eido* (NT:1492).

7 The New Testament Lexical Aids on NT:1063, *blepo*, *Hebrew Greek Key Word Study Bible*, Zondervan (1996), p. 1599.

8 International Standard Bible Encyclopedia on RIGHT HAND, revised edition, Copyright © 1979 by Wm. B. Eerdmans Publishing Co.

9 THE MESSAGE: The Bible in Contemporary Language (Genesis 26:22) © 2002 by Eugene H. Peterson. All rights reserved.

10 Theological Wordbook of the Old Testament on *'olam*, Strong's OT:5769. Copyright © 1980 by The Moody Bible Institute of Chicago. All rights reserved. Used by permission.

11 The Bible Exposition Commentary on Genesis 26:23–25: Old Testament © 2001–2004 by Warren W. Wiersbe.

12 The New American Commentary on Genesis 26:27–29.

PART TWO: ACTIVATING GOD'S ANOINTING

Chapter One: God's Holy Symphony of Doing

1 Theological Wordbook of the Old Testament on CONCIEVE (*harah*, Strong's OT:2029). Copyright © 1980 by The Moody Bible Institute of Chicago. All rights reserved.

2 Biblesoft's New Exhaustive Strong's Numbers and Concordance with Expanded Greek-Hebrew Dictionary on *shama'* (OT:8085).

3 Vine's Expository Dictionary of Biblical Words on TO HEAR, *shama'* (*Strong's* OT:8085).

4 The New American Commentary on Romans 8:5, Copyright © 1991–2007 by B&H Publishing Group. All rights reserved. For specific copyright information on each volume, see the copyright page.

5 Biblesoft's New Exhaustive Strong's Numbers and Concordance with Expanded Greek-Hebrew Dictionary on *lavah* (OT:3867).

6 Biblesoft's New Exhaustive Strong's Numbers and Concordance with Expanded Greek-Hebrew Dictionary on *epi* (NT:1909) and *strepho* (NT:4762).

7 The Brown-Driver-Briggs Hebrew and English Lexicon on *ra'ah* (*Strong's* OT:7200).

Chapter Two: Reclaiming Your Roots: The Experience of Supernatural Muchness

1 Bruce H. Lipton, *The Biology of Belief*, Hay House, New York, New York (2008), pp. 84–85.

2 The International Standard Bible Encyclopaedia on the number THREE.

3 Biblesoft's New Exhaustive Strong's Numbers and Concordance with Expanded Greek-Hebrew Dictionary on *eido* (NT:1492).

4 Vine's Expository Dictionary of Biblical Words on KNOW (*ginosko*).

5 Theological Dictionary of the New Testament on *ginosko* (*Strong's* NT:1097). Copyright © 1972–1989 By Wm. B. Eerdmans Publishing Co.

6 *Ibid.*

7. Theological Wordbook of the Old Testament on *'asah* (*Strong's* OT:4639). Copyright © 1980 by The Moody Bible Institute of Chicago.

8. The Bible Exposition Commentary on the Old Testament (Genesis 31:1–21) by Warren W. Wiersbe.

9. *Ibid.*

Chapter Three: Ability with God and Men

1. Warren W. Wiersbe, The Bible Exposition Commentary on Genesis 31:1–21.

2. Theological Wordbook of the Old Testament on VAINLY or EMPTILY (Strong's OT:7387).

3. Warren W. Wiersbe, The Bible Exposition Commentary on Genesis 31:43–55.

4. *Ibid.*

5. Matthew Henry's Commentary on the Whole Bible (Genesis 32:1–2).

6. Bruce H. Lipton, *The Biology of Belief*, p. 59.

7. The Biblical Illustrator on Genesis 32:26, Copyright © 2002, 2003, 2006 Ages Software, Inc. and Biblesoft.

8. Warren W. Wiersbe, The Bible Exposition Commentary on Genesis 32:22–26.

9. Bruce Lipton, *The Biology of Belief*, p. 159.

10. Warren W. Wiersbe, The Bible Exposition Commentary on Genesis 32:22–26.

11. The New American Commentary on Genesis 32:30, Copyright © 1991–2007 by B & H Publishing

Group. All rights reserved. For specific copyright information on each volume, see the copyright page.

12 The Bible Exposition Commentary on Genesis 32:27–32 (Old Testament) © 2001–2004 by Warren W. Wiersbe. All rights reserved.

13 Matthew Henry's Commentary on the Whole Bible (Genesis 32:24–32).

14 Barnes' Notes on Genesis 32:23–32., Electronic Database. Copyright (c) 1997 by Biblesoft.

15 C. S. Robinson on *The New Man*, *The Biblical Illustrator* (Genesis 32:28). Copyright © 2002, 2003, 2006 Ages Software, Inc. and Biblesoft, Inc.

16 J. Brewster, *The Biblical Illustrator* (Genesis 32:28).

17 *Ibid.*

Chapter Four: What Would You Do If You Knew You Could Not Fail?

1 Vine's Expository Dictionary of Biblical Words on FOOLISHNESS, Copyright © 1985, Thomas Nelson Publishers.

2 Matthew Henry's Commentary on the Whole Bible (Genesis 35:1–5).

3 Biblesoft's New Exhaustive Strong's Numbers and Concordance with Expanded Greek-Hebrew Dictionary on yashab (OT:3427).

4 Vine's Expository Dictionary of Biblical Words on DWELL (*Strong's* OT:3427).

5 The Bible Exposition Commentary: Old Testament (Genesis 35:1) by Warren W. Wiersbe.

6 F. B. Meyer in *The Biblical Illustrator* on "The Putting Away of Idols" (Genesis 35:2–4). Copyright © 2002, 2003, 2006 Ages Software, Inc. and Biblesoft, Inc.

7 *Ibid.*

8 Matthew Henry's Commentary on the Whole Bible (Genesis 35:1–5), PC Study Bible Formatted Electronic Database Copyright © 2006 by Biblesoft, Inc.

9 Warren W. Wiersbe, The Bible Exposition Commentary: Old Testament (Genesis 35:1).

10 The Essex Congregational Remembrancer as quoted in *The Biblical Illustrator* on Luke 10:38–42, Copyright © 2002, 2003, 2006 Ages Software, Inc. and Biblesoft, Inc.

11 *Ibid.*

12 E. Craig, *The Biblical Illustrator* on Genesis 35:1–15.

13 W. Roberts, *The Biblical Illustrator* (Genesis 35:9–10).

14 International Standard Bible Encyclopedia on GOD, NAMES OF; revised edition, Copyright © 1979 by Wm. B. Eerdmans Publishing Co. All rights reserved.

Chapter Five: The Heritage of Israel

1 Warren W. Wiersbe, The Bible Exposition Commentary: Old Testament (Genesis 35:5).

2 The New American Commentary on Genesis 49:3–4, Copyright © 1991–2007 by B & H Publishing Group. All rights reserved. For specific copyright information on each volume, see the copyright page.

3 Biblesoft's New Exhaustive Strong's Numbers and Concordance with Expanded Greek-Hebrew Dictionary on *cowd* (OT:5475).

4 Vine's Expository Dictionary of Biblical Words on SOUL (*Strong's* OT:5315), Copyright © 1985, Thomas Nelson Publishers.

5 Nelson's Illustrated Bible Dictionary on SOUL, Copyright © 1986, Thomas Nelson Publishers.

6 Matthew Henry's Commentary on the Whole Bible (Genesis 49:5–7).

7 Deepak Chapra, The Book of Secrets, Harmony Books, New York, NY (2004), p. 90.

8 Chapra, p. 91

Chapter Six: The Secret Things of the Lord

1 Biblesoft's New Exhaustive Strong's Numbers and Concordance with Expanded Greek-Hebrew Dictionary on *Israel* (OT:3478).

2 Matthew Henry's Commentary on the Whole Bible (Genesis 49:1–4).

3 *Ibid.*

4 *Ibid.*

5 Matthew Henry's Commentary on the Whole Bible (Genesis 49:5–7).

6 Matthew Henry's Commentary on the Whole Bible (Genesis 49:8–12).

7 *Ibid.*

8 *Ibid.*

9 Biblesoft's New Exhaustive Strong's Numbers and Concordance with Expanded Greek-Hebrew Dictionary on *yadah* (OT:3034) and *yad* (OT:3027).

10 McClintock and Strong Encyclopedia on PRAISE, Electronic Database. Copyright © 2000, 2003, 2005, 2006 by Biblesoft, Inc. All rights reserved.

11 International Standard Bible Encyclopedia, revised edition on PRAISE, Copyright © 1979 by Wm. B. Eerdmans Publishing Co. All rights reserved.

12 *Ibid.*

13 Warren W. Wiersbe, The Bible Exposition Commentary on Genesis 49:8–12 © 2001–2004.

14 Adam Clarke's Commentary on Genesis 49:10, Electronic Database. Copyright © 1996, 2003, 2005, 2006 by Biblesoft, Inc. All rights reserved.

Chapter Seven: Commitment Determines Destiny!

1 Vine's Expository Dictionary of Biblical Words on EYE (*'ayin*), *Strong's* OT:5869; Copyright © 1985, Thomas Nelson Publishers.

2 Warren W. Wiersbe, The Bible Exposition Commentary on the Old Testament (Numbers 13:26–33) © 2001–2004.

3 Adam Clarke's Commentary on Numbers 13:33, Electronic Database. Copyright © 1996, 2003, 2005, 2006 by Biblesoft, Inc.

4 Matthew Henry's Commentary on the Whole Bible (Numbers 14:1–4), PC Study Bible Formatted Electronic Database Copyright © 2006 by Biblesoft, Inc. All Rights reserved.

5 Theological Wordbook of the Old Testament on *'asah* (*Strong's* OT:6213). Copyright © 1980 by The Moody Bible Institute of Chicago. All rights reserved.

6. Biblesoft's New Exhaustive Strong's Numbers and Concordance with Expanded Greek-Hebrew Dictionary on *witness* (OT:5749).

7. The Teacher's Commentary on Deuteronomy 27–34. Copyright © 1987 by Chariot Victor Publishing.

Chapter Eight: The Wind Ran Out of Breath

1. The Bible Exposition Commentary on Mark 3:13–19. Copyright © 1989 by Chariot Victor Publishing, and imprint of Cook Communication Ministries. All rights reserved. Used by permission.

2. *Ibid.*

3. Biblesoft's New Exhaustive Strong's Numbers and Concordance with Expanded Greek-Hebrew Dictionary on *optanomai* (*Strong's* NT:3700).

4. Biblesoft's New Exhaustive Strong's Numbers and Concordance with Expanded Greek-Hebrew Dictionary on *eido* (*Strong's* NT:1492).

5. Biblesoft's New Exhaustive Strong's Numbers and Concordance with Expanded Greek-Hebrew Dictionary on *ginosko* ((NT:1097).

6. Exegetical Dictionary of the New Testament on NT:1097 © 1990 by William B. Eerdmans Publishing Company. All rights reserved.

7. Warren W. Wierbe, The Bible Exposition Commentary: Old Testament (Psalms 63:1–2); © 2001–2004.

Chapter Nine: Divine Conceptions: God's Conclusion

1. Nelson's Illustrated Bible Dictionary on PEACE; Copyright © 1986, Thomas Nelson Publishers.

2 Warren W. Wiersbe. The Bible Exposition Commentary Genesis 29:31–35 © 2001–2004.

3 Theological Wordbook of the Old Testament on *hara* (*Strong's* OT:2029). Copyright © 1980 by The Moody Bible Institute of Chicago. All rights reserved.

4 *Ibid.*

5 Biblesoft's New Exhaustive Strong's Numbers and Concordance with Expanded Greek-Hebrew Dictionary on *lavah* (OT:3867).

6 Dr. Ironside's Commentary in *The Fourth Dimension* by Dr. Paul Yonggi Cho; Logos International, Plainfield, New Jersey (1979), p. 91.

7 Paul Yonggi Cho, *The Fourth Dimension*, Logos International, Plainfield, New Jersey (1979), p. 90.

8 Cho, p. 91.

9 Cho, p. 87.

10 Cho, pp. 9&23, emphasis mine.

11 Cho, p. 23.

12 Cho, p. 24.

13 Cho, p. 31, emphasis mine.

14 Cho, p. 31.

15 Biblesoft's New Exhaustive Strong's Numbers and Concordance with Expanded Greek-Hebrew Dictionary on *yadah* (OT:3034).

16 The New Unger's Bible Dictionary on Praise. Originally published by Moody Press of Chicago, Illinois. Copyright © 1988.

17 Charles Swindoll, *Fascinating Stories of Forgotten Lives*, Thomas Nelson, Nashville, Tenn., (2005), p. 139.

18 *Ibid.*

APPENDIX: THE SCIENCE OF "SEEING"
Genesis By Observership:

1 Wikipedia on John Archibald Wheeler, October 30, 2009.

2 John Archibald Wheeler, 1990, Information, physics, quantum: The search for links" in W. Zurek (ed.) Complexity, Entropy, and the Physics of Information. Redwood City, CA: Addison-Wesley.

3 John Wheeler, Information, physics, quantum: The search for links" in W. Zurek (ed.) Complexity, Entropy, and the Physics of Information. Emphasis added.

4 Tim Folger, "Does the Universe Exist if We're Not Looking?" DISCOVER, Vol. 23 No. 06, June 2002.

5 *Ibid.*

6 *Ibid.*

7 *Ibid.*

8 *Ibid.*

9 *Ibid.*

The Reubenic Principle of Seeing:

1 Evan Harris Walker, The Physics of Consciousness, Perseus, Cambridge, Mass. (2000), p. 54.

2 Tim Folger, "Does the Universe Exist if We're Not Looking?" DISCOVER, Vol. 23 No. 06, June 2002.

3 Quoted in *Dennis Brian's, The Voice of Genious: Converstations with Nobel Scientists and other Luminaries*, 127. From the Dictionary of Science Quotations and Scientist Quotes; http://www.todayinsci.com/W/Wheeler_John/WheelerJoh-Quotations.htm.

4 Keil & Delitzsch Commentary on the Old Testament (Genesis 1:2–5), New Updated Edition, Electronic Database. Copyright (c) 1996 by Hendrickson Publishers, Inc.

5 The Bible Exposition Commentary on Genesis 49:3–15: Old Testament © 2001–2004 by Warren W. Wiersbe.

6 Fritjof Capra, *The Tao of Physics*, Shambhala Pub., Boston, Mass. (1999), pp. 68–69.

7 Paul Davis, *God & The New Physics*, Simon and Schuster, New York, New York. 1984, p. 135.

8 F. Capra, *The Tao of Physics*, p. 68.

9 Paul Davis, *God & The New Physics*, p. 135.

The Simeonic and Levitic Principles

1 Biblesoft's New Exhaustive Strong's Numbers and Concordance with Expanded Greek-Hebrew Dictionary on *suniemi* (NT:4920).

2 Bruce H. Lipton, *The Biology of Belief*, Hay House, New York (2008), p. xiv.

3 Lipton, *The Biology of Belief*, p. xxi.

4 Lipton, *The Biology of Belief*, pp. xiv-xv.

5 Lipton, *The Biology of Belief*, p. xxv.

6 Lipton, *The Biology of Belief*, p. 59.

7 Matthew Henry's Commentary on the Whole Bible (Genesis 3:6–8), PC Study Bible.

8 *Ibid.*

9 *Ibid.*

10 *Ibid.*

11 The Bible Exposition Commentary: Old Testament (Genesis 3:9–13) © 2001–2004 by Warren W. Wiersbe. All rights reserved.

12 The Theological Dictionary of the New Testament on *metanoe* (Strong's NT:3340). Copyright © 1972–1989 By Wm. B. Eerdmans Publishing Co. All rights reserved.

13 F. Capra, *The Tao of Physics*, p. 140.

14 *Ibid.*

15 Neils Bohr, *Atomic Physics and the Description of Nature*, Cambridge, Egn.: Cambridge University Press (1934), p. 57.

16 Werner Heisenberg, *Physics and Philosophy*, p. 107.

17 F. Capra, *The Tao of Physics*, p. 139.

18 Thayer's Greek Lexicon on *diablepo* (Strong's NT:1227)., PC Study Bible formatted Electronic Database. Copyright © 2006 by Biblesoft, Inc. All rights reserved.

19 Keil & Delitzsch Commentary on the Old Testament (Genesis 1:2–5).

20 Biblesoft's New Exhaustive Strong's Numbers and Concordance with Expanded Greek-Hebrew Dictionary on *telaugos* (NT:5081).

21 Vine's Expository Dictionary of Biblical Words on CLEAR (Strong's NT:5081), Copyright © 1985, Thomas Nelson Publishers.

22 Thayer's Greek Lexicon on Strong's NT:5081, PC Study Bible formatted Electronic Database. Copyright © 2006 by Biblesoft, Inc. All rights reserved.

23 Biblesoft's New Exhaustive Strong's Numbers and Concordance with Expanded Greek-Hebrew Dictionary on *auge* (NT:827).

24 Lipton, *The Biology of Belief*, p. xv.

25 Biblesoft's New Exhaustive Strong's Numbers and Concordance with Expanded Greek-Hebrew Dictionary on *cowd* (OT:5475).

26 Theological Wordbook of the Old Testament on COUNCEL, COUNSIL, ASSEMBLY (Strong's OT:5475). Copyright © 1980 by The Moody Bible Institute of Chicago. All rights reserved.

27 Vine's Expository Dictionary of Biblical Words on PEACE (*shalom*, *Strong's* OT:7965); Copyright © 1985, Thomas Nelson Publishers.

28 Fritjof Capra, *The Tao of Physics*, Shambhala, Boston, MA, (2000), p. 39.

29 Capra, p. 35.

The Judaic Principle of Requisite Action

1 Fritjog Capra, *The Tao of Physics*, p. 141.

2 J. A. Wheeler, in J. Mehra (ed.), *The Physicist's Conception of Nature*, p. 244.

3 Biblesoft's New Exhaustive Strong's Numbers and Concordance with Expanded Greek-Hebrew Dictionary on OT:270 (*'achaz*).

4 Theological Wordbook of the Old Testament on Strong's OT:270 and OT:272. Copyright © 1980 by The Moody Bible Institute of Chicago. All rights reserved.

5 Wiersbe's Expository Outlines on the Old Testament on Exodus 35:30–39:43 © 1993 by Victor Books/SP Publications. All rights reserved.

6 *Ibid.*

7 William A. Tiller, Walter E. Dibble, Michael J. Kohane, *Conscious Acts of Creation*, Pavior Publishing, Walnut Creek, Calif., (2001), xvii.

8 Tiller *et al*, p. 11.

9 Tiller *et al*, p. 37.

10 W. Hudson in The Biblical Illustrator on Acts 1:12–14, Copyright © 2002, 2003, 2006 Ages Software, Inc. and Biblesoft, Inc.

11 T. S. Dickson in The Biblical Illustrator on Acts 1:12–14.

12 Tiller *et al*, p. 37.